FRIEDRICH SCHLEIERMACHER'S
Essay on a Theory of Sociable Behavior
(1799)

Friedrich Schleiermacher's
Essay on a Theory of Sociable Behavior
(1799)
A Contextual Interpretation

Peter Foley

The Edwin Mellen Press
Lewiston•Queenston•Lampeter

Library of Congress Cataloging-in-Publication Data

Foley, Peter.
   Friedrich Schleiermacher's essay on a theory of sociable behavior (1799): a contextual interpretation / by Peter Foley.
      p. cm.
   Includes bibliographical references and index.
   ISBN-13: 978-0-7734-5623-5
   ISBN-10: 0-7734-5623-6
   I. Title.

hors série.

A CIP catalog record for this book is available from the British Library.

Copyright © 2006 Peter Foley

All rights reserved. For information contact

    The Edwin Mellen Press   The Edwin Mellen Press
          Box 450   Box 67
      Lewiston, New York   Queenston, Ontario
      USA 14092-0450   CANADA L0S 1L0

             The Edwin Mellen Press, Ltd.
             Lampeter, Ceredigion, Wales
           UNITED KINGDOM SA48 8LT

Printed in the United States of America

Dedicated to my wife Pia Cuneo, the love of my life

Contents

Acknowledgements	i
1. Introduction	1
1.1. State of the Research	2
1.2. Approaching the Salon	9
1.2.1. The Literary and the Salon	9
1.2.2. Methodological Innovation	11
1.2.3. Authorship and Social Network Theory	15
1.3. "Salon" as a Pejorative Term	19
2. Henriette Herz's Salon	27
2.1. Perceptions of Tradition	27
2.1.1. Symposium	27
2.1.2. Renaissance Texts	34
2.1.3. France/Not France	46
2.2. Sexuality	52
3. Dialogue and Dialectic	69
3.1. Intimacy	69
3.2. Philosophy and the Salon	75
4. Philosophical Content of the *Essay*	81
4.1. Rejecting Fichte	81
4.2. Natural Law from Fichte's *Some Lectures on the Vocation of the Scholar*	88
4.3. Resolving Fichte's Challenge on Freedom	95
4.4. Rousseau's General Will	99
4.5. Morality and Law	105
4.6. Kant's Kingdom of Ends	112
4.7. Reciprocity and Schiller's Free Play	118
5. The Unfinished *Essay*	125
5.1. Précis of the Completed Arguments	126
5.2. Schleiermacher's Notes for the *Essay*	133
5.2.1. Translations from the *Notebooks of Thoughts*	133
5.2.2. The Arguments of the Uncompleted Portions	141
5.3. Abandoning the *Essay*	146
Appendix: *Essay on a Theory of Sociable Behavior*	153
Bibliography	177
Indexes	187

Acknowledgements

I owe a debt if gratitude to a number if scholars and institutions with whom I have had the privilege to work during the completion of this study. I count myself among the fortunate researchers who have enjoyed on several occasions the particular hospitality afforded by the Herzog August Bibliothek in Wolfenbüttel and am thankful Dr. Gillian Bepler for the use I have enjoyed of their splendid collections.

I am thankful to my colleagues Professors Ann Weekes and Janice Dewey of the former Humanities Program at the University of Arizona. They provided support during the years that we sailed the high seas of academic life together.

I owe gratitude also to the National Endowment for the Humanities for a Summer Institute on Literature and Philosophy after Kant in 2001 organized by Professors Karl Ameriks (University of Notre Dame) and Jane Kneller (Colorado State University) who, along with my fellow participants Greg Johnson (Pacific Lutheran University), Professors Ted Kinnaman (George Mason University), John Moore (Lander University), and Michael Vater (Marquette University) helped me develop my thoughts on Schleiermacher's philosophy in context.

In the realm of Schleiermacher studies I would like to thank Professor Terry Tice (University of Michigan) and Dr. Ruth Richardson (Edwin Mellen Press) for their collegiality and their consistent support and encouragement.

I would like to thank in particular Professor Monika Nenon of the University of Memphis for her input and encouragement on the subjects of salons and sociability. We organized many academic conference sessions together during which a great number of the ideas in this book first took shape; our discussions in those meetings helped develop my ideas beyond their embryonic forms.

My final word of gratitude goes to my wife Professor Pia Cuneo of the University of Arizona who has accompanied my work with patience and immense insight. Her input to my academic work has been invaluable.

1. Introduction

In the January and February editions of the 1799 *Berlinisches Archiv der Zeit und ihres Geschmacks*, two installments of an anonymous article appeared entitled *Versuch einer Theorie des geselligen Betragens* (*Essay on a Theory of Sociable Behavior*).[1] Its author was Friedrich Schleiermacher, then chaplain at the Charité hospital in Berlin. Schleiermacher's theory of sociability issued from the lived experience of the salon. In the salon he witnessed what he thought could be an ideal of interpersonal relationships that had consequences for ethics and society. His interests and concerns ranged widely during the execution of the *Essay on a Theory of Sociable Behavior* (1799), his work was interrupted, and he was ultimately distracted from completing what he had sketched out.

I shall argue at the end of this book that Schleiermacher's distraction from his original task was a logical ultimate consequence of developing his theories on secular sociability into the religious sociability of his more famous *On Religion: Speeches to Its Cultured Despisers* (1799). The concerns of the *Essay* are secular and they issue from the realm of what we have come to know as the literary salon. To understand Schleiermacher's interest in sociability this study must start by looking at the phenomenon of the salon.[2]

---

[1] Friedrich Daniel Ernst Schleiermacher, *Kritische Gesamtausgabe*. Part I, vol. 2. *Schriften aus der Berliner Zeit 1796–1799*, ed. Günter Meckenstock (Berlin: de Gruyter, 1984). Hereafter cited as *KGA*, I/2

[2] All translations are mine, unless otherwise indicated. The only exception to this rule is Richard Crouter's translation of the 1799 edition of Schleiermacher's *On Religion*: Friedrich Schleiermacher, *On Religion: Speeches to Its Cultured Despisers*, trans. and ed. by Richard Crouter (Cambridge:

1.1. State of the Research

Increased interest in the literary salon has meant that the theologian and philosopher Friedrich Schleiermacher's 1799 *Essay on a Theory of Sociable Behavior* has now received serious attention as a work concerned with this sociable phenomenon. An article by Konrad Feilchenfeldt, published in 1987, highlighted Schleiermacher's *Essay* as a theoretical underpinning for the salon, and it was from this article that most of the interest in the *Essay* for those working on the salon was derived.[3]

Much work has been done since then, and some of it is compendious in scope. Petra Wilhelmy's 1987 dissertation lists and describes the salons of Berlin from 1780–1914,[4] while from a literary and social historical perspective, Peter Seibert's *Der Literarische Salon* of 1993 gives a broad and thoroughgoing examination of the salon and of the published works of consequence to the salon.[5] Deborah Hertz's *Jewish High Society in Old Regime Berlin* of 1988 is one of the few such works in English, but it is also different in its purely historical approach, relying on statistics and public records to create a social picture of the salons of that period.[6] All of these broad works are valuable tools in seeking to examine the *Essay* in context.

One story of the salon that has yet to be told is of particular relevance to Schleiermacher and his *Essay*. It concerns the influence of German Protestant Pietism on the salon, a subject that has been neglected in the literature. When the courtly sociability of the academies spread from Germany to Italy, it came first to the court at Köthen. Here, the Fruit-Bearing Society developed parallel groups for women. By the end of the seventeenth century, the *Collegia pietatis* of the Pietist Philipp August Spener made similar strides for bourgeois women, eventually admitting them to its

---

Cambridge University Press, 1996).
[3]Konrad Feilchenfeldt, "Berliner Salons der Romantik," in *Rahel Varnhagen. Die Wiederentdeckung einer Schriftstellerin*, ed. Barbara Hahn and Ursula Isselstein. *Zeitschrift für Literaturwissenschaft und Linguistik*, Beiheft 14 (Göttingen: Vandenhoek und Ruprecht, 1987), 152–163.
[4]Published as: Petra Wilhelmy, *Der Berliner Salon im 19. Jahrhundert (1780–1914)* (Berlin and New York: de Gruyter, 1989).
[5]Peter Seibert, *Der literarische Salon. Literatur und Geselligkeit zwischen Aufklärung und Vormärz* (Göttingen: Metzler, 1993).
[6]Deborah Hertz, *Jewish High Society in Old Regime Berlin* (New Haven: Yale University Press, 1988).

circle.[7] In the eighteenth century the moral weeklies took up the sword of propriety and, wielding it, carved out models of dialogues and good company for woman, much as Georg Phillip Harsdörffer's *Playful Colloquies for the Ladies*, published in eight volumes between 1641 and 1649, had done for the Fruit-Bearing Society and for those who sought to emulate that group.

Over the course of the eighteenth century, the public coffeehouses became the bête noire of writers on good sociability; these authors were at pains to make a place for appropriate sociability for women. This inclusion of women was a particular problem for the Protestant tradition, as it had rejected the monastic tradition of turning one's back on society, and yet did not entirely insist that women remain closeted in the home. Thus, there is a disparity between the frivolous baroque courtly sociability seen to stem from France and a German Protestant sociability that is the successor to a struggle for virtuous public sociability for women. In this light the name for Henriette Herz's early sociable circle—"Tugendbund," or "Virtuous League"—makes a connection with this hitherto much neglected tradition of the salons.

Such concerns are significant to Schleiermacher as a minister of the Reformed Church and as someone who had grown up in the neopietist traditions of the Moravian Brotherhood. Schleiermacher's *Essay* must be seen within this context, and thus, this neglected area must be examined.

Work that has focused more particularly on the salon of Henriette Herz has not only come in the form of various editions of her memoirs, the latest of which has been of invaluable assistance to me in preparing this manuscript,[8] but also from current scholarship. Martin Davies has given the best sketch of what Herz's salon might have been like for Schleiermacher,[9] and his work on Marcus Herz has proved valuable in discerning more clearly elements of the intellectual environment of the

---

[7]Martin Brecht, "Pietismus als alternative Geselligkeit," in *Geselligkeit und Gesellschaft im Barokzeitalter*, ed. Wolfgang Adam. Wolfenbüttler Arbeiten zur Barokforschung Band 28. (Wiesbaden: Harrasowitz Verlag, 1997), 263.

[8]I have relied upon the most recent and complete *Henriette Herz in Erinnerungen und Briefen und Zeugnissen*, ed. Rainer Schmitz (Frankfurt am Main: Insel, 1984) (hereafter cited as *Herz*). On the issue of the various editions, see Peter Seibert "Henriette Herz: Erinnerungen. Zur Rekonstruktion einer frühen Frauenautobiographie," *Der Deutschunterricht* 41 (1989): 37–50.

[9]Martin L. Davies, "Sociability in Practice and Theory: Henriette Herz and Friedrich Schleiermacher," *New Athenaeum/Neues Athenaeum* 2 (1991): 18–59. I also agree wholeheartedly with his use of *Essay* both to describe this work as well as to translate the title.

Essay.[10]

I will attempt in this book to establish the intellectual environment of the *Essay*, both in terms of the salon sociability with which Schleiermacher would have been familiar and in terms of the philosophical influences that would have impinged directly on his thinking in 1799. In looking at the salon, it will be important to look in particular at the realm of Jewish sociability in Berlin and at the traditions and environment in which participants in this sociability would have understood themselves to have existed. With Herz's memoirs as a significant touchstone, it will be possible to look at this sociability as something constructed within the texts that describe it. In this study I will take the innovative approach of examining the phenomenon of the salon as a textual construct. In this sense the textual social historical examination of the salon will fit seamlessly with the examination of various philosophical texts that can be seen to be relevant to Schleiermacher's *Essay*.

Most general philosophical approaches to Schleiermacher spend little time examining the *Essay* because they understand his philosophy as determined by its development toward the more acclaimed later Hermeneutics and Dialectics. To give such studies their due, the *Essay* is but a small and fragmentary work when seen in the light of Schleiermacher's complete oeuvre.[11] The *Essay* is neither strictly an early work nor a mature work. Additionally, Schleiermacher's achievements at this period of his life are overshadowed by the enormously successful *On Religion: Speeches to Its Cultured Despisers*.

Still, serious and concentrated attention to the *Essay* has been provided by a number of authors, each taking very differing approaches. Although it is of value as a starting point, the examination by Wolfgang Hinrichs published in 1965 of Schleiermacher's development of the Enlightenment notion of "Bildung" as fundamental for Schleiermacher in 1799 has since then proved to be more illuminating for education rather than for philosophical or historical analyses of the *Essay*.[12] In general, such attempts to read the *Essay* as a pedagogical work have

---

[10]Martin L. Davies, *Identity or History? Marcus Herz and the End of the Enlightenment* (Detroit: Wayne State University Press, 1995).

[11]This observation is true for such works as Gunter Scholtz, *Die Philosophie Schleiermachers* (Darmstadt: Wissenschaftliche Buchgesellschaft, 1984); Wolfgang Pleger, *Schleiermachers Philosophie* (Berlin: de Gruyter, 1988); and Christian Berner, *La Philosophie de Schleiermacher. «Herméneutique», «Dialectique», «Éthique»* (Paris: Les Éditions du Cerf, 1995).

[12]Wolfgang Hinrichs, *Schleiermachers Theorie der Geselligkeit und ihre Bedeutung für die Pädagogik* (Weinheim/Bergstraße: Beltz,1965). Another shorter study also make a contribution in this

proved to be too limiting. A rather more successful approach to this subject matter has been produced by Detlef Gaus, who also provides an enlightening and valuable contribution to the examinations of salon culture from the viewpoint of social change at the turn to the nineteenth century.[13]

My examination of Schleiermacher and the salons will differ in several important respects. Whereas Gaus looks at the issue of sociability as a matter of interest for contemporary cultural and educational thinking, I shall be looking at sociability as a historical construct produced by texts, as well as looking at the connections among the writers of such texts. This same form of intertextuality will act as the basis for looking at the philosophical content of the *Essay*. The present study will thus differ from the existing examinations of the *Essay* significantly in the matter of the specificity of the materials examined therein. All of these materials will be within the immediate proximity of Schleiermacher's activity and that of Henriette Herz because of the importance of her salon and the sociability she provided for Schleiermacher. Consequently, in comparison to Gaus, I will focus more directly and more specifically on Herz and Schleiermacher's philosophical interests documented in the *Essay*. Gaus places more emphasis on a general social and pedagogical context for the *Essay* and sociability. Ultimately, my conclusions about the *Essay* will differ from those of Gaus by providing an examination of the traditions in which Herz declares her salon to be founded and by illuminating the philosophical interests of the *Essay*.

There are also more strictly theoretical and social interpretations of the *Essay*. Many studies read the *Essay* as primarily concerned with conversation and language and see the relationship of the work to social issues as being attained through the social context in which conversation is embedded. Yorick Spiegel's work is the most starkly and self-consciously methodologically sociological of such studies. He attempts to understand communication as a social activity grounded in Adam Smith's concepts of economic exchange and then to apply this understanding to Schleiermacher's *Essay*.[14]

---

vein and should be mentioned here: Stefanie Antonie, "Bildung und Geselligkeit: Zur 'Theorie der Geselligkeit'," in *Gesellige Bildung. Studien und Dokumente zur Bildung Erwachsener im 18. Jahrhundert*, ed. Arnim Kaiser (Bad Heilbrunn/Obb: Klinkhardt, 1989).

[13]Detlef Gaus, *Geselligkeit und Gesellige. Bürgertum und bildungsbürgerliche Kultur um 1800* (Stuttgart: Metzler, 1998).

[14]Yorick Spiegel, *Theologie der bürgerlichen Gesellschaft: Sozialphilosophie und Glaubenslehre*

Karl Heinz Göttert examines communication and, like Spiegel, takes a sociological approach; he also considers, along with other matters, the psychological ramifications of the *Essay*. Göttert's study has the distinct advantage of making a concerted turn toward Kant's moral philosophy. Göttert, however, still interprets Schleiermacher's *Essay* as being a mere stepping-stone to the latter's hermeneutics. In this way Göttert can maintain the concentration on communication and conversation that is after all the focus of his book.[15]

This interest in Kantian matters is also reflected in studies that concern themselves with Schleiermacher's early works. Both Albert Blackwell and Günter Meckenstock look at the early influences on Schleiermacher.[16] Despite the fact that the *Essay* lies outside the realm of interest in these works, Blackwell's examination is generally of more specific advantage to my study because he paints with a broader brush than does Meckenstock. Meckenstock, however, has the virtue of encouraging a vigorous and critical turn toward Kant in the scholarship.

Since Meckenstock published his study, much more specific work detailing the connections to Kant's philosophy in the *Essay* has been done by Andreas Arndt. Arndt's work is fundamental to any analysis of the philosophical influences on the *Essay*. Included with other Arndt studies on Schleiermacher is a very important and thorough article that argues that the *Essay* concerns itself with ethics and that autonomy, as determined by Kant, is the final mover for Schleiermacher in ethical questions.[17] I have the advantage of being able to develop arguments with the precise and carefully argued work of Arndt as a base. I shall disagree with Arndt by turning

---

bei Friedrich Schleiermacher (Munich: Kaiser Verlag, 1968), 25.

[15] Karl Heinz Göttert, *Kommunikationsideale der frühen Neuzeit. Untersuchungen zur europäischen Konversationstheorie* (Munich: Cella, 1988). I especially recommend chapter 7, "Vom Kommunikationsmodell zur hermeneutischen Verstehenskritik: Friedrich Schleiermacher," 163–94.

[16] Albert Blackwell, *Schleiermacher's Early Philosophy of Life: Determinism, Freedom, Phantasy*. Harvard Theological Studies no. 33 (Chico: Scholars Press, 1982); Günter Meckenstock, *Deterministische Ethik und Kritische Theologie: Die Auseinandersetzung des frühen Schleiermacher mit Kant und Spinoza 1789–1794* Schleiermacher-Archiv, vol. 5 (Berlin: de Gruyter, 1988). The earlier study by Eilert Herms, *Herkunft, Entfaltung und erste Gestalt des Systems der Wissenschaften bei Schleiermacher* (Gütersloh: Mohn, 1974), did not directly influence this work because of Herms's interest in a scientific system for Schleiermacher rather than in the specifics of his intellectual development.

[17] Andreas Arndt, "Geselligkeit und Gesellschaft. Die Geburt der Dialektik aus dem Geist der Konversation in Schleiermachers "Versuch einer Theorie des geselligen Betragens," in *Salons der Romantik. Beiträge eines Wiepersdorfer Kolloquiums zu Theorie und Geschichte des Salons*, ed. Harwig Schultz (Berlin: de Gruyter, 1997), 52.

from Kant's autonomy to his "kingdom of ends" in order to explicate the reasoning of the *Essay*. This approach will permit an interpretation of the *Essay* that remains fully within the work's social concerns and yet still leaves the arguments within the ethical realm.[18]

Informed by a completely different set of concerns, Katherine Faull's consideration of the *Essay* from the perspective of feminist philosophy develops a notion of personhood that makes a valuable differentiation between Schleiermacher's and Kant's notions of the person. By looking very carefully at the *Essay* in a collection of writings on that work, Faull has been able to make arguments about notions of ethical communities that are entirely commensurate with what I shall say about Schleiermacher and Kant's kingdom of ends.[19] Faull treats Schleiermacher's work as committed to a uniquely progressive ethics and avoids embedding it deeply in the thought of its time, thus enabling her to examine Schleiermacher on his own terms. I will seek to apply that same spirit of interpreting Schleiermacher's progressive ethics that Faull relies upon from the work of Ruth Richardson and that she pursues in declaring Schleiermacher's to be a "truly human ethic."[20] In my study, however, the agenda is not to evaluate Schleiermacher's applicability to feminist philosophy but to acknowledge his independent thinking while still considering his connections to other bodies of thought.

Such acknowledgment of Schleiermacher's independence avoids the pitfall of according Johann Gottlieb Fichte a defining role in Schleiermacher's thought. Such

---

[18] A book-length study but a few years older than Arndt's article, by Bernd Oberdorfer, *Geselligkeit und Realisierung von Sittlichkeit. Die Theorieentwicklung Friedrich Schleiermachers bis 1799*, Theologische Bibliothek Töpelmann, vol. 69 (Berlin: de Gruyter, 1995), also sees the *Essay* as a realization of the ethical realm, but Oberdorfer limits this realization to speech and conversation. His study provides lengthy expositions on the works of others, such as Schleiermacher's teacher, Johann August Eberhard. Such interests would be of potential value if Oberdorfer's expositions were not sometimes less lucid than the original works. In general the study would have benefited from greater focus and the closing of certain gaps, such as the omission of the consideration of Schiller as an influence; Blackwell has already examined this influence. Oberdorfer's lengthy study shows intelligence and offers a broad overview of existing material. His method is almost dialectical at times.

[19] Katherine M. Faull, "Beyond Confrontation? The Early Schleiermacher and Feminist Moral Theory," in *Friedrich Schleiermacher's Toward a Theory of Sociable Conduct, and Essays on its Intellectual-Cultural Context*, ed. Ruth Drucilla Richardson. *New Athenaeum/Neues Athenaeum*, vol. 4 (Lewiston: Edwin Mellen Press, 1995), 48.

[20] Ibid., 43. Faull is here citing Ruth Drucilla Richardson, "Schleiermacher's 1800 'Versuch über die Schaamhaftigkeit': A Contribution Toward a Truly Human Ethic," in *Schleiermacher and Feminism. Sources, Evaluations, and Responses*, ed. Iain G. Nicol (Lewiston: Edwin Mellen Press, 1992), 49–85.

an assignment for Fichte is a perennial problem in examining the work of Romantics. Fichte's ideas are applied post hoc as a legitimate and legitimating interpretation of the philosophy of his times, even encompassing the work of Kant, who is not even seen as a legitimate interpreter of his own work (supposedly only Fichte understood it).[21] All too often philosophical work on Schleiermacher is founded on such indiscriminate reading of the history of philosophy in his time, with Fichte being found to lurk everywhere, prompting such statements regarding Schleiermacher's *On Religion* as "[t]he argumentative proximity to the later manifestations of the philosophy of Fichte and Schelling in which this aporia seeks to escape the circularity of the self-positing self-consciousness should be obvious."[22] Such connections are never obvious and should startle anyone were they to be discovered; Schleiermacher made his distaste for Fichte—both personally and philosophically—abundantly clear.

This insistence on Schleiermacher's independence does not mean that Fichte played no role in Schleiermacher's thinking. On the contrary, Fichte served as a challenge and a foil, and only very subtle analyses can serve to illuminate this relationship. Arndt is the scholar who has been the most discerning in making these very fine distinctions. When I reflect on what he has written and choose to differ, I do so with sincere appreciation for the distance he has brought us in our understanding of Schleiermacher's philosophy.

Schleiermacher is not only a philosopher. The man who wrote that "we should do everything with religion"[23] saw religion as an integral part of human existence. We should not be surprised, then, to learn that a work with such putatively secular concerns as those of the *Essay* was abandoned in favor of the celebrated *On Religion*. There is a continuity between Schleiermacher's concerns about human society in the *Essay* and his understanding of humanity and sociability in *On Religion*. Gaus talks of the *Essay* as being concerned only with issues of liturgy,[24] but already in 1927 Heinrich Töllner argued that religion represented the highest form of

---

[21] Karl Ameriks, *Kant and the Fate of Autonomy: Problems in the Appropriation of Critical Philosophy* (Cambridge: Cambridge University Press, 2000), esp. 234–64.

[22] Gunther Wenz, *Sinn und Geschmack fürs Unendliche. F. D. E. Schleiermachers Reden über die Religion an die Gebildeten unter ihren Verächtern von 1799* (Munich: Verlag der Bayerischen Akademie der Wissenschaften, 1999), 23f.

[23] To which, incidentally, he added "nothing because of religion." Friedrich Schleiermacher, *On Religion: Speeches to Its Cultured Despisers*, trans. and ed. by Richard Crouter (Cambridge: Cambridge University Press, 1996), 30.

[24] Gaus, *Geselligkeit und Gesellige,* 112.

completion of human sociability for Schleiermacher.[25] Consequently, I shall argue that, as a secular work, the *Essay* was bound to fail.

My concentration here will be on the *Essay* itself, and so, it shall not be my goal to reconstruct all of Schleiermacher's sociability. Instead, I shall attempt to reconstruct the uncompleted portions of the *Essay* as they are projected in Schleiermacher's *Gedankenhefte* (*Notebooks of Thoughts*). Of course, I shall make references to Schleiermacher's sociability elsewhere, but the limits of this work are circumscribed by the *Essay* itself.

1.2. Approaching the Salon

1.2.1. The Literary and the Salon

In a recent review of the studies carried out on salons, Seibert notes many distinct approaches to the salon that have in the main failed to cross-fertilize. Although he discerns several different methodological approaches,[26] these can be boiled down to two essential groupings that appear mutually exclusive: they are the historico-sociological approaches and the biographic literary studies. One can readily agree with Seibert's view that a lack of an integrating interdisciplinary approach to the subject has invariably resulted in the neglect of significant material. His conclusion is that an examination of the salon has yet to make a significant contribution to the project of a social history of literature.[27] This desire finds its realization in his book *Der literarische Salon: Literatur und Geselligkeit zwischen Aufklärung und Vormärz*. This work is the most recent academic study to concern itself broadly and exclusively with the German salon, and it stands alongside an increasing number of studies dealing with various aspects of this salon.

Seibert's interest in salons is informed by a traditional view of literary history,

---

[25]Heinrich Töllner, *Die Bedeutung der Geselligkeit in Schleiermachers Leben und Schriften* (Erlangen: Junge, 1927), 55. This opinion is shared by Petra Röder, "Individualität und Geselligkeit. Schleiermachers 'Versuch einer Theorie des geselligen Betragens,'" *Prima Philosophia* 3 (1990): 33.

[26]Peter Seibert, "Der Literarische [sic.] Salon–ein Forschungsüberblick," *Internationales Archiv für Sozialgeschichte der Literatur*, 3. Sonderheft 2. Folge (1993): 159–220. The headings cover different approaches: biographical, historico-cultural and -moral, local historical, Jewish historical, history of sociability, sociological, and literary sociological.

[27]Ibid., 206 ff.

and his book leads to a concept of the salon as an aesthetic happening that should be seen as a genre unto itself. His study is a thoroughgoing piece of research with a broad spectrum of meticulously examined material, and it provides a wealth of information and analyses not available elsewhere. The resolution of the conflict between literary and historical approaches to the salon would perhaps have led in different directions if a methodologically more self-critical review of certain essential issues were carried out; these are issues that are already clear in Seibert's initial article reviewing the studies of the salon.

Traditional literary history places the literary text in a relationship to events surrounding the text, such that the text reflects the world external to it. This placement results in a view of the text as interpretation and history as the real. The same is true for sociological approaches to literature, inasmuch as the text reflects the sociological reality around it. These approaches assume a fundamental dichotomy between reality, which surrounds the text, and the text, which is a reflective, interpretive document.

Such documents as memoirs, reports, and notes that have been used to explore the phenomenon of the salon are called secondary materials by Seibert.[28] The texts thus reflect passively on events that took place, and their function of constituting the phenomenon of the salon as an ideal is given no attention at all. Ingeborg Drewitz states that the sources are a problem endemic to the study of the salon, as it was a fleeting phenomenon, lost as soon as it came about.[29] This performative and ephemeral characteristic of salon interaction is something that has led Feilchenfeldt to describe the salon as essentially theatrical in nature.[30] Seibert gives this notion a great deal of potential value in affording the salon an aesthetic dimension, otherwise denied by social historical inquiry.[31] For Seibert this aesthetic valuation would be important in providing the grounds to study the salon that would motivate a literary historian. I will abandon such stalwart allegiance to a specific discipline here in order to avoid the very problems of exclusive discipline orientation

---

[28]Ibid., 161.

[29]Ingeborg Drewitz, *Berliner Salons* (Berlin: Haude und Spenersche Verlagsbuchhandlung, 1965).

[30]Feilchenfeldt, "Die Berliner Salons der Romantik," 158f. Elsewhere, the dramatic self-vision Feilchenfeldt suggests for Rahel Levin has been applied more broadly to issues of influence in the salon and to the works of Heinrich von Kleist in particular: Peter Foley, *Heinrich von Kleist und Adam Müller. Untersuchung zur Aufnahme idealistischen Ideenguts durch Heinrich von Kleist* (Frankfurt am Main: Lang, 1990).

[31]Seibert, *Der literarische Salon*, 214

that Seibert himself points out. The result of Seibert's attachment to a narrowly defined view of his own work as a literary historian is his attempt to construct the salon as a real aesthetic event with its own genrelike parameters. I will draw upon many of the same sources as are available in Seibert's study, but I will construe their meaning in a way that places history and texts in a much more reciprocal relationship. This construction makes the relationship between history and the text a rather symbiotic one. Still, it should not be deemed a plaidoyer for a relativist view of history; rather, what I am seeking here is the realization that our sources need to be read as texts that construct history.

The salon offers a case study in the constitution of meaning and history by texts. The texts that are produced with the salon as their locus *are* what constitute the salon. The texts go about constituting the institution of the salon, and Schleiermacher's *Essay on a Theory of Sociable Behavior* can be firmly positioned among these texts, inasmuch as it projects an ideal of salon sociability. My concern in the present study is, therefore, with the construction of a cultural institution by means of texts. Rather than telling us about the institution in Rankean terms of "wie es eigentlich gewesen," Schleiermacher's text is part of the very material that works to construct a projected ideal space.

1.2.2. Methodological Innovation

New methodological approaches offer the possibility of viewing history as something existing as an interpretive textual phenomenon, and in the tradition of New Historicism, it is possible to apply the tools of the literary critic to those texts that make history. The texts that make up what Seibert calls "secondary material" fit this method extremely well, although as these texts actually construct the salon, his nomenclature must be deemed faulty because in this way they are, at least to some extent, primary sources. The division between the events and the texts cannot be made with such supposed clarity; they are integrally linked.

The richest sources of information on salons are memoirs and autobiographies. Such works go about constructing events to place the author at the center of significant cultural activity. Questions of reliability and truth arise that can never be satisfactorily dealt with, but they are significant only if one adheres to a more traditional vision of the nature of historiography. A New Historicist view acknowledges that all historical writing is a construct, and in this study I will examine the salon from that viewpoint.

Thus, the salon becomes a vision appearing in the writing of those who have experienced it. It is no longer an issue that salon gatherings lacked minutes, as such records would only reflect that which the scribe wished them to reveal. Drewitz's lament of the unreconstructability of the salon thus becomes a lament over the very nature of history; no events can ever be reconstructed entirely as they happened. One of the things that we as historians can most readily do is to examine the nature of the narratives that combine to provide us with our image of the salon.

Recent approaches to the salon have begun to acknowledge the status of this social phenomenon as a construct. Barbara Hahn in her analysis of Rahel Levin Varnhagen's correspondence, *Antworten Sie mir*, points out that the salon of Rahel's letters is nothing but a chimera: "The salon proves to be…a dream, a wishful image, that is projected back into time around the turn of the nineteenth century."[32] Hahn's assiduous attention to the narrative strategies employed in the writing of the correspondence and her examination of the ruptures in the texts (produced either by omission or by erasure) open the biography of Rahel Levin Varnhagen to a new breadth of understanding. Hahn's approach is closest to that which I apply here, though her concern is with Rahel and, in particular, with her correspondence. In my study the focus with respect to the salon will be on Henriette Herz and other forms of writing.

Biographical approaches to the salon have long been a mainstay of inquiry. Much of this material is illuminating, but it is also often tainted by an enthusiasm for the subject that supports the construction of the myth of the salon. This myth, as Hahn has pointed out for Rahel, has its origin in the letters of those associated with the salon. The secondary materials begin with Rahel's husband Karl August Varnhagen von Ense, who in 1833 was the first to publish letters and reminiscences associated with his wife, at first as a handwritten manuscript.[33]

This writing represents the initiation of a tradition that reaches to some of the

---

[32] "Der Salon erweist sich…als ein Traum, ein Wunschbild, das in die Zeit um die Wende zum 19. Jahrhundert zurückprojiziert wird." Barbara Hahn, *Antworten Sie mir* (Frankfurt am Main: Stroemfeld/Roter Stern, 1990), 53.

[33] *Rahel. Ein Buch des Andenkens für ihre Freunde*, Berlin, 1833. This manuscript is now in the Biblioteka Jagiellońska in Krakau, Poland. Cf. Hahn, *Antworten Sie mir*, 14ff.

most recent works, such as Rolf Strube's *Sie saßen und tranken am Teetisch* and Verena von der Heyden-Rynsch's *Europäische Salons*.[34] These latter books both support the tradition that the salon was an ideal, yet real, space consisting of a sociability now lost. The subtitle of von der Heyden-Rynsch's book explains that the salons mark the "Highpoint of a Subsided Feminine Culture." For Strube, the explanation comes on the flyleaf to the book: "In autobiographical statements, letters, and scenes from novels of the time, Rolf Strube permits the lustrous age of the great Berlin salons to come alive again."[35] While this statement is intended as figurative, it is literally true because through this very material, which constructs that lustrous age and its great salons, the salon lives with us still. Through neglecting the fact that the material is constantly constructing the salon, the studies have misconstrued the value of period documents. In this misconstruction they are continuous with part of the original tradition that emanates directly from the leading protagonists of the salons. Nonetheless, Strube brings together a valuable collection of documents concerning the salon that are not readily available elsewhere, and thus, he makes a significant contribution to furthering interest in the salon. The intention of von der Heyden-Rynsch's book is to reach a broad public, and she provides a clear exposition of the standard view of the salon's development. My study will differ from these two in that it will carry a new awareness of the method of narrative construction of the salon in the type of material used to examine this phenomenon.

In addition to the above concerns, von der Heyden-Rynsch and Strube make an important contribution to feminist studies by making the work and sphere of women's activity accessible to a broad audience. An extension of the original mythmaking tradition exists in those works on the salon that see it as an ideal, yet real, sphere in which women were able to interact with men on an equal footing.[36] This perceived equality is highly unlikely, despite all the Enlightenment sentiments

---

[34]*Sie saßen und tranken am Teetisch. Anfänge und Blütezeit der Berliner Salons 1789–1871*, ed. Rolf Strube. Serie Piper, vol. 1204 (Munich: Piper, 1991); Verena von der Heyden-Rynsch, *Europäische Salons. Höhepunkt einer versunkenen weiblichen Kultur* (Munich: Artemis und Winkler, 1992).

[35]"In autobiographischen Zeugnissen, Briefen und Szenen aus Romanen der Zeit läßt Rolf Strube die Glanzzeit der großen Berliner Salons wieder lebendig werden." Strube, 2.

[36]Exemplary work of this nature, such as that by Silvia Bovenschen and Dana Goodman, needs to be seen within the context of first-generation feminism. Such studies helped spur interest in the subject of the salon, and without them, scholars would not have been able to progress to a more sophisticated understanding of the material.

of the times. The salon frequently had a woman as its focus, but the structure of friendship was such as to promote that between men and that between women and men. Women were able to play the role of facilitator and mediator, whereas men had a much broader spectrum of roles in society that made them the primary focus for each others' friendships.[37]

Nonetheless, many studies concur with the idealizations of the narratives surrounding the salons. They project the salon as a realm in which the Enlightenment reigned supreme and offered an island of emancipation for women. Drewitz offers such an idealized interpretation in *Berliner Salons* (1965), which has continued to be influential. Silvia Boveschen in *Die imaginierte Weiblichkeit* (1979) suggests that the salons were islands in which the otherwise enforced rule of silence for women was lifted.[38] Dana Goodman has made much the same point for French salons, indicating that in the salons the values of the Enlightenment were used "to shape a serious working space for the women who led them and for the men who frequented them."[39] Still, while Jewish salons doubtless played a significant role in mediating assimilation of the Jews in Berlin, this emancipation did not extend to the women as a distinct category in the salons.

The continuing interest in both Henriette Herz and Rahel Levin Varnhagen is an issue of consequence for feminist consideration of their importance. Herz's memoirs have appeared in numerous editions since the first in 1850. Seibert has carried out a detailed study of these editions, carefully examining the strategy of each editor.[40] All of the editors, who were male, variously engage in issues of authenticity by deleting material from the original manuscript or by adding their own remarks. Seibert suggests that there has been hesitance in terms of studies concerned with Herz because of this continuous vein of interest.[41] However, there has also been continuous interest in Rahel, and she has been given substantially more academic

---

[37]Barbara Becker-Cantarino, "Zur Theorie der literarischen Freundschaft im 18. Jahrhundert. Zu ihren traditionalen Voraussetzungen," in *Frauenfreundschaft-Männerfreundschaft: literarische Dikurse im 18. Jahrhundert,* ed. Wolfram Mauser and Barbara Becker-Cantarino (Tübingen: Max Niemeyer Verlag, 1991), 69f.

[38]Silvia Bovenschen, *Die imaginierte Weiblichkeit. Exemplarische Untersuchungen zu kulturgeschichlichen und literarischen Präsentationsformen des Weiblichen* (Frankfurt: 1979). Cf. Seibert, "Forschungsüberblick," 207.

[39]Dena Goodman, "Enlightenment Salons: The Convergence of Female and Philosophic Ambitions," *Eighteenth-Century Studies* 22 (spring 1989): 329–50, esp. 331f.

[40]Seibert, "Henriette Herz: Erinnerungen."

[41]Ibid., 38.

attention than Herz.

Such uninterrupted interest has generally not stopped female figures from being supposedly rediscovered. Writing about artists, Whitney Chadwick states, "[d]espite regular exhibitions, Gwen John (1876–1939), like [Suzanne] Valadon, was until recently most often presented as 'unknown,' to be regularly 'rediscovered' by subsequent generations of curators and critics."[42] Elsewhere, Seibert questions the use of the "Wieder [Re-]" in *Rahel Levin Varnhagen. Die Wiederentdeckung einer Schriftstellerin (The Rediscovery of an Authoress)*,[43] which was the 1987 title given to the published papers of an extremely influential symposium held in Turin the previous year. On the one hand, this subtitle can be defended in terms that its view of Rahel as a writer is new. On the other, the appeal of published proceedings that would provide information on someone forgotten must have influenced the choice of title. Just as with the painters mentioned by Chadwick, such a supposed rediscovery undermines the position of someone like Rahel Levin Varnhagen and presents her as having been more marginalized than she actually was or even as having been totally forgotten. Such a rediscovery, then, is part of a patriarchal structure that actively places a productive and acknowledged female figure such as Rahel into the category of lost or forgotten.

The same would be true if in this study I were to present Henriette Herz as a forgotten figure. The continuous interest in her autobiographical sketches detailed by Seibert illuminates a fairly seamless tradition of interest, even though the present study is the first monograph other than the various editions of her edited memoirs to give such concentrated attention to Herz.

1.2.3. Authorship and Social Network Theory

In order to illuminate the profound significance of Herz and her salon for Schleiermacher's thinking in 1799, I will place Friedrich Schleiermacher's *Essay on a Theory of Sociable Behavior* into the very specific context of the social networks within which it was produced. This placement can most readily be seen as constructing the intellectual space in which Schleiermacher was moving at the time

---

[42]Whitney Chadwick, *Women, Art and Society* (London: Thames and Hudson, 1990), 275.
[43]Seibert, "Forschungsüberblick," 175.

of the composition of the *Essay*. In the examination of this intellectual space, I will make close reference to a number of social institutions and debates that constitute what we can now reconstruct of that intellectual environment. Working from textual sources, I will establish the immediate environment in which the *Essay* and Schleiermacher operated and which is the intellectual surroundings in which meanings were constituted and constructed. Taking such an immediate and close-knit view of the intellectual environment of the *Essay* will facilitate my examination of this work within a tightly fixed intrapersonal and intratextual environment in which meanings are constituted by specific individuals with specific viewpoints. Thus, the vagaries of intellectual historical approaches that draw on such concepts as the spirit of the age and the general social forces will not play a role here. Historical information commensurate with such approaches will, however, play a role in this study, but only when such information is drawn from the very specific environment delimited by the institutions and debates relevant to the social networks in operation here.

Perhaps first in significance of these institutions is what is now known as the salon. We know Schleiermacher frequented the social gatherings in the home of Henriette Herz, and from various sources including, but certainly not limited to, memoirs and correspondence, a close interaction can be deduced. This book thus also marks a first self-reflexive moment for social network theory in textual studies, as I investigate the constitution of what has so far been the source of its material information: the discursive communities that are synonymous with salon interaction.

Social network theory enables me to structure this book in such a way as to place the production of Schleiermacher's *Essay* in a broad, but nonetheless specific, field of ideas. The *Essay*, thus, becomes a focal point of influences, the most concrete of these influences being the acknowledged author. Schleiermacher exists in a network of influences that we learn about; these networks include the people with whom he is known to have associated, his other literary works, and his library that is a source of his readings. This intellectual environment is what constitutes the author of the *Essay*, at least as far as my perspective in this book as a piece of early-twenty-first-century intellectual historiography is concerned, In short, Schleiermacher is completely synonymous with his intellectual environment. Social network analysis permits us to draw on the sociable circles as the foundation of the ideas developed in the texts: Schleiermacher is, consequently, no extrahistorical genius, but rather a member of a group of individuals, each contributing to the meanings and interpretations that find their way into the final text.

Herz's role in this regard cannot be overemphasized. As a leading figure in the singularly most significant salon that Schleiermacher is known to have frequented, she takes on a position that brings her into such close proximity to the writing of the *Essay* that her intellectual environment can be seen as providing input to it.

Perhaps one of the most potent arguments for the significance of this Schleiermacher - Herz connection is the incomplete nature of the *Essay*, which was published in two sections in the January and February 1799 editions of the journal *Berlinisches Archiv für die Zeit und ihres Geschmacks*. At least one more section was to follow, and although some ideas for the continuation exist in note form,[44] it never appeared. In February Schleiermacher had moved a few miles from Berlin to Potsdam to substitute for a minister there; he stayed until May. Meckenstock, the editor of the *Essay* in the *Kritische Gesamtausgabe*, indicates in his notes that Schleiermacher broke off work on the *Essay* because of his lack of company. Vigorous correspondence between Schleiermacher and Herz took place, and in a letter dated February 14, Schleiermacher laments that lack of company: "I have read one of Plato's dialogues, I have done a little piece on religion, I have written letters. In short, I have tried everything but the good way of life—and what should I do with that without company?"[45] This lament very much sets up the context for the broken-off work. Plato is mentioned, *On Religion* takes over as a task, and the emphasis is clearly on Schleiermacher's lack of company.

Schleiermacher's *On Religion* is often the subject of his correspondence with Herz; he wants to hear her opinion and her commentary, but nonetheless, he pursues his task quietly in social exile. With the *Essay* the situation is different. His work stops completely without Herz's proximity, and this cessation indicates that she was more of a necessary component to producing the *Essay* than she was for *On Religion*. For the *Essay* to have progressed, the interaction would have had to have been greater. Since this interaction was not possible, the project terminated. Certainly, this

---

[44] These are in the first *Gedankenhefte* (*Notebooks of Thoughts*). Between nos. 92 and –117, there are numerous indications by means of marginal jottings that some of these notes belong to a third part ("zu III"). Other notes from the *Notebooks* found their way into the published section of the *Essay*. See *KGA*, I/2, 26–29. Cf., ibid., lii.

[45] *Herz*, 281.

view is what Schleiermacher's comments are at pains to construct.

There is, however, another interpretation to explore concerning the abandoning of the *Essay*. This view is a revisionist take on the concept of "author." The author is not an isolated genius performing miraculous acrobatic feats of the mind, nor is he or she a medium with his or her spirit in tune with the ethereal soul of the age. Such notions are entirely anathema to a theory seeking to pinpoint precise references in the history of ideas. While, on the one hand, this revisionism can be seen as a kind of social positivism, on the other, social network theory has a keen sense of history as a narrative construct. In this book I will seek to illuminate the construction of salon activity as a narrative in the *Essay* and texts with which it can be linked. I draw upon all connections and information that could be construed as positivist to explain what the authors and involved individuals experienced in their immediate environments.

Schleiermacher's *Essay* appeared when the author was working on a number of other projects, all of which contribute to an illumination of Schleiermacher's environment at this time. His response to the story of the affair between Friedrich Schlegel and Dorothea Veit appeared both in a review of the work *Lucinde* and in the longer *Vertraute Briefe über Friedrich Schlegels Lucinde* (*Confidential Letters on Friedrich Schlegel's Lucinde*) of 1799. At the same time Schleiermacher also published a contribution to an ongoing debate on Jewish emancipation and a review of Kant's *Anthropologie in pragmatischer Hinsicht* (1799). All of these projects can be shown to be of significance for Schleiermacher's position on the salon. They contribute to the marking out of the intertextual space in which the *Essay* operates.

Schleiermacher's interest in the salon is, however, not restricted to the fixed date of the *Essay*, 1799. In 1806 his novella *Die Weihnachtsfeier* (*Christmas Eve*), his only fictional work, appeared. This work is a series of conversations among family and friends based on salon interactions. As a work that projects the possible practical reality of salon interaction, it takes up a position in Schleiermacher's oeuvre that the theoretical and philosophical works of a later date do not share. For this reason I will make an exception by drawing on this later work to explore his earlier considerations in the *Essay*.

We are also fortunate to have a record of the contents of Schleiermacher's library at his death in 1834.[46] While this record does not exhaust the possibility of what he might have read at the time of his involvement in the salon, it provides valuable corroboration that particular texts were a focus of his interest at some point in his life. These works then, along with Schleiermacher's and Herz's extending network of friends and antagonists, provide the initial points of reference for an examination of the *Essay* within the social network of its composition.

As far as reception of this work goes, there is much less that can be done with the *Essay* in social networks. The *Essay* was published anonymously and not acknowledged to be a work by Schleiermacher until the early twentieth century when its authorship was discovered by Hermann Nohl as part of the project by Otto Braun and Johannes Bauer to publish between 1910 and 1913 a selection of Schleiermacher's selected writings.[47] Thus, it is not surprising that there is no significant indication of the reception by Schleiermacher's contemporaries of this work.[48]

However, the *Essay* is a single marker in the construction of the institution of the salon itself, and the reception of the salon can at least be followed within the social networks existing at the time. Thus, the purview of my book is not limited to Schleiermacher's *Essay* but extends to other works involved in the construction of the salon in debates of the period. Still, my emphasis will be on Herz's salon since it is with this specific context for the *Essay* of her salon that I will proceed.

1.3. "Salon" as a Pejorative Term

In their own time, what we now call "literary salons" were known variously as "tea evenings," "tea societies," "a house," or just by the name of the host family in whose home the gathering took place. Salons grew out of the more formal academic or reading societies and took over some of the latter's roles. While the academic

---

[46]Günter Meckenstock, *Schleiermachers Bibliothek: Bearbeitung des faksimilierten Rauschen Auktionskatalogs und der Hauptbücher des Verlages G. Reimer.* Schleiermacher-Archiv, vol. 10 (Berlin: de Gruyter, 1993).

[47]*Schleiermachers Werke*, ed. Otto Braun and Johannes Bauer (Leipzig: Meiner, 1910–1913). Cf. *KGA*, I/2, liii.

[48]The only remarkable exception is the response of sociologist Georg Simmel, who seems to have taken on board some of Schleiermacher's ideas on sociability at the time of their rediscovery by Nohl.

societies with state legitimation grew into something new—most notably the university of Berlin—the reading societies were gradually replaced by the salons, which took over reading while mixing this activity with lighter forms of entertainment, such as tableaux vivants, musical and other performances, and various parlor games. Such salons continued into the twentieth century, eventually to die out except for the rare musical soiree or at-home of European households.

In this study I will examine the particular situation of Jewish salons of late-eighteenth-century Berlin. I will also examine the narrative that was constructed around these events in an environment in which Jews had become economically a part but which still marginalized them.

The concord between assimilation and this kind of sociability is found in the person of silk manufacturer Moses Mendelssohn (1729–1786), one of the leading proponents of social integration of the Jews into Berlin society. He was a writer and a thinker of some standing who believed in the principle of religion based on reason that would bring Jew and Christian together in a spirit of enlightened tolerance.[49] Mendelssohn's activities made him a leading figure in the Enlightenment in Berlin: it was his essay that came first in the series of replies to the question concerning the meaning of enlightenment; Immanuel Kant's "What is Enlightenment?" came second.[50]

Mendelssohn opened his household for evenings of entertainment that were based loosely on the reading-society model. However, he focused on the opening up of his family sphere to welcome like-minded spirits.[51] His wife and daughters were

---

[49] David Sorkin, *The Transformation of German Jewry 1780–1840* (Oxford: Oxford University Press, 1987), 161.

[50] Kant's "Answer to the Question: What is Enlightenment?" appeared in the November and December issues of the *Berlinische Monatsschrift* of 1784. On Mendelssohn's essay, see Norbert Hinske, "Mendelssohns Beantwortung der Frage Was heisst Aufklärung? Oder Über die Aktualität Mendelssohns," in *Ich handle mit Vernunft: Moses Mendelssohn und die europäische Aufklärung* (Hamburg: Meiner, 1981), 85–117. This debate was sparked by a question in the footnote of an article in the December 1783 issue of the *Berliner Monatsschrift* by the Berlin pastor Johann Friedrich Zöllner. Moses Mendelssohn contributed frequently to the *Berliner Monatsschrift*. The preponderance of defenses of the Enlightenment led to the journal being equated with the Berlin Enlightenment clique ("Berlinischen Aufklärungsclique," or "Aufklärungsbande"). It is interesting to note that the participation of Mendelssohn and other Jews in the *Berliner Monatsschrift* likely brought about the nickname for the journal as "Berliner Aufklärungssynagoge." Ehrhard Bahr, ed., *Was ist Aufklärung* (Stuttgart: Reclam, 1974), 72. This kind of pejorative jocularity is entirely in the vein of the argument offered below that seeks to explain the movement of the term "salon" from commercial uses to the social sphere.

[51] Feilchenfeldt, "Die Berliner Salons der Romantik.".

involved, and daughter Brendel (later known as Dorothea) went on to become one of the leading lights in the Romantic salons of Berlin. The main figures involved in this sociable culture were members of an economic elite within the Jewish community[52] who aspired to an interaction of this nature with gentile fellows in order to exhibit in their homes a form of leisurely pursuit common to all of their economic status regardless of ethnic origin or religious identification.

At the meetings in the Mendelssohn home, Brendel shared the company of two young Jewish women of her generation, Rahel Levin and Henriette Herz. Rahel was the daughter of a wealthy banker and jeweler, while Herz was the daughter of a university-educated physician Benjamin de Lemos and the wife of another physician, Markus Herz, who was also a famed student of Kant's.[53] These two women later ran the two most famous salons of Romantic-era Berlin.

Herz was a member of this group by virtue of her education and background: physicians were among the first to gain education outside the Jewish community in order to possess the qualifications needed to ply their trade. The encouragement her father gave her to read and write was continued by her husband after her marriage at fifteen (Markus at that time was thirty-two). The Levins also had acquired the trappings of the leisured—and therefore also implicitly cultured—classes, with an ostentatious home and with Markus Levin even having his daughter's portrait painted by the admired artist Chodowiecki.[54]

The first contacts with the gentile elites is thought to have derived from such men as Markus Levin who turned meetings with clients into social events.[55] A recollection from Henriette Herz's memoirs helps to underscore the significance of the connection between the trappings of culture and these business transactions. When the businessmen-fathers lent sums to the members of the gentile elite, the daughters took advantage of these transactions to develop and indulge an important social skill, the speaking of French: "Their aim was mainly to converse in the language of fashion with the court cavaliers and good-looking officers who only

---

[52]Hertz, *Jewish High Society*, 192–93. See also Steven M. Lowenstein, *The Berlin Jewish Community: Enlightenment, Family and Crisis, 1770–1830* (Oxford: Oxford University Press, 1994), 235f., 235n. 15.
[53]Davies, *Identity or History?* 20.
[54]Heidi Thomann Tewarson, *Rahel Varnhagen* (Hamburg: Rowohlt, 1988), 14f.
[55]Ibid., 14.

repaid the money borrowed from the fathers in attention paid to the daughters."[56] Clearly, Herz couches the acquiring of culture in the terms of a transaction, and in so doing, the value of the interaction is diminished. Implicit in Herz's comment is that true free sociability has quite a different character and must be made distant from such commercial contextualizations.

The definition of free sociability is one dimension of the task Schleiermacher sets for himself in his *Essay on a Theory of Sociable Behavior*. One element, he states, must be removed from good conversation: the subject matter of the business world. He in fact writes that sociability has the "goal of lifting a person out of the viewpoint of his or her profession for a time."[57] However, this distancing is not what invariably happened in the salon. People tended to "crystallize themselves into little circles according to classes as if some unconscious chemical attraction were driving them."[58] While the *Essay* is in nature mostly prescriptive, it draws on experience of salon conversation, and thus, Schleiermacher goes on to comment that "better sociability comes about under the eyes and upon the direction of women."[59]

As noted above, Schleiermacher's *Essay* is based on his experience of the salon of Henriette Herz. He struck up an enduring and significant exchange with her in letters and in his frequent visits to her home. The very fact that the men had to attend to the matters of the business world meant that they were less well prepared to contribute to good sociable conversation, and they thus tended to undermine interaction by discussing the world of work, a practice that inevitably excluded certain individuals from the discussion. When Schleiermacher mentions occupations as examples of this destructive tendency, he names the merchant (*Kaufmann*), the professional farmer (*Landwirth*), and the financier (*Financier*).[60] The second occupation clearly excluded Jews owing to the property laws of the time, but the other two were occupations that Jews of the economic elite either could carry out, as in the case of the merchant, or the financier. Clearly, Schleiermacher harbors an awareness of certain characteristics of sociability, and their connection with the world of Jewish business in particular, with which his *Essay* indirectly takes issue. Indeed, these characteristics are popular pejorative aimed at Jewish salons.

---

[56] *Herz*, 63.
[57] *KGA*, I/2, 178.
[58] Ibid.
[59] Ibid.
[60] Ibid., 177.

In order to examine how this popular pejorative connotation shaped the use of the term "salon," we must first look at the history of the use of the word "salon" to describe sociable gathering. The origin and use of this term has been much debated. There are, of course, the old stories of its association with a particular room the "salon," especially the salon bleu of Madame de Rambouillet of the second quarter of the seventeenth century. Seibert's 1993 study on the literary salon follows the derivation of the term through the aristocratic courts of Italy, Spain, and France.[61] The term is clearly associated with entertainment for representational purposes. Through a careful examination of correspondence between Rahel Levin and Gustav Brinckmann, Seibert shows that the former assiduously avoids the use of the term "salon" to describe her gatherings; she prefers to write of aesthetic or sociable teas.

The term "salon" does not come into use to describe this form of sociability in Germany until later in the nineteenth century, and plans of Rahel's home clearly label her salon as a *Wohnzimmer*, or living room. It is in a perplexed tone that Petra Wilhelmy's extensive and thoroughly researched study of the salons of Berlin remarks on the use of the term "salon." According to her research, the word is documented in 1798 only for the commercial contexts of the *Hotelsalon*, a hotel lounge, and the *Frisiersalon*, a hairdresser's salon. It is not until 1829 that the term is used to describe the members of a group who meet for this kind of sociability; it is then retrospectively applied to earlier sociability.[62]

I would like to suggest that the very commercial terms just mentioned indicate that "salon" gains its usage in Germany from original pejorative application to Jewish salons. My proposal underscores the very link these households made between business and pleasure. Mixing business with pleasure as a major faux pas appears to be more than just a commonplace. A stridently anti-semitic Berlin journal article of 1802 contains a passage concerning the particular *Geldgeiz*, or a mean and rapacious desire for money of the Jews in which the following connection is made to sociable behavior:

> Ever since money has become a general sign, the Jew has had to seek out the very sources of income that bring him into possession of this sign the most quickly. But how unfortunate he is in this situation that limits him to trade. Nothing remains for him but refinement of his own exclusive advantage.

---

[61] Seibert, *Der literarische Salon*, 8–24.
[62] Wilhelmy, *Der Berliner Salon*, 18.

But, this destroys all free sociality and makes him alternately the object of fear or reproach.[63]

Just as in Schleiermacher's *Essay*, this anti-semitic piece emphasizes the negative influence work has on sociability. In the above passage, in particular, it is the work of lending money that makes Jews unacceptable.

In reality, however, the very opposite was the case. Through their work and economic status, the Jews began to have contact with gentiles, and through Jews taking the opportunity for interaction with their clients, the very basis for social interaction came into being. The above article appeared in a journal edited by Ignaz Feßler, a close associate of Henriette Herz's husband. It was Feßler's Mittwochs-Gesellschaft that had originally brought forth Henriette's tea circle that eventually developed into her salon. Therefore, it can be readily assumed that such notions would have been common currency within these circles.

The very fact that Herz's autobiography is a source for the anecdotal evidence I gave above concerning the daughters of certain Jewish businessmen engaging their father's young gentlemen customers in polite French conversation indicates that she had a particular axe to grind in this ideological debate. Although she is also Jewish, she is careful to distance herself from this bound sociability in which the male customers are under some obligation to their female conversational partners. Her narrative carefully constructs a kind of Jewish sociability that is distant from the ostentatious homes in which many Jews lived and entertained.

Herz's most significant predecessor in matters of sociability is clearly Moses Mendelssohn, in whose home she was a guest. A noteworthy anecdote she recounts recalling entertainments in his home serves to highlight the limited means of his household.

> Mendelssohn practiced this extended hospitality, despite the family having to restrict itself because of this hospitality, whereby the material comforts that his house offered to its guests were, nonetheless, not permitted to transcend

---

[63]"Seitdem das Geld allgemeines Zeichen geworden ist, hat der Jude gerade diejenigen Erwerbsquellen aufsuchen müssen, welche ihn am schnellsten in den Besitz dieses Zeichens setzen.... Aber wie unglücklich ist er in dieser Lage, da sie ihn nur auf Handel einschränkt? Nichts bleibt ihm übrig, als Raffinement auf seinen ausschließenden Vorteil. Dies aber vernichtet alle freie Socialität, und macht ihn abwechselnd zum Gegenstande der Furcht und der Verachtung." Philaleth [Pseudonym], "Die Juden," in *Eunomia. Eine Zeitschrift des neunzehnten Jahrhunderts. Von einer Gesellschaft von Gelehrten.* ed. [Ignaz] Feßler and Fischer, Zweiter Jahrgang (1802), vol. 2 "IV Zeichen der Zeit," 336.

> the limits of the strictest moderation. As a close friend of the daughter, I knew that, before the salvers were brought into the reception room, the good mistress of the house would count raisins and almonds, at that time a snack de rigueur, onto the salvers in a relationship determined by the number of guests.[64]

Herz is careful to emphasize the limited means of the Mendelssohn household, although the example given appears a ridiculous intricacy or an eccentric habit. But what is most important is that this household draws the best guests and "makes a house" and sets the definition for sociability of this nature. The sentence defining this sociability ends with the comment "and according to his external calling, this individual belonged to the ranks of merchants [*dem Kaufmannsstande*]." She continues: "The house of this excellent man, whose income as chief manager of a silk-retailing business combined with the proceeds of his literary works were still of little consequence and who was responsible for the care of six children, was, nevertheless, an open house."[65] The veracity of these comments should not be the subject of our inquiry here. There appears to be a necessity to construct some kind of narrative that allows Mendelssohn a significant intellectual sociability in spite of his belonging to the ranks of merchants. The narrative of the poverty of the family as an ascetic intellectualism requires careful construction in the face of and despite Mendelssohn's position as a merchant.

Another instance of this rhetorical strategy is to be found in Rahel's term for her first salon *die Dachstube*, or the attic room. The construction of the idea that Rahel's salon was another ascetic intellectual realm is a notion that is repeated throughout the literature. As recently as 1994, Steven Lowenstein in his *Berlin Jewish Community* comments as follows on Rahel's first salon: "Although she came from a wealthy family, her salon was anything but luxurious. She prided herself on the naturalness and simplicity of her gatherings, which she referred to as gatherings in her attic (Dachstube)."[66] I suggest that the very naturalness and simplicity of her gatherings are, to cite Lowenstein again, the result of "the immortaliz[ation] by her husband in various publications."[67] Evidence to the contrary of this avowed

---

[64]*Herz*, 65.
[65]Ibid.
[66]Lowenstein, *The Berlin Jewish Community*, 106.
[67]Ibid.

simplicity can be derived from the fact that Rahel is forced to reduce her activities when the financial situation of the family changes. With the death of her father and the decline in the fortunes of Prussia owing to its defeat by Napoleon, the family business becomes debt-ridden. Tewarson admits that Rahel had not only entertained in her attic apartment but also in the reception rooms of the family residence in the Jägerstraße.[68] For a while, she maintained this household herself, but later she moved into a smaller home of her own. It was not until she was married that she could set up entertainment that came anywhere close to what had been the case in her father's home. Evidently, such entertainment was not without cost and was not as simple as fabled.

Clearly, a sociable connection between the Jews and their gentile clients is initiated by wealthy Jewish businessmen. As time passed, the connections develop a momentum of their own. Criticism of sociability on the basis of business connections becomes rife, and it is in the face of these criticisms that Rahel Levin's and Henriette Herz's salons become eulogized as simple ascetic realms, in which true free sociability excludes the subject matter of trade. I suggest that this view is a narrative carefully constructed to counteract critical voices that are intended to undermine the intellectualism of this kind of sociability. While Seibert concludes that Rahel wished to find a term that adequately described her intimate uncourtly gatherings, I propose that she carefully constructed an alternative to a perceived representational role connected with business, which was placed under erasure by the use of the term "aesthetic tea." To construct this narrative, she distanced her gatherings from the term "salon" that in the 1790s was used only in connection with commercial spheres. When Schleiermacher conceives of the salon, he positively opposes the connection between business and sociability, and he looks much further afield to establish a tradition for free sociability.

---

[68]Tewarson, *Rahel Varnhagen*, 29; "in den Levinschen Gesellschaftsräumen und Rahels Dachstube in der Jägerstraße."

2. Henriette Herz's Salon

Although the Jewish salons of Berlin were facilitated by the particulars of the social and economic position of Jews in Berlin in the eighteenth century, they sought to comprehend themselves within a broader set of traditions. Schleiermacher stands within interpretive schemes that reach back all the way to classical models for inspiration in talking about the salon. This chapter will explore the traditions and influences that formed Schleiermacher's and Henriette Herz's perceptions of their shared sociable gatherings. It is important to remember that these perceived traditions informed and shaped the way in which Herz and Schleiermacher described their experience of fashionable sociability at the end of the eighteenth century.

2.1. Perceptions of Tradition

2.1.1. Symposium

Schleiermacher's strong interest in classical ideas found a focus in his translation of the works of Plato. This project, conceived with Friedrich Schlegel as a joint endeavor, had originated in 1798 from discussions between the two men in which Plato recurred as a frequent subject.[1] Ultimately, it was Schleiermacher who delivered on the published proposals with a series of translations appearing between 1804 and 1828.

Schleiermacher's *Christmas Eve* of 1806 contains similar allusions to

---

[1]Letter to August Böckh 18 June 1808. Cf. Friedrich Wilhelm Kantzenbach, *Friedrich Daniel Ernst Schleiermacher*, Rowohlts Monographien 126 (Reinbeck bei Hamburg: Rowohlt, 1967), 45.

classical philosophy as he makes in his letter to Henriette Herz mentioned in the previous chapter. This novella constitutes the practical equivalent to the *Essay*, which is entirely theoretical. Although later in date than the *Essay*, *Christmas Eve* is very much a part of the complex of Schleiermacher's preoccupation with the issue of the conventions of conversation and can help illuminate the background to the *Essay*.

Hermann Patsch has produced a very valuable study of the nature of such classical allusions found in *Christmas Eve*.[2] Intimations of content of this classical nature were provided for an insider of the intellectual community to recognize and thus to have the feeling of being included. Among others, several allusions to Plato's *Symposium* occur. In what follows, I will make the connection between the *Symposium* and what is conceived of both broadly among the cultured of the period and more specifically among Schleiermacher and his associates as being the tradition within which the salon existed. This section will, thus, provide further information concerning the construction of tradition.

Writing in 1913, Sabine Lepsius lamented the decline of salons and emphasized the loss of tradition: "Cultural values can only be maintained if tradition is fostered and simultaneously is adapted to the needs of the times. If tradition is forcibly reduced to rubble and one forces the sensational instead, then barbarity and chaos come about."[3] While her reasons for the decline of salons focus on the mechanization of society and the change in values brought about by that process, one of her chief complaints concerns the change in the status of women.[4] According to Lepsius, women no longer seek fulfillment in the salon, but rather go out to seek it in work. Yet, it was the very balance between men and women that made the salon such a good social model.

When describing the missing balance between "male objectivity and female spontaneity…that is lacking in the gentlemen's dinner and the ladies' café," Lepsius justifies her statement by turning to the classical past: "The Greeks were the first to recognize the absolute necessity of female natures for higher culture; this is what

---

[2] Hermann Patsch, "Die esoterische Kommunikationsstruktur der 'Weihnachtsfeier.' Über Anspielungen und Zitate," in *Schleiermacher in Context. Papers from the 1988 International Symposium on Schleiermacher at Herrnhut, the German Democratic Republic*, ed. Ruth Drucilla Richardson, Schleiermacher: Studies-and-Translations, vol. 6 (Lewiston: Edwin Mellen Press, 1991), 132–56.
[3] Sabine Lepsius, "Über das Aussterben der Salons," *März* 7 (1913): 228.
[4] Cf. von der Heyden-Rynsch, *Europäische Salons*, 180–83.

brought about the change of a portion of their men into women."[5] Thus, Greek homosexuality is explained with reference to sociability requiring female natures to complement those of the men, thereby providing a nice justification for Greek homosexuality. While this statement in no way reflects role positions afforded men by Greek homosexuality, it reveals a great deal with respect to Lepsius's view of ancient Greek sociability. As an ideal of highbrow interaction, ancient Greek sociability is used as a significant reference point and measure of good sociability. Good sociability and homosexuality are combined in one significant dialogue,

The *Symposium,* unconsciously or consciously, contributes to Lepsius's view of the Greeks. No other work is so explicit concerning both what constitutes good conversational entertainment in the home and issues of homosexual love. The latter is the subject matter of the debate of this piece. The term "symposium" is the generic term for a formalized entertainment of the ancient Greeks.[6] No matter how mistaken about the status of homosexuality Lepsius might be, this dialogue by Plato can be seen to act as a benchmark in her perception of what constitutes a high level in the culture of sociability.

Lepsius attempts to introduce a feminine aspect to Greek sociability that she sees as excluding women. Similarly, Schlegel had been encouraged by Caroline Schlegel-Schelling to examine the status of women in classical times, and it is out of this interest that his piece *Über die Diotima* on Diotima was written in 1795.[7] Diotima is a character interjected into the *Symposium* by means of a dialogue within the dialogue narrated by Socrates. In this way, she, as the only female, makes a contribution to the superior dialogue on love. The project of Schlegel's *Über die Diotima* is to flesh out this marginal figure and to draw conclusions concerning the status of women in Greek society.

According to Schlegel, the common conception of most readers of the *Symposium* is that, in order to have acquired education and to have associated freely with men, Diotima must have been an *hetaira,*[8] a member of a class of women who

---

[5]Lepsius, "Über das Aussterben der Salons," 232.
[6]Michael J. Vickers, *Greek Symposia* (London: Joint Association of Classical Teachers, 1978).
[7]Baerbel Becker-Cantarino, "Schlegels *Lucinde.* Zum Frauenbild der Romantik," *Colloquia Germanica* 10 (1976/77): 130.
[8]Friedrich Schlegel, *Über Diotima,* in *Kritische Friedrich-Schlegel-Ausgabe,* ed. Ernst Behler et al., vol. 1, part 1, Studien des Klassischen Altertums (München: Schoningh, 1979), 73 [= 48].

provided entertainment to men at symposia. The hetaira's entertainment entailed providing conversation, music, and sex. Schlegel argues, however, that Diotima was not a hetaira, but a woman of independent means who possessed learning. Had she been a hetaira, she would have appeared in the lists of such or would have been mentioned by anecdotalists.[9]

Schlegel is also at pains to promote the status of at least some of the known hetaira. Aspasia, who was closely connected with Pericles, the powerful leader of Athens, is praised as gaining public recognition and political influence.[10] Thus, Schlegel's goal is to achieve a general upgrading of the opinion of the status of women among the Greeks. Aspasia is likened to the more recent mistresses of monarchs who gained similar acknowledgment and power; Schlegel must have had Madame de Pompadour in mind. Aspasia is also praised as an artist who founded a school for the art of being a hetaira and, further, as someone with a great skill in and a teacher of rhetoric.[11] Against this background, Schlegel's Diotima takes on a significant position as an independent woman of intellect.

In Schlegel's hands, the *Symposium* becomes a work that supports a changing role for women in intellectual communities such as those frequented by Schlegel and Schleiermacher. However, I cannot emphasize enough that this new role concerns idealized types rather than real women.[12] I will examine this issue later in connection with the issue of sexuality in the salon. Schleiermacher's statement "that better sociability comes about under the eyes of and upon the direction of women"[13] is commensurate with these considerations.

Schleiermacher's *Christmas Eve* has a background similar to that of the *Symposium*, inasmuch as both works purport to record the conversations of individuals gathered in connection with a religious festival. For the *Symposium* a victory in association with the Lenaian Festival in Athens in 416 B.C.E. has given rise to the gathering.[14] Additionally, *Christmas Eve* contains an interjected dialogue

---

[9] Ibid., 80 [= 51].
[10] Ibid., 79 [= 51].
[11] Ibid., 78 [= 50].
[12] For an excellent exposition of Schlegel's use of idealized types, see Becker-Cantarino, "Schlegels *Lucinde.*"
[13] *KGA*, I/2, 178.
[14] Plato, *Symposium*, translated with introduction and notes by Alexander Nehamas and Paul Woodruff (Indianapolis: Hackett Publishing, 1984), xi.

that has a sufficient number of coinciding elements to conclude that the *Symposium* acted as model here.

Women also play an active role in Schleiermacher's *Christmas Eve*. At one point the decision is reached to choose a topic to discuss: "Good, if we have decided then to wait here the night conversing and with our glasses, then I think we owe the women a reply"[15] The terms under which the challenge is set out refer both to Schleiermacher's *Essay* and to Plato's *Symposium*: "Well, what do you say friends, should we not proceed in the English fashion, not to mention the ancient fashion to which we certainly are no strangers, and choose a subject for which each of us would be responsible to say something?"[16] Here, the reference is directly to the *Symposium* as the guiding principle for "the ancient fashion to which we are certainly no strangers"; in Plato's work it is Eryximachus who makes the suggestion to have an evening of conversation. After all have agreed not to make a drinking contest of it and to drink "only as much as pleased them," he says: "Let us instead spend our evening in conversation. If you are so minded, I would like to propose a subject."[17] The reference to glasses in *Christmas Eve* signals a connection to the decision to participate in moderate drinking, just as in the *Symposium*. Both works also follow the same formalized conversation, as in each, one individual proposes a subject for general discussion. Furthermore, as in the *Symposium*, the interjected piece is a set of speeches delivered by men only.

When it comes to Eduard's turn in *Christmas Eve*, he refers to "one better than I am, who has commented at a similar opportunity that the last are worst off no matter what the subject when speech is delivered in this manner."[18] In the *Symposium* Socrates comments at the end of the speech of Aristophanes: "That's because *you* did beautifully in the contest, Eryximachus. But if you ever get in my position I'll be in after Agathon's spoken so well, then you'll really be afraid. You'll be at your wit's end, as I am now."[19] Eduard's comment reaches out of the text and is a challenge to

---

[15] Friedrich Schleiermacher, *Die Weihnachtsfeier. Ein Gespräch*, in F.D.E. Schleiermacher, *Schriften aus der Hallenser Zeit 1804-1807*, ed. Hermann Patsch, Kritische Gesamtausgabe I/5, ed. Hermann Fischer et al. (Berlin / New York: Walter de Gruyter, 1995), 83. Hereafter cited as *KGA* I/5.
[16] Ibid.
[17] *Symposium* 176E, Nehamas and Woodruff, 7.
[18] *KGA* I/5, 94.
[19] *Symposium* 194A, Nehamas and Woodruff, 30.

the reader to recognize the similarity to the *Symposium*.[20]

Another reference to the *Symposium* occurs shortly after this discourse is set up when Leonhardt starts his speech: "One can glorify and worship each and every thing in two ways. Once in that one praises it or acknowledges its type and inner nature as good, and on the other hand, one can boast about it or emphasize its excellence or completeness of character."[21] The *Symposium* also contains a discourse on praising in which Socrates contrasts these two aspects: "In my foolishness, I thought you should tell the truth about whatever you praise.... But now it appears that this is not what it is to praise anything whatever; rather, it is to apply to the object the grandest and the most beautiful qualities."[22] Leonhardt has learned from the *Symposium* and chooses to follow the second of his options, which is what Socrates learns is the way one is required to speak on such occasions.

Schleiermacher differs from Plato in that women are significant members of the dialogue, and they affect the way the men are to speak. Concerning the issue of choosing a topic, Ernst says that they are to choose one "such that we do not in any sense forget the presence of the women, rather that we regard it as the most beautiful to be understood and praised by them."[23] While this statement appears condescending, it is entirely commensurate with and can be explained by referring to the *Essay*. The *Essay* comments on the significance of women being the presiders over conversation under whose auspices the best form of sociability comes about: "Here I cannot help but make a comment; is it not true that better sociability comes about under the eyes of and upon the direction of women, and that this is, like so many other excellent matters in the affairs of humans, a consequence of exigency?"[24]

Schleiermacher is seeking to create a position for women in intellectual circles but in a rather different manner from that of Schlegel's Diotima. Women here

---

[20] Hermann Patsch refers to this point of reference as the esoteric structure of communication in Schleiermacher's novella, with Eduard's comment being one of two points Patsch uses to show reference to the *Symposium*. Indeed, to a general reader, the reference is esoteric and belongs with many other allusions throughout the text that are intended to challenge the reader who belongs to the initiated and, thus, will recognize what is being indicated. While taking some important initial impulses from Patsch, I differ in finding more references to the *Symposium* and in giving them a significant status in shaping the view of conversation.

[21] *KGA* I/5, 84.
[22] *Symposium* 198Df, Nehamas and Woodruff, 38.
[23] *KGA* I/5, 83.
[24] *KGA*, I/2, 178.

are regulators who fall readily into the line of descendent from Aspasia, who as a teacher is a facilitator for others. Further discussion in the *Essay* positions women as an instance of control by means of which topics do not run into the humdrum of daily business and political life. Consequently, topics retain a general validity and are accessible to the widest possible group.

A last point that connects the *Symposium*, *Christmas Eve*, and the *Essay* is Leonhardt's scurrilous speech. In this passage he is similar to Alcibiades whose provocative speech in praise of Socrates turns out to fit very well into the round on love. The scurrilous nature of Leonhardt's speech fulfills one of the significant demands of good sociability made by Schleiermacher in the *Essay*:

> It really is essential to the perfection of a society that its members diverge from one another in their opinion of the subject and in their manner of dealing with it in as many ways as possible. It is only thus that the subject can be exhausted in regard to sociability and the character of the society can be entirely developed.[25]

Fredericke objects to the way in which Leonhardt has made her look laughable by the "manner of his argument."[26] However, Eduard comes to the latter's defense, saying that Leonhardt has spoken like a legal counsel and praising the "way in which he has woven the disparaging together with intention to affirm."[27] Further, Ernestine commends Leonhardt for fulfilling the promise to stay away from what they would hear in church the next day. As Leonhardt has spoken in a manner that diverges so much from the others, he has helped to develop the character of the group and has contributed to the exhaustion of the subject in regard to its sociability.

Thus, Leonhardt has stayed entirely within the bounds of the rules for good sociability. What Schleiermacher terms the tone of the group is its character as determined by the subject matter. This principle is set down in the *Essay*'s rule of propriety (*Schicklichkeit*): "I must observe the tone of the society, and with regard to the material, I should allow myself to be guided and limited by that society.... Nevertheless, I remain at liberty to allow my individual manner to reign entirely free."[28] In this manner Leonhardt and Alcibiades give similar speeches: both stay

---
[25]Ibid., 175.
[26]*KGA* I/5, 88.
[27]Ibid., 88f.
[28]*KGA*, I/2, 174.

within the bounds of the subject matter of the group, and yet both allow their unique dispositions to color their respective speeches. We can see that the rules Schleiermacher has developed in some way explain the status of the *Symposium* as the high culture of sociability. If other gatherings can be made to fit the rules that apply to the *Symposium*, then those gatherings also have claim to appraisal as the high culture of sociability. The tradition in which Schleiermacher places his sociability clearly bears reference to ancient Greek sociability, at least as it appears in the philosophical dialectics in general and the *Symposium* in particular.

2.1.2. Renaissance Texts

In looking to ancient Greek models, Schleiermacher was following the example of many writers of the Enlightenment who, in turn, were continuing a tradition reaching back to the Renaissance. A work that concerns itself with dialogue and good manners and that acknowledges its debt to classical material is Baldasar Castiglione's *Il libro del Cortegiano*, or *The Book of the Courtier*, published in 1528.[29] Peter Burke's recent study on the reception and influence of Castiglione's work, *The Fortunes of the Courtier*, indicates the breadth of the influence of Castiglione's work on subjects of manners and conversation throughout Europe, not only in the sixteenth century but also well into the eighteenth.

While the *Book of the Courtier* is definitively a work concerned with the court, its readership went beyond purely aristocratic circles as it had many bourgeois readers. One way of seeing the connection between Castiglione's book and sociability is to view the text as a model or guide for sociable games. Indeed, the dialogues in the *Book of the Courtier* are supposed to be models with which the users of the text could craft their own dialogues. The justification for the suggestion that the *Book of the Courtier* was actually used as a model for games is derived from texts

---

[29] *The Book of the Courtier* declares itself to stand in the tradition of various classical precursors. Xenophon's *Education of Cyrus*; Plato's *Republic*, and Cicero's *Orator* are expressly mentioned in the text. Cf. Peter Burke, *The Fortunes of the Courtier: The European Reception of Castiglione's 'Cortegiano'* (University Park, Pa.: Pennsylvania State University Press, 1996), 82. Of course, other classical works are also mentioned that are not so obviously didactic in nature. One example is the story of Alcibiades from Plutarch's *Parallel Lives*.

that are manuals of conversational play intended for emulation. The realization of this goal and a development of this theme can be found in numerous works that take their lead from the *Book of the Courtier*. Thus, by the mid-sixteenth century in Italy, Innocenzio Ringhieri's *Cento giuochi liberali* (Bologna, 1551) and Scipione Bargagli's *Dialogo de' giuochi* (Venetia, 1574) had taken a game from the *Book of the Courtier* in which characters from the *Orlando Furioso* are discussed and made that game the basis for their own dialogues.

It is in this tradition that Schleiermacher's *Essay on a Theory of Sociable Behavior* also exists: the many references to the free play of thoughts or feelings in this work bear witness to this literary debt.[30] My goal in this section is to show how the connection can be made between Renaissance Italian traditions of sociability and those of Germany in the late eighteenth century, particularly with regard to Schleiermacher and Herz.

Along with the idea that these works are manuals for application of these dialogues is also the notion that they are pieces of literature in their own right. The veracity of dialogue is a topos associated with the genre of dialogue that goes back to classical times. An example of this topos is given in Plato's *Symposium* 172A–174A, in which Apollodorus tells his interlocutor that he was not present at the dialogue and that his knowledge of what went on is only mediated, though verified, by Socrates.[31] In the Renaissance dialogues, veracity is also an issue for most of the writers. For Castiglione, the dialogues took place at the court in Urbino, and Guazzo cites the oral testimony of the "Cavalier Bottazzo"[32] as the verifying instance.

The two notions, then, that the dialogues are, on the one hand, real reported events and, on the other, that they are guidelines to be emulated exist simultaneously. The concept of the dialogues as reports of real conversations supports their function as documents that supposedly verify the existence of conversational institutions. The idea that the dialogues are fiction supports their function and status with regard to the creation and maintenance of conversational institutions and as literary works in their

---

[30]*KGA*, I/2, 165, 170, 172, 176, 179.

[31]Aristodemus is the character referred to as the originator of the version of the speeches and dialogue that Apollodorus leaves for posterity; Plato is mentioned nowhere. Nehamas and Woodruff, 1–3.

[32]Stefano Guazzo, *La civil Conversatione del Signor S. G. Gentilhuomo di Casale Monferrato, Divisa in quattro Libri* (Vinegia, 1580), 167.

own right.

The most prominent popularizer in Germany of texts of Italian conversational games was Georg Philipp Harsdörffer (1607–1658). His *Playful Colloquies for the Ladies* appeared as a series of eight volumes between 1641 and 1649 and contained dialogues taken from various sources, the majority of which can be traced back to Italian Renaissance writers that include Castiglione, Guazzo, Ringhieri, and Bargagli.[33] Harsdörffer, however, does not frame his dialogues so as to make them appear to have really taken place.[34] Still, he does claim his collection to have real use in making conversation in sociable settings. In this way he uses the dialogues to prescribe conversational sociability in the same way Schleiermacher's *Essay* does a hundred and fifty years later. On the basis of his work on the *Playful Colloquies*, Harsdörffer was inducted into the Fruit-Bearing Society (*Fruchtbringende Gesellschaft*) under the pseudonym 'The Playing One' (*Der Spielende*).

The Fruit-Bearing Society was a German academy based on the model of the Accademia della Crusca, founded in Florence in 1582. Such academies had started to form in the fifteenth century, and almost every city had one,[35] with the Accademia della Crusca often being cited as the most important of them. According to its statutes of 1584, the Florentine academy's goal was to purify the vernacular language, for it the Italian of Tuscany: the institution's name even suggests the separation of the chaff (*crusca*) from the grain. Its members were to strive for the introduction of the vernacular language to science and literature and were to continue to develop the language. Foremost among its achievements was an edition of the works of Dante (1595) and a dictionary of Italian the *Vocabulario degli Accademii della Crusca* (Venice, 1612). It was upon this model that on August 24, 1617, the Fruit-Bearing Society was founded.

---

[33] Georg Philipp Harsdörffer, *Frauenzimmer Gesprächspiele*, ed. Imgard Böttcher, vol. 3 (Tübingen: Max Niemeyer Verlag, 1968), 101. Of 444 works cited by Harsdörffer, only 111 are written by Germans, whereas 134 are by Italians. Cf. Georg Adolf Narciss, *Studien zu den Frauenzimmergesprächspielen Georg Philipp Harsdörffers (1607–1658). Ein Beitrag zur Literaturgeschichte des 17. Jahrhunderts*, ed. Lutz Mackensen. Form und Geist Heft 5 (Leipzig: Hermann Eichblatt Verlag, 1928), 30 and 55ff. Even Harsdörffer's French models are in many cases dependent on Italian originals: 57.

[34] Rosmarie Zeller, *Spiel und Konversation im Barock. Untersuchung zu Harsdörffers "Gesprächspielen"* (Berlin: de Gruyter, 1974), 88f.

[35] The information provided here is much indebted to Karl F. Otto, *Die Sprachgesellschaften des 17. Jahrhunderts* (Stuttgart: Metzler, 1972), 7ff.

The very fact that we know this date so precisely draws attention to the intimate connection between institutions and texts. Still, we enter here a disputed territory in which issues of the connection between history and text need further evaluation: my inquiry will have consequences for the way in which we perceive the connection between the salon and those texts that are used to examine it.

In examining the Pegnitz Order of Flowers (*Pegnitzer Blumenorden*), which was a baroque society with some relationship to the Fruit-Bearing Society since both were connected to Harsdörffer, Jane Newman works through some important theoretical considerations of the link between history, text, and institution.[36] Her analysis can be brought to bear on other institutions of the period, such as the Fruit-Bearing Society, and her ideas can also be applied beyond the baroque to the salon.

What becomes evident from this application is the powerful role texts play in our perception of such institutions as these emergent societies. A problem Newman discerns with New Historicist methodologies is that they still have a fundamental dependence on the very dichotomy between text and history. Although theorists such as Stephen Greenblatt and Jonathan Goldberg have attempted to realign our understanding of what is real and what is imaginary as an interplay between the two, they, according to Newman, still "recall the previously dissolved distinction between the 'real' and the 'imaginary'."[37] The reason this distinction becomes necessary in New Historical argumentation is because a system of analysis is set up in which an interaction between the text and its social surroundings becomes part of the argument. Greenblatt's term "embedded"[38] can do little to counter arguments concerning the split between these two realms. This term has the disadvantage of indicating that literature is a secondary and dependent phenomenon that owes a debt to what is posited to be the realer realm of the social.

Newman's solution to this problem is to derive a theoretical approach to the texts of the Pegnitz Order of Flowers that recognizes their "institutionalizing function."[39] Ultimately, Jacques Derrida's *différance* provides the basis for

---

[36] Jane O. Newman, *Pastoral Conventions: Poetry, Language and Thought in Seventeenth-Century Nuremberg* (Baltimore: Johns Hopkins University Press, 1990), 1–30.
[37] Newman, *Pastoral Conventions*, 6.
[38] Stephen Greenblatt, *Renaissance Self-Fashioning: From More to Shakespeare* (Chicago: University of Chicago Press, 1983), 5.
[39] Newman, *Pastoral Conventions*, 13.

understanding the texts without needing to rely on any notion of reality beyond the texts. "Différance" is a term Derrida produces in order to resolve a difficulty he perceives with Saussure's distinction between the signifier and the signified. Whereas Saussure wishes to eliminate the distinction between the sign and its meaning, the terms he uses still appear to be caught in this area of conflict. Rather than postulating a relationship of meaning between two areas, différance designates movement that produces such difference as language leads us to believe exists between such areas as have been discussed here. Thus, the sign can have meaning independent to what it refers. For Newman, différance allows her to analyze the texts of the Nuremberg language society "as institutions, as foundational/originary and monumental/regulatory, at one and the same time."[40]

Returning to the Fruit-Bearing Society, the date that is given for its founding is from a text recording the event.[41] Considering the relationship between the text and the institution with this theoretical framework in place, we can see the significance of the role of the text in bringing the institution to life. The text of Carl Gustav von Hille's *Der teutsche Palmenbaum* (1644) recounts in detail what the Fruit-Bearing Society was intended to be and under what circumstances it came into being. The relationship between the text and the Society cannot just be a mimetic one, and already Greenblatt's notion of being embedded can be seen to herald a reciprocity between the two. For Newman, applying différance allows the text an institutional life of its own. The date given in von Hille's text projects out to an actual event and a founding meeting, but the portrayal of the institution in the text has a richness and fullness that goes beyond a singular founding moment. It is in the text itself that the institution becomes fully developed.

Harsdörffer's *Playful Colloquies* has a similar founding role in creating conversational institutions. His text is both a collection of written dialogues and, purportedly, the locus for the performance of dialogues. This dual function sits well with Newman's deliberations, as the *Playful Colloquies* can exist as a literary piece

---

[40] Ibid., 29f.

[41] Carl Gustav von Hille, *Der teutsche Palmbaum: Das ist / Lobschrift von der hochlöblichen Fruchtbringenden Gesellschaft Anfang / Satzungen / Vorhaben / Namen / Sprüchen / Gemählen / Schriften und unverwelklichen Tugendruhm. ...* Nürnberg, 1647. Reprinted as: *Die Fruchtbringende Gesellschaft: Quellen und Dokumente in vier Bänden*, ed. Martin Bircher, vol. 2 (München: Kosel, 1970), 11.

of active institutionalization in its own right.

What I wish to add to the theoretical discourse reported above is that we have here also a particular form of dialogic tract that has at least the preliminary outlines of being its own genre. This existence as a literary genre also has consequences for the way in which we view the academies. A connection is evident within Harsdörffer's text in the form of the statutes of the "Intronati," a Sienese academy.

The source Harsdörffer uses most in his collection is *Dialogo de' Giuochi che nella vegghie sanesi si usano di fare. Del Materiale Intronato* (Venetia, 1574), which is cited twenty-nine times. The author of this work is identified by Georg Adolf Narciss as Scipio Bargagli, whose pseudonym was *Il Materiale* in the *Accademia degli Intronati* (The Academy of the Enthroned).[42] Harsdörffer's going as far as to include the statutes of this Sienese academy in the *Playful Colloquies* indicates a convergence of goals between the conversational games of his book and the goals of the seventeenth-century academy. This convergence becomes clear in the reasons Harsdörffer cites for including them in his book:

> This is the well-intentioned goal of the Playful Colloquies copied from the highly honorable *Enthroned* of Siena the following laws and statutes that are unprecedented, and they praise as their own invention, are also written up at the place of their meetings, and we have sufficient cause to present these to German opinion as the preface to the Playful Colloquies.[43]

While the dialogues since Castiglione's *Book of the Courtier* have included women, the membership lists of the academies excluded or only reluctantly accepted them. At the time of the Fruit-Bearing Society, there is a decided attempt to found institutions that are similar to those of the Renaissance and that yet also create space for women. It is likely Harsdörffer's publication of the *Playful Colloquies* acted as a parallel to the Fruit-Bearing Society that offered him membership in that august and mostly noble group. Thus, there appears to be a tradition of phenomena attendant to the academy that makes space for female inclusion alongside the main exclusionary

---

[42] Narciss, *Studien*, 57.

[43] "Diese ist der wolgemeinte Zweck der hochlöblichen *Bethronten* zu Siena / für solche die ihre eigene und zuvor unerhörte erfingungé ausrühmen / auch in dem Ort ihrer Zusammenkunft folgende Lehren und Satzungen angeschriebi / welche wir den Gesprächspielen Teutscher Meinung vorzusetzen genugsame Ursach haben." Harsdörffer, *Frauenzimmer Gesprächspiele*, vol. 5, Aiii [97].

institution. The pairing of these phenomena and Harsdörffer's declaration that their goals coincide offers no contradiction to those texts used to found any of these groups: where we might see inclusion and exclusion today, the writers of the times stressed complement and similarity.

The most obviously parallel organization for women was *La Noble Academie des Loyales*, also known as *L'Ordre de la Palme d'Or* (The Order of the Golden Palm), founded by Anna von Bernberg, wife of Christian I, a member of the Fruit-Bearing Society. This group is recorded to have had twenty female members, all titled and all wives of members of the Fruit-Bearing Society. Its goal was appreciation of the French language and education.[44] A second group that was also formed in association with the Fruit-Bearing Society and that also focused on French culture was the *Academie de vrais amants*, which had forty-eight members. The group was founded in association with a meeting of some members of the Fruit-Bearing Society and consisted of enthusiasts for the works of the French author Honore d'Urfé. In a communal letter, the members expressed their faith in d'Urfé's *Astreé*, a pastoral novel. Again, we see the necessity for the textual founding of the institution that gives us a precise date of its beginning as the first of March 1624.[45]

One society in particular was founded to channel the participation of the women into the legitimate and mainstream work of the academy. Klaus Conermann has examined the relationship between the Virtuous Society (*Tugendliche Gesellschaft*) and the Fruit-Bearing Society and shown their parallel roles.[46] The statutes of the former dictated that the members should pass their time "with honest and joyful exercises and conversations truly appropriate to their estate, among which the following should be: that they engage themselves in diverse languages; all kinds of beautiful handicrafts, including music, poems; and in general in all that which is honorable [*rühmlich*] for them and their kind and that is seemly, each unto their ability."[47]

---

[44]This group appears to receive no mention until its demise in 1640. Otto, *Die Sprachgesellschaften des 17. Jh.*, 19.

[45]Ibid.

[46]Klaus Conermann, "Die Tugendliche Gesellschaft und ihr Verhältnis zur Fruchtbringenden Gesellschaft. Sittenzucht, Gesellschaftsidee und Akademiegedanke zwischen Renaissance und Aufklärung," *Daphnis* 17 (1988): 13–626.

[47]"mit Ehrlichen / Ihnen und Ihrem Sande wohl anstehenden auch fröhlichen Ubungen [sic] und Gesprächen zubringen / unter welchen auch diese sein sollen / daß Sie [sic] befleißigen /

The statutes of this society also encouraged members to correspond and converse, and thus, one can readily see why Conermann suggests that these institutions need to be examined for their relevance as historical antecedents of the salon.[48] As the above discussion indicates, the path to the women's societies and orders from the older academies follows a clear route through the statutes of the various groups that all established themselves textually. These texts are carefully interconnected. Harsdörffer's use of the statutes of the Intronati of Siena in his *Playful Colloquies* presents a broad textual agenda to make the oral high culture of Italian academies available to a wide audience. What is thus available as an institution is then a textually projected orality that is enshrined in terms of the pursuit of virtue through sociability.

Sociohistorical approaches to literature have discerned a change in literary production that coincides with the movement of the locus of culture from the court and its system of patronage to a bourgeois, anonymous patronage of the unknown reader. The breadth of this new public can be used to explain the growth of the journal as a popular genre.[49] In line with this argument, sociability (albeit as textual projection) also changes its locus from courtly to bourgeois circles.

One of the earliest journals in the pietistic vein made evident in the *Playful Colloquies* was edited by Christian Thomasius and appeared in 1688 and 1689. His *Monathsgespräche* led the way for the somewhat later moral weeklies of the early eighteenth century. These publications were a popular medium elsewhere in Europe; British moral weeklies included such well-known journals as *The Tatler*, *The Spectator*, and *The Guardian*. In Germany the journals carried short identifying titles, such as *Die Vernünftige Tadlerinnen* (*The Sensible Chastisers*),[50] *Der Patriot* (*The Patriot*), *Die Matrone* (*The Matron*), and *Der Biedermann* (*The Honest Fellow*). In

---

unterschiedlicher Sprachen / allerhand schöner Hand-Arbeit / auch andrer feiner künstlicher Sachen / darunter auch die Musick / Gedichte / und ingemein in allem dem / was ihnen und ihres gleichen rühmlich is / und wohl anstehet / nach einer jeden Fähigkeit." Johann Christoph Beckmann, *Historie des Fürstentums Anhalt*. 7 Tle. (Zerbst, 1710), Tl. 5, 336. Cited after Conermann, "Tugendliche Gesellschaft," 547.

[48]Conermann "Tugendliche Gesellschaft," 547. The statutes are in Beckmann, *Historie des Fürstentums Anhalt*, 335–39. I am happy to pursue Conermann's valuable suggestion here.

[49]Hildburg Herbst, *Frühe Formen der deutschen Novelle im 18. Jahrhundert*. Philologische Studien und Quellen; Heft 112. (Berlin: Erich Schmidt Verlag, 1985), 55.

[50]Narciss indicated in his work on the *Playful Colloquies* that he discerned its influence in both the *Monthly Conversations* of Thomasius and in Gottsched's *Sensible Chastisers*. Narciss, *Studien*, 161.

observations that come precariously close to acknowledging a projected oral ideal of communication, Hildburg Herbst notes that these titles had the function of making the journals appear to be a familiar person who would at regular intervals intervene in the life of the reader. Indeed, she goes on to point out that each issue had a fictional author who supposedly bore responsibility for the entire issue and who addressed the reader directly.[51] Just as the German academy the Fruit-Bearing Society had brought forth attendant phenomena that were more inclusive of women, so along with academic journals[52] other publications appeared that also projected an oral form of communication as their ideal. Like Harsdörffer's *Playful Colloquies*, these journals contributed to a projected oral realm that fulfilled pietistic goals of virtuous activity for women.

It is not surprising, then, that Henriette Herz called her first gathering of friends a Tugendbund, that is, the Virtuous League. In her memoirs she writes that "[t]he purpose of this league, a kind of virtuous league, was mutual moral and spiritual development as well as performing acts of charity." She clearly has a particular type of institution in mind when writing and goes on to describe what form this institution took: "It was a league with all the formal aspects, as we had statutes and even our own ciphers, and in later years I still owned quite a few things of Wilhelm von Humboldt's, handwritten in these ciphers."[53]

This secretive group had many of the aspects of the institutions mentioned above. Although the statutes of the group do not survive, its pietistic virtuous goals of self-improvement and good works bring it into close relationship with the older, chiefly Protestant orders of the sixteenth century. Indeed, Varnhagen von Ense refers to the Tugendbund as an order. When looking back at Herz's invitation to his wife Rahel Levin to join the Tugendbund in or about 1792, he writes:

> Henriette had revealed to Rahel (in 1792?) that she belonged to a league, a kind of order, which she had founded along with Wilhelm von Humboldt, Kunth, her sister Brenna, Göckingk, and several other women and men for

---

[51] Herbst, *Frühe Formen*, 65.

[52] For example, the *Acta Eruditorum* that survived from 1682–1782. Cited after Herbst, *Frühe Formen*, 63.

[53] "Der Zweck des Bundes, einer Art Tugendbund, war gegenseitige sittliche und geistige Heranbildung sowie Übung werktätiger Liebe. Er war ein Bund in aller Form, denn wir hatten auch ein Statut und sogar eigene Chiffern, und ich besaß noch in späteren Jahren manches von der Hand Wilhelms von Humboldt in diesen Chiffern Geschriebene." *Herz*, 82.

their mutual ennobling and improvement, and she invited her to pledge membership herself.[54]

The semisecretive nature of this order, as well as the statutes enshrining the institution, indicates that the Tugendbund followed at least some aspects of such baroque academies and orders as the Fruit-Bearing Society and the Pegnitz Order of Flowers. All of these groups had mutual advancement and the pursuit of virtue as common goals within a sociable context.

Harsdörffer's important promotion of Italian Renaissance influence via his membership in the Fruit-Bearing Society and the Pegnitz Order of Flowers and through his book *Playful Colloquies* is not the last sign of Italian influence on German sociability. Herz certainly acknowledges other European cultural influences After discussing learning French and Lessing's contribution to making French drama accessible to a reading public by means of his critical work, Herz next explains how she learned English in order to read Shakespeare in the original, owing to the inadequacy of translations. Herz's representation of her knowledge of things literary is founded on matters of taste or aesthetics dictated by journal literature. In this section, it is Lessing's *Hamburgische Dramaturgie* that she ranks so highly. But Herz makes reference to Italian literature in a highly significant passage of her memoirs. The paragraph in her memoirs following the discussion of this learning from different European literary cultures starts by indicating that she and her social compatriots learned to read Italian: "Several members of our circle learned to read Italian authors in the original."[55] The paragraph continues with a discussion of the members' Jewish intellectual sociability and its lack of tradition. This entire enterprise develops a unique spirit that has arisen out of the literature they have read:

> And this spirit was indeed unique. While it was on the one hand born of the literature of the modern peoples, the seed had, nevertheless,

---

[54]"Henriette hatte Rahlen (1792?) eröffnet, sie gehöre einer Verbündung an, einer Art Orden, den sie mit Wilhelm von Humboldt, Kunth, ihrer Schwester Brenna, Göckingk und noch einigen anderen Frauen und Männern, zu gegenseitiger Veredelung und Förderung gestiftet habe, und sie bot ihr an, selber auch in diese Verbündung zu treten." Karl August Varnhagen von Ense, *Nachlaß* (1867), vol. 1 [= Ludmilla Assing, ed., *Briefe von Chamisso, Gneisenau, Haugwitz, w. v. Humboldt, Prinz Ioius Ferdinand, Rahel, Rückert, L. Tieck u.a. Nebst Briefen, Anmerkungen und Notiizen von Varnhagen*, vol. 1 (Leipzig, 1867)]. Cited after *Herz*, 464.

[55]"Auch die Kenntnis der italienischen Dichter in der Ursprache eröffneten sich mehrere aus unserm Kreise." *Herz*, 63.

fallen on original soil. All mediation by any tradition, by education that proliferated from generation to generation...was entirely missing.[56]

Thus, Herz concludes this paragraph by discussing the unique nature of Jewish sociability. The tradition of sociability is here entirely derived from literature. Her choice of the words "von Geschlecht zu Geschlecht sich fortpflanzend" is literally "breeding from estate to estate" and emphasizes the fact that these people are not members of the nobility practicing this intellectual sociability. The fact that she chooses to combine the Italian authors with her information on sociability is an indication that the authors she had in mind had some bearing on this subject, just as the preceding paragraph concerning the French and English authors made reference to Lessing's *Hamburgische Dramaturgie*. The Italian authors mentioned above would have some affinity with the oral sociability she mentions sharing with her Jewish friends. The very fact that she cites a lack of tradition and that the shared sociability of her circle grows in some way naturally out of the literature is a further indication of this affinity. Many of those Italian authors wrote in the form of dialogues and cyclical narratives, such as Boccaccio's *Decameron*.[57] Thus, Herz constructed her sociability out of the Italian literature she read.

Another link between Italy and German sociability lies in the person of Anna Amalie, dowager duchess of Saxony-Weimar. In her book on the salon, Verena von der Heyden-Rynsch makes the common assumption that sociability in Germany is entirely of French origin when she states that Anna Amalie introduced French sociability to the court at Weimar. Still, von der Heyden-Rynsch provides a useful summary of the duchess's activities and acknowledges the latter's great enthusiasm for all things Italian.[58]

Anna Amalie's circle in Weimar included Sophie von La Roche, Christoph Martin Wieland, and Goethe. The last of these three wrote what for many years was

---

[56]"Und dieser Geist war in der Tat ein eigentümlicher. Er war allerdings einerseits aus der Literatur der neueren Völker hervorgegangen, aber die Saat war auf einen ganz ursprünglichen Boden gefallen. Hier fehlte jede Vermittlung duch eine Tradition, durch eine von Geschlecht zu Geschlecht sich fortpflanzende...Bildung." Ibid., 63f.

[57]I would like to thank Prof. Kablitz (Universität Köln) who provided me with many insights into the breadth of Italian literature pertinent to this discussion as well as pointing me to useful information on this subject that I have incorporated elsewhere in this volume.

[58]von der Heyden-Rynsch, *Europäische Salons*, 97ff.

thought of as the earliest German novella, *Conversations of German Exiles* (*Unterhaltungen deutscher Ausgewanderten*) (1794/95), in which a baroness sets up sociability for a group of Germans fleeing from the war and turmoil that the French Revolution had brought to their estates on the Rhine. Schiller complimented this cyclical narrative work by stating that it belonged to the tradition of Boccaccio,[59] thus recognizing its debt to Italian traditions of narrative, of which the *Decameron* is but one of the earliest and most widely known examples. It does not seem too farfetched to identify the baroness's striving for an ideal sociability with the dowager duchess Anna Amalie. It was Amalie who passed her enthusiasm for the Italian on to Goethe, and it was she who contributed significantly to creating the aura of an Italianate movement around the "greats" that became identified as Weimar Classicism.[60] Our best record of this sociability can be found in the directions the baroness gives in the *Conversations of German Exiles*,[61] a fictional projection of ideal sociability. In this way the work resembles the statutes mentioned above, as they also projected an ideal of virtuous activity.

A possible mediating link between Amalie and Herz can be found in Karl von La Roche, the son of Sophie von La Roche, who was a member of Herz's Tugendbund. It was through von La Roche's encouragement that a lasting correspondence was initiated between Herz and his mother.[62] It is quite possible that he contributed to bringing Weimar ideas to Herz and that these concepts might have persisted beyond the Tugendbund into her later sociability.

From the above discussion, we can see that there are clear indications that the high culture of Berlin Jewish sociability was constructed out of and into literature. I have found it fruitful to look back to Italianate Classicism in German literature and the baroque, as well as to Renaissance sources for this oral sociability.

---

[59] *Schillers Briefe* [1794–1795], ed. Fritz Jonas (Deutsche Verlags-Anstalt, 1892–1896), 54.

[60] Astrid Köhler points out the contribution made by Anna Amalie in promoting Goethe as a great figure. The dowager duchess had busts of Goethe, Herder, Wieland, and Schiller put up in the park at Tiefurt. Astrid Köhler, *Salonkultur im klassischen Weimar. Geselligkeit als Lebensform und literarisches Konzept* (Stuttgart: M und P, 1996), 39.

[61] Johann Wolfgang Goethe, *Unterhaltungen deutscher Ausgewanderten* (Stuttgart: Reclam, 1991), 17f.

[62] *Herz*, 82f.

2.1.3. France/ Not France

French salons are widely assumed to have been a fundamental influence upon, and often even the sole inspiration for, the German salons of the eighteenth century. While it can hardly be disputed that French was the language of fashion, it appears that the particularly French manifestation of sociability was broadly rejected by numerous German writers. As we have already seen, Italian models of sociability had a currency amongst various figures who considered and discussed sociability. Some clearly harbored an antipathy toward what they saw as poor sociability, which they considered a result of the influence of French culture. What was being rejected here was really a distortion of salon sociability termed préciosité. It would be a mistake to attempt to catalogue a thoroughly German salon sociability; rather, a realignment in our understanding of German sociability must be sought, such that we need no longer automatically assume a mere appropriation of French precursors. While not excluding French influence, the picture will become more complex as to include Italian models as well as the literary mediation of sociability.

Stéphanie-Félicité Ducrest de Saint-Aubin, countess de Genlis, was an important source of French culture among the women of bourgeois circles in early nineteenth-century Berlin. In particular, Henriette Herz received lessons from de Genlis in French composition that also extended to the reading of French classics together.[63] Despite this interaction, Herz was careful to distance herself in her memoirs from this woman, whom Herz describes as talented but also as a rather disheveled eccentric. She also reports in her memoirs that she met de Genlis in the home of the "rich Jewish merchant Cohen,"[64] where the latter had an opportunity to display her abilities as an actress. The circumstances indicate that the performance was of French material. Herz's comments about this performance occur within the context of her being unable to perform French tragedy in the lessons given by de Genlis. Furthermore, Herz reports that the conversation she had with de Genlis at this function was entirely in French. Elsewhere in the context of the description of the

---

[63] Ibid., 94.

[64] "Ich sah sie einmal in dem Hause des reichen jüdischen Kaufmanns Cohen...." Ibid., 96. Presumably, this reference is to the cotton merchant Ezechiel Benjamin Cohen who lived in the Münzstraße 20.

Cohen house as "elegant and striving hugely for distinction,"[65] Herz refers to the wife of the merchant as Madame Cohen. The use of the French title further emphasizes the fashionable nature and opulence of this household.

Herz associates a rich and representative form of entertainment with the French style of Madame Cohen. However, she also deems something of this French taste to be ridiculous. Not only does Herz describe de Genlis as disheveled, she also comments on the strange prudishness of the countess's attitude to the mixing of the sexes. When Herz asks to be able to take lessons together with someone else, de Genlis insists that, although she will accept male and female pupils, she will not tolerate teaching the two sexes together. Herz goes on to show the extent of de Genlis's separation of the sexes:

> She even took this separation of the sexes to the most peculiar lengths. For example, later on in Berlin, once she had come into the possession of a small supply of books, she took the greatest care to separate the male writers from the female. Not only was each sex accorded its own side in the repository, for even greater security, an empty space was left between them.[66]

Madame de Genlis stands at the very end of a tradition that had always existed as an ironization of a particular form of interaction practiced by French women known as *précieuses*. Madame de Genlis is herself attributed with having written a one-act comedy poking fun at the seventeenth-century hostesses of the salon to whom this title of précieuse was applied.[67] The concept that French sociability was in some sense not to be taken seriously has a tradition going back to Molière's 1672 *Les Femmes Savantes*, which appeared in German editions between 1752 and 1769. Polite speech under these conventions meant that issues should be alluded to rather than addressed directly; there was, therefore, much intimation and clever repartee that relied on intimation. It has been suggested that the précieux language of the salon

---

[65]"Dieses Haus war sehr elegant und gewaltig nach Vornehmigkeit strebend." Ibid., 35.

[66]"Wie sie denn überhaupt die Trennung der Geschlechter bis ins Wunderliche trieb. So trennte sie zum Beispiel, als sie sich später in Berlin in den Besitz eines kleinen Büchervorrats gesetzt hatte, die männlichen Schriftsteller aufs sorgfältigste von den weiblichen. Nicht nur wurde jedem Teile eine eigene Seite des Repositoriums eingeräumt, zu größerer Sicherheit blieb auch noch ein leerer Zwischenraum zwischen ihnen." Ibid., 94.

[67]*Le Club des dames, ou le retour de Descartes*, 1784. Erica Harth, *Cartesian Women: Versions and Subversions of Rational Discourse in the Old Regime* (Ithaca: Cornell University Press, 1992), 114.

might have originated with the secretive manner in which knowledge of the philosophy of Descartes was traded among early salon women in France.[68] The exclusion of women from the Académie Royale des Sciences had made it necessary for the women to seek refuge in a different setting. This necessity led to the founding of salons that included notable Cartésiennes, who had to hide their unseemly knowledge beneath the veil of metaphor and circumlocution that Molière and others ridiculed.

When Heinrich von Kleist came to Berlin in 1801, he also commented on the nature of the sociability of the salons:

> I hardly go to socials. The Jewish ones would be my favorites if they did not deal in such a "pretiös" manner with their education. I have made an interesting acquaintance with the Jew Cohen, not so much on his account, but rather for the splendid cabinet of physical instruments he owns.[69]

The term "pretiös" can readily be explained as meaning "affected,"[70] and the context makes it clear that Kleist is referring to a particular form of salon interaction. In applying the term, he is recalling the French "précieuse" and the long tradition of ridicule of that particular style of interaction. His comment clearly is pertinent to the salon of the Cohens, but we do not learn of any other Jewish salons that he frequented during this early period in Berlin. His contrast may in fact be limited to that with the neighbors of the Cohens, the family of Christian Friedrich Gottlieb Clausius, who lived in the Münzstraße 19 while the Cohens lived in number 20. It was through Minna Clausius, the daughter who was befriended by Kleist's fiancé Wilhelmine Zenge, that Kleist gained access to this part of Berlin's social life. Kleist's criticism of the attitude to learning being too précieuse indicates that different forms of sociability existed in parallel. What he discerned in the Jewish salons was the remnants of the need to mask education stemming from the secretive reception of Descartes.

---

[68]Harth, *Cartesian Women*, 82f.

[69]"In Gesellschaften komme ich selten. Die jüdischen würden mir die liebsten sein, wenn sie nicht so pretiös mit ihrer Bildung täten. An dem Juden Cohen habe ich eine interessante Bekanntschaft gemacht, nicht sowohl seinetwillen, als wegen seines prächtigen Cabinets von physicalischen Instrumenten." Heinrich von Kleist to Ulrike von Kleist, 5 February 1801. Heinrich von Kleist, *Werke*, vol. 4 (Frankfurt am Main: Insel, 1986), 193. See Schleiermacher's use of this term in the *Notebooks of Thoughts*, no. 146, *KGA*, I/2, 34.

[70]In the notes to the letters: "kostbar; geschraubt [precious; affected]." von Kleist, *Werke*, 552

During a discussion of reading societies, Henriette Herz offers further corroboration as she discerns a difference between her sociability and that of previous sociable gatherings. She describes Hofrätin Bauer, the wife of the bailiff of the royal castle and aulic councilor, as being at pains to act as a bel-esprit. While explaining that the activities of the participants of the gatherings went beyond reading to summertime open-air sociable games that included ball games, she comments that these activities met with Frau Bauer's disapproval: "Of course these distractions were always a disappointment to Frau Bauer for whom one could never read enough."[71] By categorizing Frau Bauer as a bel-esprit, Herz's narrative shows that this old-fashioned form of sociable practice was far too restrictive, and Frau Bauer is described as a rather inflexible hostess who wishes to enforce a rigid and retrograde set of sociable rules of behavior.

In the context of discussing that the Germans are theoretically capable of their own sociability, Madame de Staël describes what a horror it is to meet a foreigner who attempts to act in a French manner. While it is wonderful to meet with someone French and to have a conversation regarding French literature with them on their own terms, it is quite a different matter to discuss such matters with what from the context must be a German putting on a pretense to French culture, language, and customs. The contrast with the former pleasure is great:

> Not so with a foreigner *putting on a pretense of being French* [ein *französierender* Ausländer], such a one allows himself no opinion, no turn of phrase that does not carry with it the stamp of orthodoxy; and this orthodoxy is invariably out of date, and yet he or she considers it to be the opinion of the day. In some northern countries one keeps to anecdotes concerning the government of Louis XIV. One can hear foreigners who would like to emulate the French and who recount the court intrigues of Madame de Montespan and Mademoiselle de Fontanges in detail and complexity that would be tiresome even if it were a description of an event of yesterday.[72]

From this statement it is clear that some sociable practices in Germany required an exact emulation of the French salon and even a set of practices that clearly belong to

---

[71]"Diese Allotria wurden freilich stets nur zu großer Unzufriedenheit der Frau Bauer getrieben, welcher nie genug gelesen werden konnte." *Herz*, 49.

[72]Anne Germaine de Staël, *Über Deutschland* (Frankfurt am Main: Insel, 1985), 70.

the seventeenth century. Herz's criticism of what she identifies as the practices of an older generation are the ones she also links to the ideas of Madame de Genlis. In her memoirs Herz makes it profoundly clear that "Madame de Staël was, of course, a completely different type of woman from Madame de Genlis."[73] Herz goes on to point out that she had opportunity to meet with Madame de Staël on several occasions and that she was also often invited to the soirees that the latter threw every Friday in Berlin, thus giving further indication of the close contact and respect Herz had for this woman. Madame de Staël's discussion helps us to see Herz's comments less in the light of national prejudice and more clearly as a distancing from particular practices of sociability.

German had become acceptable as an academic language in the later seventeeth century, and this change led to German being acceptable as a language for courtly sociability. A tradition of furthering the national language lies at the root of the academies that brought forth the salons. Even if it were because of the exclusion of women from the academy that the salons were founded in France, the salons, nevertheless, initially stood in a close relationship to the idea of the academy. Similarly, in Germany, the Fruit-Bearing Society was a parallel to the Tugendliche Gesellschaft. Harsdörffer's *Playful Colloquies* was written by a member of the Fruit-Bearing Society who maintained the precepts of the work of the academy and made sociability open to a wider audience. Here, also, as noted earlier, the linguistic sources were Italian rather than French, and development continued along the lines of the Academia della Crusca in pursuing the goals of a written and standardized vernacular.

One of the key figures in making German acceptable as an academic language was Christian Thomasius, who was also mentioned above in the context of furthering the idea of conversation in the baroque. He is perhaps most famous for holding lectures in German. His first program of lectures held in German, and the first program to be publicly announced to the students in writing in German, was "Welcher Gestalt man denen Franzosen in gemeinem Leben und Wandel nachahmen solle?" ("Which Way to Emulate Those French in Ordinary Life and Behavior?")[74]

---

[73]"Eine Frau von ganz anderer Art als Frau von Genlis war freilich Frau von Staël." *Herz*, 117

[74]"Dieses is mein erstes Teutsches *Programma*, so ich in Leipzig *Anno* 87. verfertiget, auch vielleich das erste *Programma*, das in Leipzig in Teutscher Sprache an das schwarze Brett geschlagen worden." Christian Thomasius, *Von Nachahmung der Franzosen nach den Ausgaben von 1687 und*

This lecture discusses in detail the code of gallantry appropriate to the maxims of Gratian, though the entire breadth of such works is discussed. Thomasius warns his students against adopting too much French affectation because such an extreme can make a person laughable.[75]

The consciousness of being too French appears also in the criticism of Knigge's editor, J. G. Zimmermann, who said that Knigge "praises the social tone and the sociable virtues of the French at the expense of the Germans"[76] Knigge's *Über den Umgang mit Menschen* (1788) was a classic work for the discussion of sociability; Schleiermacher felt compelled to refer to it at the outset of his *Essay*.[77] Zimmermann's ambivalence toward the French tradition of sociability coincides with the rejection of baroque representation and decoration by German pietists.[78] Harsdörffer complains of the decline in standards in the first dedicatory poem of the *Playful Colloquies*:

> The coarse common man
>
> Makes a mess of German-Latin, that he neither knows nor commands.
>
> He wants to use French, outlandish and foreign words,
>
> That which he never understands should decorate his speech.[79]

The foolishness of the German attempting to embellish his language by applying language he does not understand becomes a morally reprehensible form of sociability for the pietist tradition. Schleiermacher's relationship to pietism is, of course, highly differentiated, but he remains educated within a tradition that absorbed the mystical aspects of baroque piety while rejecting the decorative representational aspects of the

---

1701, ed. August Sauer. Deutsche Litteraturdenkmale des 18 und 19. Jahrhunderts 51 NF 1 (Stuttgart: Behr, 1894). Kraus Reprint (Nendeln: Kraus, 1968), 38.

[75]Ibid., 7.

[76]"den französischen Gesellschaftston und die geselligen Tugenden der Franzosen auf Unkosten der deutschen zu presen." J. G. Zimmermann, "Über die Einsamkeit," *Kürschners Nationalliteratur*, vol. 73 Berlin/Stuttgart o. J., 365. Cited after Herbert Naumaier, *Der Konversationston in der frühen Neuzeit 1815-1830* (Munich: Cella, 1974) = Diss. Univ. Munich, 1972, 7f.

[77]Furthermore, this work was considered to be aimed at a female audience. At the back of Pockels's *Liebe und Ehe* of 1799, an advertisement lists Knigge among the "Frauenzimmerschriften" available from the publishers. Carl Friedrich Pockels, *Liebe und Ehe in psychologisch moralischer Hinsicht*. (Hannover: Ritscher, 1799), [446].

[78]Martin Brecht, "Pietismus als alternative Geselligkeit," in *Geselligkeit und Gesellschaft*, ed. Adam 28, part 1, 261–73: 268.

[79]"Der grobe Povelmann / zertrümmelt Teutschlatein, das er noch weiß noch kann./ Er will französisch welsch und frembe wörter füren / das, was er nie versteht, soll seine rede zieren." Harsdörffer, *Frauenzimmer Gesprächspiele*, vol. 1, 101.

courtly baroque style that were popularly understood to be French in origin.

The pietism of Francke and Spener remains twice-removed from Schleiermacher, who is an errant learned Herrnhuter. Not only did the founder of the Herrnhuter Zinzendorf ultimately find his congregation to be in direct competition with the Collegia pietatis and, thus, subject to careful differentiation between pietism and Moravianism, but also through his love of theological and secular learning, Schleiermacher's intellectual position originated within the pietist tradition, although it developed into something quite unique. The most startling evidence for Schleiermacher's own unorthodox understanding of his position comes from the way in which he confronts the scandals of the new sexual mores associated with the salon.

2.2. Sexuality

In the *Book of the Courtier* Castiglione provides sample conversations for use in Italian salons and, in so doing, presents a defining, and perhaps truly seminal, discourse on the ideal characteristics of a woman courtier at the court of Urbino. Castiglione documents the abandonment of a type of courtly pastime or sociability that was no longer restricted to a single sex as it had been throughout the medieval period when women and men interacted in two distinct spheres. Castiglione states that his dialogues are supposedly verifiable,[80] and they indeed involve contemporaneous members of the court of Urbino and take as their subject the roles of men and women in this new form of courtly sociability. The putatively verifiable nature of these dialogues indicates not that there is some Rankean truth that is "wie es eigentlich gewesen," or "as it actually was"; rather, this text should adumbrate our awareness that this orality is much more a textual projection.

Furthermore, these conversations are almost exclusively male discourses that develop the position for women in courtly interactions. There is one female voice represented that, through its conformity, acts only to substantiate the power structure established in the dialogues. Such Italian models for conversation were familiar to the courts of Germany when Georg Phillip Harsdörffer made them available to a

---

[80]Baldesar Castiglione, *The Book of the Courtier*, trans. Charles S. Singleton (Garden City, N.Y.: Doubleday Anchor, 1959), 202.

bourgeois audience.[81]

At Castiglione's court of Urbino Elizabeth Gonzaga, the duchess of Urbino presides over the dialogues described as "games, which are designed for the relaxation of minds."[82] The Third Book of the *Book of the Courtier* deals with the establishment of an ideal of the courtly woman. In describing affability as an attribute of this ideal woman, Il Magnifico (Giuliano de' Medici) brings sexuality firmly and openly into their debate when he discusses comeliness in conversation: "I say that, in my opinion, in a Lady who lives at court a certain pleasing affability is becoming above all else, whereby she will be able to entertain graciously every kind of man with agreeable and comely conversation."[83] Il Magnifico goes on to define this comeliness of conversation in terms that elucidate the sexual duplicity of the situation into which women are being forced. Speaking again of the ideal courtly woman he says:

> [S]he will show herself a stranger to all boorishness; but with such a kind manner as to cause her to be thought no less chaste, prudent, and gentle than she is agreeable, witty and discreet: thus, she must observe a certain mean (difficult to achieve and, as it were, composed of contraries) and must strictly observe certain limits and not exceed them.[84]

The very fact that Il Magnifico sets limits proves that flirtation is acceptable, nay may even be required, to draw the ideal woman's conversational companion to her. This text then establishes a tradition of the sexual tease, or flirt, which can be expected in courtly conversation.

Women who contravene the bounds of what is permitted of them can expect to be criticized. In a dialogue reproduced by Varnhagen von Ense, authorship by women is discussed by two men and a woman, representing the kind of numerical gender proportion typical of the salon. In the following excerpt Ottilie expresses

---

[81]"Unsere Gesprächspiele sind von den Italienern abgesehen / welchen auch die Franzosen nachgeahmet / und ist solche Verstandübung auch an vielen Teutschen Fürstenhöfen / mit sondrem Behagen / eingeführet worden [Our Playful Colloquies have been copied from the Italians, whom the French also immitated, and such exercises of the mind have also been introduced at many German courts with very great pleasure]." Harsdörffer, *Frauenzimmer Gesprächspiele*, vol. 8, 45 [85]. Cf. Narciss, *Studien*, 158.

[82]Castiglione, *Book of the Courtier*, 202.

[83]Ibid., 207.

[84]Ibid., 207.

annoyance at Ferdinand's dislike of works authored by women;

> Ottilie: Oh, so you belong to those that cannot abide a book that is written by a woman!
>
> Franz: Now that is still better than if he were unable to abide the women who write books.
>
> Ferdinand: I admit I prefer to read the women themselves rather than their books.[85]

Women are thus unfailingly represented as objects of desire. They can only enter the realm of the intellectual indirectly as channels for male wisdom. As Ferdinand says to Ottilie, "[y]ou must not give us entertainment that keeps your lips silent. Why not at least animate with your voice all the beautiful wisdom that might be printed there?"[86] Women are not regarded by the men as making an intellectual contribution.

Henriette Herz reinforces this notion when she casts herself in the role of pupil in the salon conversations that she reports: "But these conversations were not without advantage for me because they were mainly conducted by intelligent people. If they could not always talk with me they could talk to me."[87] In her memoirs Herz expressly states that the contribution she makes to attracting participants to the gatherings in her home lies in her physical beauty. She contrasts her sexual appeal with the serious academic and scientific interests of her husband: "Herz drew people to him by means of his spirit and his fame as a physician, and I by means of my beauty and the notion I had for everything scientific."[88]

Herz's self-image was thus not that of an intellect but of a physical beauty, and to her mind, her physical qualities overshadowed her intellectual qualities. When recollecting salon conversations, she notes that her beauty made people come to false conclusions concerning her abilities. The reason her guests liked to talk with her was "because they made me, and likely themselves too, believe that I was clever because I was pretty."[89] In other words, she sees her sexual attraction as producing an illusion of intelligence. Her comments show that she is playing her role in a strictly gendered

---

[85]"Über die Schriften der Baronin De La Motte Fouqué," in Karl August Varnhagen von Ense, *Literaturkritiken*, ed. Klaus F. Grille (Tübingen: Niemeyer, 1977), 1.
[86]Ibid.
[87]*Herz*, 28.
[88]Ibid., 51.
[89]Varnhagen von Ense, *Literaturkritiken*, 1.

society, and she insists on according herself a position as sexual object that she sees as incompatible with intelligence.

Herz is just like the objectified passive females about whom Werner complains in Ludwig Tieck's 1796 play *Die Theegesellschaft (The Tea Society)*. He describes the conversation with salon women in terms that emphasize their objectified passive nature: "For me it was like being one of those children that talks to its dolls and lets them answer back and then is greatly gratified at its own brainwork."[90] Werner's derision allows Tieck to describe the limitations of salon women's activities, which were based on the conventions derived from older models of sociability.

In Schlegel's *Lucinde* the positive description of the new sociability produced for the young people's salon still affords the key female figure a role as facilitator for the key male figure: "Julius had also altered his outward behavior; he was more sociable... Lucinde bound and maintained it all, and thus a free society came about."[91] Whereas research has generally judged the Romantic salon as a revolutionary and even emancipating space, the old limiting prejudices and restricted roles clearly held true. Lucinde plays a mostly passive—at best augmenting—role for the main protagonist Julius, who remains the focus of the novella.[92]

Indeed, the eroticized nature of the novella, named after Lucinde, places her in a tradition of female literary figures that reaches back to a time before Harsdörffer's *Playful Colloquies*. Barbara Becker-Cantarino has shown convincingly that Harsdörffer promotes an innovative sociable scheme in which women can act as paragons of virtue. Harsdörffer consciously constructs his model in opposition to the idea of the woman as an erotic object and a locus of sin: "Von den Weibern ins gesamt sagt man: Sie sind ein Paradies der Augen / ein Fegfeuer des Beutels und eine Hölle der Gedanken [One says of women in general that they are paradise for the eyes, / purgatory for the wallet, and hell for the thoughts.]."[93] In contrast with this

---

[90] Ludwig Tieck, *Die Theegesellschaft*, in *Ludwig Tieck's Schriften*, vol. 12 (Berlin: Reimer, 1829), 359.

[91] "Julius hatte auch sein äußeres Betragen verändert; er war geselliger,...Lucinde verband und erhielt das ganze, und so entstand eine freie Gesellschaft." Friedrich Schlegel, *Lucinde. Ein Roman. Mit Friedrich Schleiermachers »Vertrauten Briefen über Friedrich Schlegels >Lucinde<«*, ed. Ursula Naumann (Goldmann: München, 1993), 64.

[92] Becker-Cantarino, "Schlegels *Lucinde*," 128–39: 135.

[93] Harsdörffer, *Frauenzimmer Gesprächspiele*, vol. 8, 215. Cited after Barbara Becker-Cantarino

traditional idea of women, he promotes Sophie Elisabeth, duchess of Brunswick and Luneburg, as "der Tugend Ebenbild [the very image of virtue.]."[94] The agenda of educating women to virtue next moved from Harsdörffer's *Playful Colloquies* to the moral weeklies and became integrated with the Enlightenment's moral engagement.

In response to the revision of the Enlightenment sexual morals of Schlegel's *Lucinde*, Friedrich Nicolai wrote and published *Vertraute Briefe von Adelheid B an ihre Freundin Julie S*** (*Confidential Letters from Adelheid B to Her Friend Julie S***). This work is a parody of *Lucinde* and a critique of the ideas of the Romantic clique from which Schlegel's work issued. Direct quotations from the *Atheneaum* are put into the mouth of the sharmanlike Dr. Pandolfo,[95] and the nine-year difference between Adelheid and Gustav identifies these two as Dorothea Veit and Friedrich Schlegel, respectively.[96] But, apart from the complete indictment of Romantic ideas, Nicolai offers a moral and virtuous alternative to the sensuous and erotic indulgences of *Lucinde*.

Nicolai's Adelheid is contrasted throughout his work with Frau von C., who runs a salon that is derisively referred to as "a weekly joke shop."[97] Frau von C. is only concerned with making herself the center of an erotic menagerie; all her efforts to bring about sociability in her home are focused on gathering a flock of devoted young men about her:

> She makes her house into a gathering place for good society so that she can shine in it. She always has worshipers around her a half dozen at a time, and they have to look out that they get on as best they can. If she sees a young man who excels in some way, then she does not rest until he is harnessed to a triumphal carriage. She offers up everything to make him hers: beauty, talents, innocent kindnesses. In this way she leads the inexperienced youth to the point at which he falls head over heels in love and can no longer live

---

"Frauenzimmer Gesprächspiele. Geselligkeit, Frauen und Literatur im Barockzeitalter," in *Geselligkeit und Gesellschaft*, ed. Adam; 28, part 1, 19.

[94]Harsdörffer, *Frauenzimmer Gesprächspiele*, vol. 5, 9. Cited after Becker-Cantarino "Frauenzimmer Gesprächspiele," in *Geselligkeit und Gesellschaft*, ed. Adam; 28, part 1, 17.

[95][Friedrich Nicolai], *Vertraute Briefe von Adelheid B an ihre Freundin Julie S*** (Berlin: Friedrich Nicolai, 1799), 79.

[96]Ibid., 202. It was an open secret in Berlin that *Lucinde* was based on the relationship between Veit and Schlegel.

[97]"Frau von C. hat seite einem Monate in ihrem Hause jeden Freytag einen wöchentlichen Witzmarkt angsetzt." Ibid., 64.

without her. She, however, remains cold, or should she ever be affected by some emotion, then it is not heartfelt love but what the French refer to as *amour de tête* that a pretty woman can discard like a skirt for which she no longer cares.[98]

Adelheid, on the other hand, wishes to use the affection Gustav feels toward her to improve her young suitor: "But I wish to use this attachment, contrary to his own philosophical laws, to make him more complete. Through his love for me, I wish to become an emblem for him for what is good and honorable."[99] Adelheid's virtuous motivation provides a startling contrast with the licentious abandon of the relationship between Schlegel's Lucinde and Julius. In the "Dithyrambic Fantasy," Julius describes the all-encompassing nature of their relationship as both spiritual/intellectual and sensuous: "You go through all the stages of humanity with me from the most indulgent sensuousness to the most spiritual intellectuality."[100]

Far from falling into such a wanton full scope of human relations, Adelheid provokes strong emotions that still remain within the bounds of accepted ethical standards. When Gustav leaves Adelheid, we are told of the heartfelt but ethical attachment his eyes express: "As he left, he pressed my hand, and his dark eyes looked into mine with due propriety [sittsam]. We were both silent. When he left, I felt unusually moved."[101] The German "sittsam" here expresses that the feelings of Adelheid's suitor Gustav are entirely ethical and have not succumbed to the unethical intermingled sweep of the spiritual and the physical that characterizes the relationship between Lucinde and Julius. Adelheid's emotional response then remains within the

---

[98]"Sie macht ihr Haus zu einem Sammelplatze feiner Gesellschaft, damit sie darin glänzen kann. Sie hat immer die Anbeter zu halben Dutzenden um sich, die sich vertragen mögen so gut sie können. Sieht sie einen jungen Mann der sich auf irgend eine Art auszeichnet; so ruht sie nicht eher bis er an ihrem Triumphwagen zieht. Sie bietet alles auf, um ihn sich eigen zu machen: Schönheit, Talente, unschuldige Gefälligkeiten; und so führt sie den unerfahrernen Jüngling bis dahin, daß er sterblich verliebt wird und ohne sie nicht leben kann. Sie aber bleibt kalt, oder wird sie ja von einer Empfindung hingerissen, so ists nie Herzensliebe, sondern was die Franzosen *amour de tête* nennen, die eine hübsche Frau ablegen kann, wie einen Rock der ihr nicht mehr gefällt." Ibid., 51.

[99]"Aber ich will diese Verbindung brauchen, um ihn, wider sein eigenes philosophisches Gebot, vollkommener zu machen. Ich will ihm ein Hauptmotiv zum Guten und Edlen werden, durch seine Liebe gegen mich." Ibid., 165.

[100]"Durch alle Stufen der Menschheit gehst Du mit mir, von der ausgelassensten Sinnlichkeit bis zur geitigen Geistigkeit". Schlegel, *Lucinde*, 15.

[101]"Beym Abschiede drückte er mir die Hand, und sein schwarzes Auge sah sittsam in das meinige. Wir schwiegen beide. Als er mich verließ, fühlte ich mich ungewöhnlich bewegt." Nicolai, *Vertraute Briefe*, 153.

realm of ethical and appropriate behavior because it rests on ethical feelings on the part of Gustav. The insincere erotic games played by the likes of Frau von C. are the foil and counterexample for the relationship between Adelheid and Gustav.

Nicolai's direct indictment of Schlegel's *Lucinde* comes when we discover that, unlike Dorothea Veit, alias Lucinde, Adelheid has gained experience that guides her actions. Although her love is as fiery as it was when she was eighteen, she can now handle it more consciously: "It is the advantage of several more years of experience that one knows oneself and that one takes the consequences of one's actions into consideration ahead of time."[102] Dorothea Veit's marriage was destroyed, and she and Friedrich Schlegel fled the public scandal first to Jena and, later, Vienna. In Nicolai's judgment, Veit should have been able to foresee the consequences of her actions and should have exercised the restraint of his heroine Adelheid. After setting up Gustav with a more appropriate match and having assured herself of the correct upbringing for Gustav's child, the self-sacrificing Adelheid goes to an early grave. While this sentimental ending is worthy of criticism, a broader criticism and a defense of Schlegel's original project was composed by Schleiermacher.

Friedrich Schleiermacher's 1799 *Vertraute Briefe über Friedrich Schlegels »Lucinde«* (*Confidential Letters on Friedrich Schlegel's* Lucinde) represents a careful discussion of the essential revision of traditional morality presented in *Lucinde* and attacked by Nicolai. Schleiermacher's title indicates that his response includes taking Nicolai's work to task. According to Schleiermacher, in his "Dedication to the Uncomprehending," the moral system underlying Nicolai's *Confidential Letters from Adelheid B to Her Friend Julie S*** was outdated and barbarous, thus accounting for the various negative responses to *Lucinde*: "Above all, as far as love is concerned, you have a constitution to defend to which centuries have contributed and which is the ripest fruit of the tidy bond between barbarity and falseness."[103] His belief is that a new set of moral values will present itself and that

---

[102]"aber es ist der Vortheil einiger Jahre Erfahrung mehr, daß man sich selbst kennen lernt und auf die Folgen seiner Handlungen vorher achtet." Ibid., 161.

[103]"Vorzüglich habt Ihr in Absicht der Liebe eine Konstitution zu verteidigen, an der Jahrhunderte gearbeitet haben, die die reifste Frucht ist von dem schönen Bunde der Barberei und der Verkünstelung." Schleiermacher, *Vertraute Briefe über Friedrich Schlegels »Lucinde«* in, Friedrich Schleiermacher, *Vertraute Briefe über Friedrich Schlegels Lucinde*, in F.D.E. Schleiermacher, *Schriften aus der Berliner Zeit 1800-1802*, ed. Günter Meckenstock, Kritische Gesamtausgabe I/3, ed. Hans-Joachim Birkner et al. (Berlin / New York: Walter de Gruyter, 1988), 147. Hereafter cited as

this arrival will mean that all previous systems will become obsolete: "Thus, it could readily come about...that your descendants...will need to honor quite different rules in matters of ethics from those that you would like to see made valid for all eternity. This would be the case even if your sense for these things would be theirs ten times over."[104]

To Schleiermacher, then, Nicolai and his cohort think in structures that will prove themselves outdated and morally invalid. Their unfortunate dedication to this old system of ethical thinking leaves them closed to the challenging and thought-provoking content of *Lucinde*, which presents love in a more profound way than its detractors can accept. Their view of love is superficial and weak. For Schleiermacher, Schlegel has grasped the issue and presented a stronger, more profound notion of love than the recent moralists are generally able to accept: "I welcome the fact that something is being done to counteract the supposedly moral weakness that only allows love to play on the surface."[105]

One aspect of this weakness is the inability to accept the sensual as potentially intermingled with spiritual love. This lack of acceptance robs the notion of love of its full capacity and presents a diminished and disfigured truth. A major culprit leading to this failure is the prudery of most people. If some matters are considered a violation of decorum even to discuss, then proper human relationships cannot come about. There are various passages in which Schleiermacher attacks prudery. His strongest against it is perhaps where he defends himself against the putative arguments of an English Miss:

> Our Mistress B., at whose truly English "Good God how can you speak of garters in the presence of girls?" we have laughed so heartily, would be more careless, and the most narrow measure of decorum would be that other Englishwoman who maintained that it would be unchaste to evince the word "chaste" in mixed company; yes even "decent" already had a ring of indecency about it.[106]

KGA I/3.
[104]"So könnte es leicht dahin kommen,....daß Eure Nachkommen,...in allem was sittlich ist, und wenn Euer Sinn zehnfach auf ihnen ruhen sollte, ganz andern Formeln zu huldigen genötigt werden, als diejenigen sind, welche Ihr gern für alle Ewigkeiten geltend machen möchtet." Ibid.
[105]"Mir ist es schon recht, daß etwas geschieht gegen die moralisch sein wollende Weichlichkeit, die Liebe immer nur auf der Oberfläche spielen läßt." Ibid., 163.
[106]"Unsere mistreß B., über deren echt englisches 'Guter Gott, wie können Sie doch in Gegenwart

These comical examples serve to illustrate how the limits of ethical decency (*Sittlichkeit*) can be taken to a debilitating extreme.

More relevant, however, is that this information highlights the difficulty with which lovers can even talk about subjects that will be of significance to them and the relationships they are seeking to develop. In his review of *Lucinde*, Schleiermacher calls this need "a demand for unrestricted freedom of communication."[107]

Apart from defending Schlegel's *Lucinde* as a worthy moral conversation piece, Schleiermacher was also fulfilling a moral duty to defend his friend in a time of need. In this enterprise Schleiermacher reveals his indebtedness to older views of sociability that reached back to Cicero's work on sociability, *De officiis*. Schleiermacher's superior, Court Preacher Sack, took issue with *On Religion* and prefaced his remarks in a letter to the young preacher at the Charité with his general misgivings about the company Schleiermacher was keeping: "I was not able to bring into line with my ideas of what a preacher owes to himself and his station the predilection you appear to have toward more intimate ties with persons of dubious principles and ethics."[108] Although the record we have of Schleiermacher's reply leaves out the names, other than that of Schlegel, it is beyond suspicion that Schleiermacher knew this comment to refer to Henriette Herz and Dorothea Veit (Schlegel). The whole paragraph in which Schleiermacher defends his strategy to stand by his friend reveals a great deal concerning his ideas about sociability:

> I shall never be the friend of anyone with reprehensible tendencies: but fear of other people shall never incite me to withdraw the comfort of friendship from someone who is unjustly repudiated; I shall never, just because of my station, allow myself to be swayed by some appearance that others see before them,

---

der Mädchen von Strumpfbändern reden' wir so oft unsäglich gelacht haben, wäre noch unvorsichtiger, und der geringste Maßstab der Sittlichkeit wäre jene andere Engländerin, welche behauptete, es sei unkeusch, in einer vermischten Gesellschaft das Wort 'keusch' auszusprechen, ja auch 'unanständig' habe schon etwas Unanständiges." Ibid., 158.

[107]"die Forderung einer unbedingten Freiheit der Mittheilung." *Ein Jahrhundert deutscher Literaturkritik. Vol. 4: Das grosse Jahrzehnt in der Kritik seiner Zeit*, ed. Oscar Fambach (Berlin: Akademie-Verlag, 1958), 520.

[108]"Den Geschmack, den Sie an vertrauteren Verbindungen mit Personen von verdächtigen Grundsätzen und Sitten zu finden scheinen, konnte ich mit meinen Vorstellungen von dem, was ein Prediger sich und Seinen Verhältnissen Schuldig ist, nicht vereinen." Friedrich Schleiermacher, *Briefwechsel 1801-1802 (Briefe 1005-1245)*, ed. Andreas Arndt & Wolfgang Virmond, in Kritische Gesamtausgabe V/5, ed. Hermann Fischer et al. (Berlin / New York: Walter de Gruyter, 1999), #1005, 3. Hereafter cited as *KGA* V/5.

rather than acting in accordance with the facts of the matter. According to such a maxim, we preachers would be given unlimited freedom in the realm of sociability; every slander brought against a friend, if it was well enough thought out to gain credibility, could make us shun him or her. On the contrary, the goal I have set myself is this: by living an irreproachable, regular life to achieve a point, by and by, such that an unjustly acquired bad reputation of my friends will not be able to cast a poor light on me, but rather that my friendship will be advantageous for their reputation.[109]

Cicero's view of friendship and justice in *De officiis* emphasizes the sociable duties of a friend. For him the second type of injustice within sociable duties is to fail to combat offense given to others.[110] In taking up the sword for his friend, Schleiermacher is proving himself to be a sociable fellow in the older, traditional sense that Nicolai and even Sack would understand. His familiarity with a representative philosopher of this generation, Garve, is documented by his correspondence with his uncle Samuel Stubenrauch. Schleiermacher also reviewed Garve's last edited works and rejected Garve's own philosophy (including that on sociability). The former did make positive remarks about the latter's ability to produce individual commentary or notes on the works of other philosophers.[111]

Schleiermacher possessed both a copy of Garve's translation of and commentary on Cicero's *De officiis* as well as the original Latin text.[112] The duty to

---

[109]"Nie werde ich der vertraute Freund eines Menschen von werferlichen Gesinnungen sein: aber nie werde ich aus Menschenfurcht einem unschuldig geächteten den Trost der Freundschaft entziehen, nie werde ich meines Standes wegen, anstatt nach der wahren Beschaffenheit der Sache zu handeln, mich von einem Schein, der Anderen vorschwebt, leiten lassen. Einer solchen maxime zufolge würden ja wir Prediger die Vogelfreien sein im Reiche der Gesellgkeit; jede Verläumdung gegen einen Freund, wenn sie gut genug ersonnen war um Glauben zu finden, könnte uns von ihm verbannen. Vielmehr ist das Ziel welches ich mir vorgestetzt habe dieses, duch ein untadelhaftes gleichförmiges Leben es mit der Zeit dahin zu bringen, daß nicht von einem unverschuldeten üblen Ruf meiner Freunde ein nachtheiliges Licht auf mich zurückfallen kann, sondern vielmehr von meiner Freundschaft für sie ein vortheilhaftes auf ihren Ruf." Ibid., #1065, 130.

[110]Marginalia: "9.b. Zweyte Art der Ungerechtigkeit: Beleidigungen anderer nicht wehren." Marcus Tullius Cicero, *Abhandlung über die menschlichen Pflichten in drey Büchern aus dem Lateinischen des Marcus Tullius Cicero übersetzt von Christian Garve*, fourth complete edition (Breslau: Wilhelm Gottlob Korn, 1792), 19.

[111]*KGA*, 1/3, 65–72. The essence of the evaluation that Garve was unable to produce significant synthesis of ideas in his work on sociability (69) will shed light on Schleiermacher's own intentions in writing such a work.

[112]Meckenstock, *Schleiermachers Bibliothek*, 164

combat offense given others belongs in the section on sociable duties and the subsection on justice. Garve discusses the validity of including under the heading of justice what appears to be merely a consequence of the duty to carry out acts of charity. He feels that Cicero has correctly given this duty a higher position than the duty to carry out acts of charity and says that it is positioned "between the absolute and relative duties, equitably in the middle," and that, thus, "Cicero was not without reason in placing it among the articles of justice."[113] Clearly, this discussion is one that Schleiermacher took very seriously in creating his own theory of sociability, and his staunch support of his friend Schlegel was demanded by the older universal rules of sociability to which he still felt strongly indebted. By standing by his decision to come to his friend's aid, Schleiermacher had proclaimed to Sack his belief in ideas with which his superior should have been able to identify.

Schleiermacher's indebtedness to older ideas of sociability extends also to the notion of female roles. Just as for Castiglione comeliness was a necessary constituting element of conversation, so also for Schleiermacher there was a need for a mixing of the sensual and the spiritual. He allows Ernestine to describe "how the sensual can gain completely new qualities and can be carried beyond the danger of becoming dulled and old by a profound interweaving with the spiritual."[114]

The expression of such sentiments allowed detractors to identify the salon culture with sexually scandalous behavior, but for Schleiermacher the discourse in which he was engaging was one that was designed to give love a role in marriage.[115] Unfortunately, a practice of decrying the salon as a sphere of sexual profligacy was established, and Schleiermacher's association with the salons could be held against him by his superior Friedrich Samuel Sack. This view of the salon was evinced by Karl Gutzkow when he republished Schleiermacher's *Confidential Letters on Friedrich Schlegel's* Lucinde in 1835. Gutzkow's aim was to embarrass the memory

---

[113]"da sie zwischen den vollkommenen und uvollkommenen Pflichten gleichsam in der Mitte steht, vom Cicero nicht ohne allen Grund, unter den Artikel der Gerechtigkeit gezogen worden." From Garve's notes (Anmerkungen), Cicero, *Abhandlung über die menschlichen Pflichten*, 75.

[114]"wie das Sinnliche durch seine innige Verwebung in das Geistige ganz neue Eigenschaften erhält und über alle Gefahr des Abstumpfens und Veraltens hinausgeschoben wird." *KGA* I/3, 164.

[115]For a discussion of the literature on this subject with copious quotes from contemporary sources, see Julia Bobsin, *Von der Werther-Krise zur Lucinde-Liebe. Studien zur Liebessemantik in der deutschen Erzählliteratur 1770–1800.* Studien und Texte zur Sozialgeschichte der Literatur, vol. 48 (Tübingen: Niemeyer, 1994).

of the recently deceased Schleiermacher and the Prussian Protestant hierarchy.[116] The claims expressed in Gutzkow's work and insinuated in contemporary remarks about Jewish women and their sociability by Helene Unger[117] were taken to an extreme later in a thoroughly disreputable work on the salons written in Nazi Germany in 1940. Relying on the existing tradition of the salon as eroticized space, Kurt Fevers produced a tirade of the boldest and most disturbing anti-semitic stripe that expanded on the innuendo of the existing materials, none of which bears repeating.[118]

These considerations indicate that the salon remained a sphere in which women functioned as erotic, spiritual muses for male conversation. This notion of female function, derived from the Renaissance and the early baroque, found its place in the attempts to develop a sociability that included women; inevitably, older models of sociability came into play. What at first appears to be an entirely new form of sociability for women can, in fact, be seen as much more in line with older views of that role in which women function as mediators between men. Significant relationships then form between the men in the salons, with women facilitating and animating learning rather than counting as creators and teachers. This tradition extends to the courts of France and Germany and to the salons and academies associated with them and by extension to the bourgeois salons in Germany.

A play by Ludwig Tieck about a salon, roughly contemporary with Schleiermacher's *Essay*, displays relationships between the sexes that exemplify this surviving tradition that saw woman as animating men's learning. The play shows the way in which a woman is used to make connections between men. Ludwig Tieck's 1796 *The Tea Society* is a play that contextualizes several conversations at a German salon, presided over by a young woman named Julie. The scene at the beginning of the play is pointedly placed in Berlin, where the high culture of salon sociability is acknowledged to have had its seat in such salons as those of Henriette Herz and Rahel Levin Varnhagen. "On the Literary Works of the Baroness de la Motte Fouqué: A Conversation at the Tea Table," the other conversation mentioned as a dialogue in

---

[116] I am indebted to Martin L. Davies for his analysis concerning this edition of Schleiermacher's *Vertraute Briefe*. Davies, *Identity or History*, 173f.

[117] Helene Unger "Ueber Berlin. Aus Briefen einer reisenden Dame an ihren Bruder in Ha." *Jahrbücher der Preußischen Monarchie* Mai bis Juni 1798 Bd. 2: 17–33, 133–43, 287–302.

[118] Kurt Fevers, *Berliner Salons. Geschichte einer großen Verschwörung* (München: Deutscher Volksverlag, 1940).

which authorship by women is discussed, is a report by the husband of Rahel Levin, Karl August Varnhagen, of a dialogue that is supposed to have been based on the experience of his wife's salon. Neither of these works claims to be an accurate record of actual dialogues. In fact, *The Tea Society* is nothing but a spoof of the salon. Ultimately, though, the dialogues presented, though not actually claiming to be real conversations, have a similar truth value as the dialogues of Castiglione, even if he does claim his dialogues are based on real conversations. None of these dialogues should be accepted as conveying a naive notion of originary truth.

In terms of a literary theory as a basis for this discussion, I am closest here to the ideas of Stephen Greenblatt and his New Historicism. New Historicism helps draw our attention to the literary nature of documentary evidence and the need to interpret evidence in order to discern the various agendas active in such material. The self-fashioning of writers and their times as Greenblatt determines it for the Renaissance is something we can also seek out for the eighteenth century.[119] Furthermore, we can see this self-fashioning working not only for individuals but also for institutions, and here, I am looking at the institution of the salon.

The status of the salon as an eroticized space can be underscored by the great difficulties the Protestant pastor Friedrich Schleiermacher experienced when it became public that he was associated with Henriette Herz's salon. The reputation of such places was so scandalous as to move Schleiermacher's superiors to threaten him with dismissal from his post. Further, Schleiermacher's defense of Friedrich Schlegel's relationship with Dorothea Veit, the married daughter of Moses Mendelssohn, became a matter of broad public debate through the publication the novel *Lucinde* and in Schleiermacher's 1799 essay on this work. But the Schlegel-Veit affair was by no means the only scandalous relationship forged in the atmosphere of the salon. Adam Müller's elopement with his employer's wife was preceded by her socializing in his company in the salons of Dresden, and Heinrich von Kleist's suicide pact with Madam Vogel was regarded to have been a consequence of the bond they formed in the salons of Berlin.

The salon was generally presided over by a central female figure, who provided the identification and focal point of the gatherings. In Moses Mendelssohn's protosalon, his daughters, who went on to marry salon attendees, provided the

---

[119]Greenblatt, *Renaissance Self-Fashioning*, 8.

comeliness so significant to the courtly conversation of Castiglione's the *Book of the Courtier*. Konrad Feilchenfeld has pointed out that this original Berlin salon gathering was essentially an opening up of the family sphere.[120] As other salons appeared, they continued to follow a pattern in which a woman was the central figure and in which a male family member of the same or a preceding generation was a background figure of authority. In terms of sexual theory, the salon thus manifests an Oedipal home-away-from-home for young postpubescent males. This alternative structure is what Sandor Ferenzci would call transference[121] and what later theorists would see as commensurate with the symbolic realm.

Another much discussed element of the salons, especially those of Berlin, was the fact that many of them offered the newly emancipated bourgeois Jews the opportunity to interact with Prussian nobility. This interaction provided a path to social integration with the higher classes. In Henriette Herz's memoirs, the young daughters of wealthy Jews are reduced to the status of a commodity in a transaction that takes place between men. The daughters of wealthy Jews learnt French and took the opportunity to practice it whenever the young men of court called; Herz implies that these calls concern money the men borrowed but never returned. She says of the young women: "Their aim was mainly to converse in the language of fashion with the court cavaliers and good looking young officers who only repaid the money borrowed from the fathers in attention paid to the daughters" (63). In this way, as exemplified in the work by Gayle Rubin in "The Traffic in Women" and by Eve Sedgwick in *Between Men,* women became the objects or a commodity of significance in the interaction between men.

In Tieck's the *Tea Society*, a transaction of this kind is carried out to attain respectability. The family constellation is comprised of an uncle, Ahlfeld, and his niece, Julie, the salon hostess. Ahlfeld has found a husband for his niece, a baron, who has promised to provide him with a title. Ahlfeld explains to Julie that she has no need to love her husband because he has a sufficient relationship with the man: "You are a clever girl, and it'll work out. Men like the Baron are rare nowadays; I delight in him uncommonly, because he delights in me, and thus we have, I believe,

---

[120] Feilchenfeld, "Die Berliner Salons der Romantik," 52ff.
[121] Sandor Ferenczi, *Sex in Psychoanalysis* (Boston: Badger, 1922), 35–93.

come into a certain parallelism of friendship."[122] This passage reveals that it is the relationships between men that are significant. These relationships determine and motivate the power behind the attraction of women. In the *Tea Society*, the surrogate daughter is to be traded for a title for the surrogate father. Elsewhere in the play, the purpose of marriage is to integrate a man into society: "A person is still not—how shall I put it—yet quite happy, yet quite a citizen of the world, until such time as he is married."[123] The happiness brought by marriage is the ability to become a full citizen of society. Possession of power is a male attribute; women can at best augment a man's power.

Thus, women in the salons fit neatly into a patriarchal society. Such a clearly defined gender separation "can be even more homosexual than gay male culture" to use a phrase from Eve Sedgwick's *Epistemology of the Closet* and that she took from Craig Owens. The bonds between men that are at least homosocial, if not homoerotic, are not broken by women in such a man's world. The homoerotic structure of mentoring is not a sphere women have been able to break, and the significant and powerful bonds remain between men.

The classical ideal of intellectual mentoring is based on the homoerotic relationship between Socrates and Alcibiades as described in Plato's *Symposium*. Castiglione's *prima genitor* the *Book of the Courtier* refers to Alcibiades several times as having human qualities that are to be emulated. The information on the Socrates-Alcibiades relationship is presented in Plato's work in such a way as to praise the continence of Socrates and to explain the attraction this old man holds for his young student because of the elder's intellectual prowess. The story tells us of the erotically charged desire Alcibiades has for Socrates and of the various attempts by the young man to place his teacher in sexually provocative situations.[124] In one particular instance, Plato alludes to the continence of Socrates in his rejection of the advances made by Alcibiades. It is a trope of this story that the homoeroticism is emphasized by Socrates's placing his urges under erasure. The relationship remains a sexualized instance of homoerotic attraction and the ideal of intellectual mentoring—one that excludes women.

---

[122]Tieck, *Die Theegesellschaft*, 377.
[123]Ibid., 367.
[124]Plato, *The Republic and Other Works*, trans. B. Jowett (New York: Doubleday Anchor, 1973), 355–65.

This examination of the sexual dynamics of the German salon at the end of the eighteenth century and the beginning of the nineteenth does not provide any evidence of a changed status for women in the circulation of sexuality within intellectual communities. In the differentiated network of sexual roles in the salon, women took a submissive and passive position in interaction—even to the point of being a commodity traded for power and honor. Doubtless many women made significant contributions to intellectual exchange, and Ferdinand indicates that women were at times violating these sexual norms by writing. The dialogues examined here show that the tone of salon conversation as reported, however, afforded women a highly sexualized and objectified role that by its very nature excluded them from intellectual input, and this situation is even acknowledged by Herz in her memoirs. Violations of the norms notwithstanding, salon sociability does not offer us a feminized sphere of women's emancipation as some research would like present it.

Instead, we have a structure of relationships that continues to emphasize homosocial bonds between those involved in the salons. The ideal of salon sociability is constructed as sexualized in Schlegel's *Lucinde*, in which the male protagonist discovers a new form of intimacy in the salon: "Julius had also changed his external behavior; he was more sociable.... [H]e rejected some [participants] entirely in order to be all the more intimately bound to a few." And it is Lucinde who manages this sociability: "Lucinde bound and maintained it all, and thus, free sociability, or rather a big family, came about."[125] The notion of individuals playing surrogate family roles is closely bound with issues of Freudian and post-Freudian sexuality.

Eve Kosofsky Sedgwick has explored the sexuality of such surrogate groups. In her paper "Tales of the Avunculate," published in the 1993 *Tendencies* collection, this model is applied to Oscar Wilde's *The Importance of Being Ernest*.[126] Relationships do not turn out to be what they first appear, and in her analysis, the secret Bunburying excursions take on a focal significance.

The relationship between Jack and Algernon has a parallel in that between Werner and Ehlert in Tieck's *Tea Society*. Here also their friendship is central, and as

---

[125]Schlegel, *Lucinde*, 64.
[126]Eve Kosofsky Sedgewick, "Tales of the Avunculate," in *Tendencies* (Durham, N.C.: Duke University Press, 1993), 52–72.

indicated above, the restoration of good order with the betrothal of Werner and Julie also revives the old friendship between the young men. What had disturbed the good order was a bogus aristocrat who had interloped as a suitor to Julie. His position had been achieved by promising the uncle, Ahlfeld (Julie's surrogate father), a title. The daughter is being traded for a name for the father. Only by cross-dressing as a fortune-telling gypsy is Werner able to achieve a position that allows him to reveal the truth. The real connection that makes a difference in this salon is that between the father and the bogus baron.

The description by the uncle "Er gustiert mich und ich gustiere ihn" means literally that "he tastes me and I taste him." But what has been contravened here is not a rule about sexuality; rather, it is one of class, in that the baron is not what he pretends to be. Power and influence are what matter in the relationships mapped out in the salon; comical transgressions of sexual taboos help highlight Ahlfeld's ridiculous pursuit of the title Julie's marriage to the baron promises. The dutiful Julie does not object to the match and, as far as the intellectual or artistic life of the salon is concerned, is only significant as a marker in the relationships Werner forges with others. Ahlfeld is the real power broker in the marriage game.

Henriette Herz tends to see herself in a similar passive role between powerful men although, in reality, she was eventually an active translator and intellectual in her own right. In Henriette Herz's salon the intellectual focus for the young attendees is at least initially her husband, who is fifteen years her senior. Just as Herz is self-deprecating about her intellectual position in the salon, so too must have been other salon women, whose assessment must often have been that they were present in order to stimulate male learning.

3. Dialogue and Dialectic

Concerns about the intimacy of the gatherings in the Herz household were countered in Schleiermacher's mind, as evidenced by his writing, through the very positive value he gave to close friendship. His ideas on friendship were not matters of mere visceral experiential phenomena for him, instead he sought to formulate philosophically and live publicly what he saw as an exemplary life of loyalty to his intimate circle of friends. This circle brought him into contact with significant philosophical persons and ideas that circulated in Berlin at the end of the eighteenth century. For Schleiermacher it was only natural that intimacy, friendship and philosophy should be linked in such explicit ways

3.1. Intimacy

Early on Henriette and Markus Herz had experienced sociability together in the home of Moses Mendelssohn. Here, one of the daughters of the house, Brendel—later known as Dorothea—had presided over a salon, with her father providing patriarchal approval in the background. Originally, there had only been a more traditional reading society in the home over which Mendelssohn presided and at which his wife and children were present. Henriette Herz's recollections about these gatherings make it clear that it is through the daughters that she and Rahel Levin became active participants. The family of Moses Mendelssohn, thus, provided the original locus for these gatherings at which were various well-known literati.

Konrad Feilchenfeldt has pointed out that salon sociability began as family sociability,[1] specifically with the significant Mendelssohn family. With the opening up of the Mendelssohn household and the inclusion of all members of its immediate family in this sociability, participation in Mendelssohn gatherings can be seen as entering the family sphere. Ingeborg Drewitz has made the very plausible suggestion that this family sociability may, in the first instance, have extended to other Jewish families for the purpose of celebrating religious festivals together.[2] Such celebrations would bring the families Levin, de Lemos, Herz, Veit, and possibly Cohen together with the Mendelssohns at various times, as they were all members of an economic elite among Berlin Jews.

In the second generation, this familial space opens further, and its religious basis erodes entirely, for the salon takes on an entirely gentile focus. For Dorothea Mendelssohn, her Jewish husband is replaced by a gentile, Friedrich Schlegel, and by conversion to Roman Catholicism. For Rahel Levin, marriage to a gentile of noble status, Varnhagen von Ense (even if his claim to the title was dubious), is accompanied by baptism. Henriette Herz, however, remains within Judaism, although even she converts to Christianity upon the death of her mother.

In the end, the common factor of Jewish identity is replaced by intimate friendship between individual members of the salon. In Schlegel's *Lucinde*, Julius displays this link between intimacy and his new-found sociability: "Julius had also changed his external behavior; he was more sociable....[H]e rejected some [participants] entirely in order to be all the more intimately bound to a few." And, it is Lucinde who manages this sociability: "Lucinde bound and maintained it all, and thus, free sociability, or rather a big family, came about."[3] Lucinde's sociability creates a large family out of an intimately connected few.

In light of this familial intimacy, Schleiermacher's opening statement in the *Essay* concerning free sociability as "neither fettered nor determined by any external end is demanded vociferously by all educated people as one of their primary and most cherished needs" can readily be connected with these early models of family sociability that the Mendelssohn family provided. For Schleiermacher sociability combines friendship and community with the religious, in a manner similar to the

---

[1] Feilchenfeldt, "Die Berliner Salons der Romantik," 152–56.
[2] Drewitz, *Berliner Salons*, 22.
[3] Schlegel, *Lucinde*, 64.

original sociability in Moses Mendelssohn's home. Inge Hoffmann-Axthelm has pointed out that Schleiermacher must have been influenced by his experiences in the community of Herrnhuter Brothers in Niesky and Barby where he was educated and trained for the priesthood.[4] In this community, however, sociability was not free, but rather bound by a highly restrictive conventional morality, a morality very much at odds with the natural ethics Schleiermacher expresses in the *Confidential Letters*.

Free sociability is available to Schleiermacher in the friendships he makes among his Berlin associates. This friendship system also carries over to his letters: his correspondents functioning as a family with relationships based on intimacy. When he sets up a common household with Schlegel, the union is both jokingly and at times seriously referred to by Schleiermacher as a "marriage" (*Ehe*).[5] By applying this term, Schleiermacher's daily life possesses something of the sociable ideal of intimacy that he sought.

Schleiermacher also expresses this ideal when he writes of preferring intimate settings with Henriette Herz over interactions with other visitors:

> My favorite time to see Herz is between lunch and the hour for tea. This is because anyone other than an intimate friend of the house will not readily visit at this time. If toward the end I am surprised by strangers, then I stay for another hour or so, depending on whether I find them agreeable or not, or I take my leave right away.[6]

Some others can contribute to this close group if they are members of the intimate circle. In this presentation of his preferences Schleiermacher reveals that he does not require exclusive contact with Herz because the time he chooses to be with her is a period of the day in which other intimate friends might call.

Both Schleiermacher's *Christmas Eve* and his *Confidential Letters* show family to be the core of meaningful sociability. The basis for the dialogue of the *Christmas Eve* is a family, with close friends being added to the circle established by the family gathering. This work has been convincingly interpreted as being based on the von Willich home on Rügen: several of the characters are identifiable as various family members. It was such an ideal for Schleiermacher that he adopted it as his

---

[4] Inge Hoffmann-Axthelm, „*Geisterfamilie*". *Studien zur Geselligkeit der Frühromantik* (Frankfurt am Main: Akademische Verlagsgemeinschaft, 1973), 121.
[5] *KGA* V/2, 219. Cf. Hoffmann-Axthelm, „*Geisterfamilie*", 124.
[6] *KGA* V/4, 376. Cf. Hoffmann-Axthelm, „*Geisterfamilie*", 145.

own by marrying the von Willich widow, thus taking on the family as a fait accompli.

The subject matter of the *Confidential Letters* concerns Schlegel and Dorothea Veit, née Mendelssohn, who later marry, thus taking the intimacy of the salon to its logical conclusion. Schleiermacher approves of this conclusion, and he applies his literary skills to defend it in the *Confidential Letters*.

At the time of his reading *Lucinde* and preparing his *Confidential Letters*, Schleiermacher was also considering various works of classical philosophy. Further, around this time, he was considering the *Essay*. In his note collection, *Notebooks of Thoughts* III (*Gedankenhefte* III), his comments on *Lucinde* and Plato's *Lysis* come close together and are followed by further observations concerning Aristotle's *Nicomachean Ethics*.[7] Schleiermacher made these notes at the most only some months after similar notes found their way into the *Essay*. The project to translate Plato had been an enterprise planned between Schleiermacher and Schlegel for some time. Here, Schleiermacher is preparing ideas connected with Aristotle by taking clearly referenced notes from his own edition of the *Nicomachean Ethics*.[8]

The subject matter of the *Nicomachean Ethics* brings together the issues of ethics and friendship, and Schleiermacher is still steeped in these issues when he writes to Henriette Herz declaring that he lacks company. He writes in a way that also reflects his philosophical interests at that point: "I have read one of Plato's dialogues, I have done a little piece on religion, I have written letters. In short, I have tried everything but the good way of life—and what should I do with that without company?"[9] A dialogue by Plato could be any one of many. Still, it could well be *Lysis*, which is referred to in note 65 of the *Notebooks* III. The February 14 date of the letter would place this part of the *Notebooks* somewhat earlier than generally thought, but it does not contradict the other dating information for them.[10]

---

[7] *KGA*, I/2, 119–39.

[8] The notes are so clear here that it was possible to identify the very edition from which Schleiermacher was taking them (See *KGA*, I/2, xxxf). He was thus preparing these references in order to be able to refer back to them at a later date.

[9] *Herz*, 281.

[10] Notes 79 and 80 must come after 1801 as they refer to a posthumous autobiography of Hippel that appeared in that year (*KGA*, I/2, xxix). However, the date of 1799 for note 41 (ibid., xxx), which refers to atheism, need not be placed far into the year. The atheism controversy certainly reached its zenith in the spring of 1799, but it had been gaining momentum for some time. It started in October 1798 with essays by Fichte and his student Forberg in the *Philosophisches Journal*, edited by Fichte.

The good life, which is useless without company, also has points of reference with the *Notebooks* III. At least some of the references to the *Nicomachean Ethics* occur at a point in the notes that likely postdates the writing of Schleiermacher's letter to Herz, but it is safe to assume familiarity with this material at the time of the composition of the *Essay*. In the *Notebooks* III Schleiermacher refers to happiness that is represented by the good life and of which friendship is a component.

Schleiermacher's friend Friedrich Schlegel knew of the importance of friendship for Schleiermacher, and in *Lucinde* Schlegel explained what sociable friendship was about. The second letter to Antonio in *Lucinde* deals with two kinds of friendship. Antonio represents Schleiermacher, and Julius, the author of the letter, is a thinly disguised Schlegel, such that Schleiermacher can be expected to reflect on this letter in particular:

> My feeling is that there are two kinds of friendship.
>
> The first is completely external. It rushes insatiably from deed to deed and accepts every worthy man into the great federation of united heroes. It ties the old knot tighter with each virtue and is always seeking to win new brothers; the more it has, the more it desires....The other friendship is completely internal. A wonderful symmetry of the most unique, as if it were all determined ahead of time that one was to complement one's self everywhere. All thoughts and feelings become sociable by means of mutual encouragement and development of the most sacred.[11]

The first kind of friendship is worthy in its own right and is like a civil organization that is based on mutual virtue. The second variety is sociable and intimate. The self is developed and absorbed, thus taking it to a new sacred level of being. The second is a new type of friendship, based on a new motivational codex. For Aristotle it is the deed that determines virtue: as Julius says in the same letter comparing these two forms of friendship:

An anonymous reply appeared as a pamphlet in November of that year. In January 1799 Fichte's defense against his indictment for atheism appeared. Although the bulk of material was published in response to this latter work, a sufficient case can be made to place this fragment as early as late 1798 or January 1799. As a theologian Schleiermacher is likely to have been interested in such a subject at an early stage in the dispute. For an exposition of the events surrounding this controversy, see Peter Rohs, *Johann Gottlieb Fichte* (Munich: Beck, 1991); Beck'sche Reihe: Große Denker, vol. 521: "Atheismusstreit 1798//99": 111–21.

[11] Schlegel, *Lucinde*, 85.

The deed will teach whether the virtue of a man holds true. However, whoever feels and sees humankind and the world internally will not readily be able to seek universal spirit where it is not to be found.[12]

As Aristotle puts it in the *Nicomachean Ethics*, "we become just by doing just acts" (1103b1). The test for virtue lies in action. He explains at the beginning of Book II that ethics has its root in habit: "[M]oral virtue comes about as a result of habit, whence also its name *ethike* is one that is formed by a slight variation from the word *ethos* (habit)" (1103a16f.).[13]

Clearly, Schlegel's view of virtue is entirely commensurate with Aristotle's. What then of friendship, which also figures as a subject of the *Nicomachean Ethics*? Once more, Schlegel is telling Schleiermacher something similar to Aristotle. Friendship for Aristotle figures in two ways, both of which are external goods.[14] Friends can be useful in achieving ends as other tools and instruments can (1099b27). The second way in which friendship is an external good, however, is quite different, having to do with friendship being valuable in its own right. This notion is expressed in Book VIII:

> For without friends no one would choose to live, though he had all other goods; even rich men and those in possession of office and of dominating power are thought to need friends most of all; for what is the use of such prosperity without the opportunity of beneficence, which is exercised chiefly and in its most laudable form towards friends? (1155a5-9)[15]

Schlegel is aware of the general nature of Aristotle's view and applies a roughhewn model of it to his theories on friendship. His view of the second kind of friendship is a more self-focused formulation and bears something of a Fichtean ego. Still, Schleiermacher has the greater fidelity to classical models; it is Schleiermacher, not Schlegel, who made good on the promise to complete translations of the works of Plato. Aristotle's definition of friendship is on Schleiermacher's mind when he writes

---

[12] Ibid., 85f.

[13] *Introduction to Aristotle*, ed. Richard McKeon (New York: Random House, 1947), 331. For a broader and specific analysis of Schleiermacher's use of Plato's dialectics see: Julia A. Lamm, "Reading Plato's Dialectics: Schleiermacher's Insistence of Dialectics as Dialogical," *Zeitschrift für neuere Theologiegeschichte/Journal for the History of Modern Theology* 10 (2003): 1-25.

[14] The exposition of this issue follows Nancy Sherman, "Aristotle on the Shared Life," in *Friendship: A Philosophical Reader*, ed. Neera Kapur Badhwar (Ithaca: Cornell University Press, 1993), 92ff.

to Henriette Herz complaining of the lack of society: "In short, I have tried everything except the good life—and what should I do with the latter without company."[16] The similarity to Aristotle is striking. The editor of Schleiermacher's letter in the critical edition is right to point out that this statement refers to the writing of the *Essay*.[17] Yet, it is more: it is Schleiermacher's acknowledgment of the profound debt that he owes Aristotle for his own conception of friendship and virtue. A good life is a life of virtue, and happiness can only be achieved through external goods among which friends figure prominently. The intimation (and one could expect Henriette Herz to be aware of the reference to Aristotle) is that life is not worth living without friends.

3.2. Philosophy and the Salon

Moses Mendelssohn represented a new phenomenon among the Jews: he was a publicly acclaimed individual participating in the mainstream of gentile intellectual debate. His contribution to discussions concerning the ideas of his time earned him broad respect. As a young man, Mendelssohn, by studying German, violated the strictures of the Jewish community of Berlin set by the elders. It was his translation of the Pentateuch into German that laid a foundation for the Jewish community to emulate his example. He also published widely on philosophy and became a close associate of Lessing and Nicolai.

Lessing left a monument to him in the figure of Nathan in *Nathan the Wise*, in which the eponymous hero preaches religious tolerance. Mendelssohn espoused a doctrine that allowed for various forms of belief within a political state. Moral personhood within a state was achieved through a compact between the individual and the state: by means of this compact, the individual resigned his authority to the political power. For Mendelssohn, religion was a matter for individual conscience and was voluntary. No religion had the authority to coerce belief.[18] He believed in achieving a closing of the gap between Jews and gentiles by renewing the

---

[15] Ibid., 471.
[16] *KGA*, V/3, 10n. 23.
[17] Ibid.
[18] Sorkin, *The Transformation of German Jewry*, 69.

commitment to religion through a reflection upon the rational basis of such belief systems. Thus, Mendelssohn made a move toward emancipation and assimilation based upon the tenets of Enlightenment rationality. Mendelssohn and his Berlin home became a focal point for those with similar philosophical leanings, and his hospitality was enjoyed by both educated Jews and notable gentiles.

One of the few Jews in the second half of the eighteenth century to have had the benefit of a university education was Mendelssohn's physician, Markus Herz. Herz had studied at the University of Königsberg and had become Immanuel Kant's most distinguished student. It was he whom Kant chose as respondent to his inaugural dissertation, delivered as a public defense upon being elected to the chair of logic and metaphysics at the university of Königsberg in 1770 (Kant had waited fifteen years with the status of *Privatdozent* for this professorship).

When Herz came to Berlin, he continued to correspond with his former teacher and provided an important link between the distinguished philosopher and cultural developments in Berlin. It was through Herz, for example, that Kant learned of the work of Solomon Maimon, another Jewish philosopher residing in Berlin. In Berlin Maimon had found refuge from a destitute life and had taken advantage of the liberalized attitude toward learning available to a small group of Jews there. The manuscript he produced as the result of his studies offered what amounted to a skeptical defense of Kant's critical philosophy, showing that he had submerged himself in the newest philosophical ideas.

Henriette Herz's memoirs tell us that Markus Herz gradually made a name for himself in Berlin by publishing on philosophy, by holding seminars on physics in the home he shared with Henriette, and by lecturing publicly.[19] Many of the social contacts he initially made were with those to whom he ministered as a physician, but his fame spread and so did his acquaintances. His lectures on physics, for instance, with their displays of experiments were visited by the younger brothers of the King and the five-year-old crown prince. A connection was made with the Humboldt family when the construction of a lightening conductor was under consideration for the house of that family at Tegel. Initially, the household tutor Gottlob Kunth came to seek Markus's advice, and eventually the two boys, Wilhelm and Alexander,

---

[19] *Herz*; the comment on publishing is on p. 24; the rest of the information in this paragraph is from p. 27f.

accompanied Kunth to view Herz's experiments and listen to his lectures.

Markus Herz also lectured as a member of Ignaz Feßler's Mittwochs-Gesellschaft, and it is as an offshoot of this group that the Herz household became "one of the most highly regarded and sought after of Berlin."[20] Further analysis of the section of Henriette Herz's autobiographical narrative from which this information is drawn offers a greater understanding of the way in which she constructed her salon sociability such that it was different from that of some contemporaneous sociable phenomena.

After mentioning a number of reading societies, the last of which is the Teekränzchen,[21] Henriette Herz writes about Feßler's Mittwochs-Gesellschaft. This group was still in existence at the time of her writing, and she runs through an impressive list of men who were among its first members. When she writes of the group's intellectual program, she first mentions her husband (as she did with the list of original members) who read (*wissenschaftliche*) papers from various disciplines. Next she comes to a famous actor:

> Neither the belles lettres [*Schönwissenschaftliches*] nor dramatic material were lacking here, and no one read the latter more poorly than Fleck, who was the most bright star in what was then a truly dazzling heavenly array in the theater of those times. He was only inspired by the stage. There, he spoke compellingly, expressing every feeling with inimitable truth and irresistibly evoking every one of the same feelings in the listener.[22]

Through Fleck the whole of literary appreciation is denigrated in the environment of the Mittwochs-Gesellschaft. It is neither the material nor the presenter so much as the organizational structure that fails to allow the members' abilities to come to full fruition. Culture of this nature is clearly out of place in such surroundings.

Herz reaches this conclusion in the introductory sentence of the next paragraph and then goes on to undermine the institution further:

> In this group, also, one naturally had to be undemanding with regard to one's spiritual nourishment from time to time. However, one always needed to be undemanding with regard to one's bodily nourishment because, after the

---

[20]Ibid., 51.
[21]Ibid, 50. Cf. Seibert, *Der literarische Salon*, 184ff.
[22]*Herz*, 50f.

reading, one ate incredibly badly. This took place under the light of a few tallow candles that cast little more than a dusky glow over a room that was long and narrow like a piece of intestine.[23]

The whole ambiance is lowered rhetorically to that of a rather impoverished sphere in which nothing comes up to scratch. Not only is the food and the lighting poor, but even the space in which one eats is uncomfortable and as uncouth as a piece of intestine.

Herz ends her discussion of this group on a note that leaves an impression that the Mittwochs-Gesellschaft was an unimpressive organization: "But nobody was demanding, nobody was pretentious, and thus, these external matters did not disturb us."[24] These difficulties failed to disturb those attending because nobody expected very much of the meetings.

At this point in her memoirs, Herz turns to the subject of the gatherings in her home. She tells us that "[s]everal members of Feßler's society came to our house," and in the same sentence, she writes that "almost every intellectually significant outsider [non-Berliner]" also came. It is this combination that makes her household significant: "Under such auspicious circumstances our house developed, of which I can say without exaggeration, that, within a short space of time, it became one of the most respected and sought after of Berlin."

A connection with the Mittwochs-Gesellschaft is evident, but Henriette Herz is at pains to contrast the meager offerings of that group with the standing her home has in Berlin sociability. By means of the contrast, her home clearly possesses those elements that were lacking in the Mittwochs-Gesellschaft: "[Markus] Herz drew people to him by means of his spirit and his fame as a physician, and I by means of my beauty and the notion I had for everything scientific."[25] The words she uses here are "alles Wissenschaftliche," which cover the belles lettres as well as the natural sciences. The former were referred to in her text earlier, as mentioned above, as "Schönwissenschftliches," which is evoked again here by her juxtaposition of "Schönheit" (beauty) with "alles Wissenschaftliche." Thus, she is able to offer something that is presented rhetorically as being very much an improvement upon

---
[23]Ibid., 51.
[24]Ibid.
[25]*Herz*, 51.

the dull environment of the Mittwochs-Gesellschaft, which is even detrimental to such cultural phenomena as drama. Under these auspices, Henriette Herz's salon stands out as a true alternative to the older forms of sociability in Berlin.

4. Philosophical Content of the *Essay*.

Those close to Schleiermacher provided an invigorating context for his philosophical development in Berlin. Schleiermacher had found a Kantian ally in Markus Herz and in Friedrich Schlegel and Henriette Herz he had found younger compatriots who had accompanied him into a more modern world of ideas. Schleiermacher made this combination of Enlightenment and Romantic ideas his very own. This chapter will examine the specifics of the philosophical path Schleiermacher chose in negotiating various texts that contributed to his formulation of the *Essay*.

4.1. Rejecting Fichte

The *Essay* has seen increasing scholarly interest as a work concerned with literary salons, but it has garnered scant attention as a philosophical work in its own right. Two philosophical interpretations of the *Essay* in German see Schleiermacher as developing ideas derived from Johann Gottlieb Fichte's *Grundlage der gesammten Wissenschaftslehre* (*Basis of the Entire Doctrine of Science*) of 1794/95. In his edition of the *Essay* for the *Kritische Gesamtausgabe*, Günter Meckenstock reads Schleiermacher as developing Fichte's three basic propositions (*Grundsätze*).[1] Andreas Arndt also sees Schleiermacher deriving his thought from the *Basis of the Entire Doctrine of Science*, but he identifies the opening of the practical section five, the second doctrinal proposition (*Zweiter Lehrsatz*), as key to the *Essay*.[2]

Fichte's philosophy, therefore, warrants close examination as Schleiermacher uses language in the *Essay* that clearly resonates with that of Fichte. A stronger case

---
[1] *KGA*, I/2, li.
[2] Arndt, "Geselligkeit und Gesellschaft," 59.

than those of Meckenstock and Arndt, however, can be made for sources other than the *Doctrine of Science* as producing Schleiermacher's resonance with Fichte. This case can be made in a way that is entirely consonant with Schleiermacher's, at times underestimated, rejection of Fichte's philosophy. In specifically concentrating on Schleiermacher's formulation of the notion of freedom, I propose that his philosophical position in 1799 is a reaction to the unresolved antinomies of freedom in Fichte's 1796 *Grundlage des Naturrechts* (*Basis of Natural Law*) in particular.

According to Meckenstock, the three basic propositions of the *Doctrine of Science* can be seen to coordinate with the three laws of Schleiermacher's *Essay*: the general concept of society taken together with concrete individualized sociability leads to Schleiermacher's formal, material, and quantitative laws.[3] Certainly, this propositional approach echoes that of Fichte, and Meckenstock's brief remarks are intentionally limited as a historical introduction to the *Essay*; thus these comments do not come close to developing an argument about Fichte's and Schleiermacher's respective sets of propositions. In seeking parallelism in this instance between these two writers, one should keep in mind that the method of developing propositions in this manner is characteristic of all philosophers who followed Spinoza, who used this method most boldly in his *Ethics*. It is likely that both Fichte and Schleiermacher were likewise influenced. Thus, the fact that both philosophers have three propositions may be no more than a coincidence.

Still, there are certainly other indications in Schleiermacher's text to lead to the suspicion that Fichte played some role. The very fact that Schleiermacher uses such characteristically Fichtean terms as "Wechselwirkung" (mutual affecting), and "Selbsttätigkeit" (self-activity, or independent action) to illuminate his philosophy should make a historian of philosophy look closely at the works of Fichte to find impulses that led to the *Essay*. Meckenstock's notion is certainly worthwhile, but the scope of the comments in the *Kritische Gesamtausgabe* did not leave him room for a more nuanced development and analysis of Schleiermacher's application of Fichte's ideas. In a longer study like the present one, any indication that Schleiermacher is applying Fichte's ideas needs to be examined closely and skeptically, especially in light of the fact that Schleiermacher was adamant about rejecting Fichte's philosophy.

---

[3]*KGA*, I/2, li.

In a letter to Friedrich Heinrich Christian Schwarz, who had reviewed his *Speeches on Religion,* Schleiermacher makes the case that his work is to be differentiated very sharply from that of Fichte: "Within idealism...one cannot make a greater contrast than between him [Fichte] and me."[4] While aligning himself with philosophical idealism, Schleiermacher made it clear that he did not see it as a unified movement. He had made some references to Fichte's philosophy in *On Religion* and was now careful to make the point, not only that there were differences, but that there was in fact a powerful contrast to be made.

Schleiermacher had been reading Fichte at least since Friedrich Schlegel had encouraged him to do so. For evidence of this reading, one mostly has to rely on Schlegel's 1798 letters because those from Schleiermacher during this period are lost. Schlegel's letters reveal that Schleiermacher is reading Fichte (and Kant) intensely at this time: "That you [Schleiermacher] are so diligently at your Kant and Fichte is not just a matter that pleases me as such, but it is also worth a lot to me because I think you are doing it for my sake."[5] Schleiermacher had possibly been familiar with Fichte before this time, but Schlegel certainly encouraged him to deepen his knowledge of the philosopher. A note in Schleiermacher's *Notebooks of Thoughts* I (*Gedankenhefte* I) from September 1797 indicates that he was already reading or discussing Fichte's *Wissenschaftslehre* or some other work by Fichte, derived from the *Wissenschaftslehre*'s principles, and finding with which elements to take issue:

> There are only two virtues: 1) Philosophical virtue, or pure love of humanity, i.e., striving to posit the I absolutely to bring about humanity and to raise it up; 2.) heroic virtue, or pure love of freedom, i.e., striving to give the I dominance over nature allied with it.... Scientific development [*Bildung*] [does] not belong to virtue at all, but historical development does because it leads to the development of the absolute. That is why the sciences are only of historical interest to philosophical natures. Maintaining life or increasing knowledge by positing the components of virtue involves lots of contradictions. In so far as philosophical virtue is sociable, it is called religious virtue—a striving to help other individuals also to posit their

---

[4]Schleiermacher to F. H. C. Schwarz, March 28, 1801. Cited after Andreas Arndt, "Gefühl und Reflexion. Schleiermachers Stellung zur Transcendentalphilosophie im Kontext der Zeitgenössischen Kritik an Kant und Fichte," in *Der Streit um die Gestalt einer Ersten Philosophie (1799–1807)*, ed. Walter Jaeschke (Hamburg: Meiner, 1999), 110.

[5]*KGA*, V/2, August 6, 1798, 384.

absolute I. In so far as the heroic virtue is sociable, it is called cosmopolitan virtue. It has been a mistaken abstraction to see sociable virtue as something special because a person is not possible without others, and so, there could be no virtue that is not already sociable of its own accord.[6]

Schleiermacher was acquiring a differentiated view of Fichte's *Doctrine of Science* by September 1797. Because of the specific references to virtue in this passage, Schleiermacher is possibly discussing Fichte's *Bestimmung des Menschen* (*Vocation of Man*), which he later reviewed for the *Atheneaum*, but the references to positing the "I absolutely" are sufficiently general that he appears to be talking about the *Doctrine of Science* in the broadest possible terms. Elsewhere, in this section, he even compares his assessment of these ideas with Kant, whom he would like to include among the empiricists. Schleiermacher expresses frustration with philosophy in general when he says this positing merely achieves maintaining the I over time—what he calls the "historical interest" of the philosophical natures.

He preempts both the *Essay* and *On Religion* by moving the discussion to sociability and then religion. It will prove valuable to look at this passage again when attempting to evaluate the reasons why Schleiermacher abandoned the *Essay* and turned to religious matters in *On Religion*. At this point, it is sufficient to say that philosophy did not hold the answers he sought, particularly as formulated by Kant and Fichte. The solutions he saw offered were fraught with "lots of contradictions." Philosophical virtue ends as being something that is religious virtue, and Schleiermacher is willing to consider it under that rubric—this sociable virtue has been mistaken as something virtuous in its own right when it is actually virtuous merely because it is sociable. Heroic virtue as pure love of freedom is sociable and virtuous in a secular, or he put it "cosmopolitan," way. Heroic secular sociability, the love of pure freedom, is the subject of the *Essay*'s "free sociability." This view is contrasted in the above passage with a Fichtean "striving to posit the I absolutely" that proves itself to be nothing special. The contradictions that Schleiermacher sees are thus the subject of a practical approach to philosophical matters rather than a theoretical or abstract approach to philosophy. For Schleiermacher, virtue is to be achieved as a philosophically practical matter in society, rather than through mere

---

[6]*KGA*, I/2, 9f. As this passage (note 15) comes between note 10, dated September 10, 1797, and note 20, dated September 29, 1797, we are justified in assuming a date in mid-September 1797 for this section.

positing of the I.

However, this notion does not mean that he is against philosophical approaches; indeed, he has disdain for both a purely empirical and a purely intellectual approach. Calling the empirical approach one that concentrates on life, he writes:

> This interest in life is not virtuous at all; it produces not virtuous people but only those who live virtuously. Similarly, intellectual interest is not virtuous either. It is focused on maintaining the existence of the I in its mediated connection with external nature through reflection, namely through necessary reflection.[7]

Schleiermacher's position, then, is carefully differentiated as a rejection both of the practical Aristotelian approach to ethics in the first instance and in the second as a disapproval of Fichte's focusing on the reflexive positing I as self-serving or uninteresting. Schleiermacher's antiphilosophical ire is here formulated in singularly philosophical language, but his rough thoughts in this writing will ultimately develop into cogent positions in the *Essay* and in the *Speeches on Religion*, in which sociability and philosophy are again joined.

These critical positions can be drawn on to illuminate comments Schleiermacher made about meeting Fichte. This juxtaposition will clarify Schleiermacher's desire to see philosophy dealt with not in complete (or "absolute") abstractions but as a scientific tool to bring perspectives together and thus to synthesize new ideas. Schleiermacher criticizes Fichte's approach and yet praises the form of the latter's work in a letter to his friend Carl Gustav Brinckmann as 1799 turned to 1800:

> Fichte—who is also no longer here now—was, of course, someone I got to know—but he hardly affected me much. For him philosophy and life—as he lays it out theoretically too—are quite separate. His *natural way of thinking* [*natürliche Denkart*] is not at all extraordinary, and thus, he has nothing that would make him interesting for me as long as he remains on the level of that *general perspective* [*gemeinen Standpunct*]. Before he came, I had a mind to let him know that I thought that his way of differentiating a general perspective from a philosophical one did not work properly. But, once I saw

---

[7]*KGA*, V/2., 10.

how determined he is about his natural way of thinking, I soon struck that sail because I have nothing of that sort to criticize within his philosophy, and as far as I am concerned, admiration is no subject for discourse. Apart from that, there were no other connections than the most ordinary ones, so we didn't get to know each other well at all. He is not instructional because he doesn't seem to have detailed knowledge of other fields (not even in philosophy inasmuch as there is knowledge in philosophy), and instead, he has general overviews just as I might be capable of, too. It's a great shame by the way because he has a quite wonderful gift of making himself clear and is the greatest dialectician I know. I didn't notice any original opinions or connections, and he also completely lacks any wit or fantasy.[8]

Schleiermacher has nothing to disagree with within Fichte's philosophy that matches his disagreement with the nature of the perspective Fichte adopts to generate his philosophy. In the *Vocation of Man*, Fichte contrasts a "natural way of thinking" with the skeptical worries of someone trying to philosophize: "I wish to take up the viewpoint of natural thinking [*Dem Standpuncte des natürlichen Denkens*]…and to banish from my thoughts all brooding and ponderous argumentation that might only cause me to doubt its truth."[9] If this is the choice, then this very "brooding and ponderous argumentation" are what Schleiermacher considers to be the philosophical perspective.

This "viewpoint of natural thinking" is fundamental to the success of the *Doctrine of Science*. Fichte spends the entire second section (Knowledge) of the *Vocation of Man* creating a dialogue between a spirit and its human interlocutor in which the interlocutor becomes convinced of the necessity of this perspective of natural thinking. Schleiermacher is referring to this dialogue when he writes to Brinckmann crediting Fichte with being the greatest dialectician that he knows; this assessment is honored in Schleiermacher's review of the *Vocation of Man* when he makes part two of the review a dialogue. In fact, other elements of the form of Fichte's *Vocation of Man* are followed throughout Schleiermacher's review, three numbered sections with an introduction. The form of the work is what Schleiermacher admired most, and in this way, he emulated Fichte's clarity in exposition.

---

[8] Ibid., 5/3, 313 f.
[9] *Johann Gottlieb Fichtes Sämmtliche Werke*, ed. I. H Fichte, vol. 2 (Berlin: Veit, 1845), 253.

On substance though, the differences in philosophical approach are profound if Schleiermacher is making such a decided rejection of the fundamental perspective from which Fichte's unencumbered positing I is meant to operate. The first section of Fichte's *Vocation of Man* shows how this fundamental perspective is derived from his rejection of determinism. Fichte argues against a body of thought that sees destiny predetermined by some other natural force. Such a determinism assumes the existence of some eternal force that determines one's destiny:

> Such a freedom that is not *my own* at all but that of *some other force* external to me, and even for this force, it was merely determined and a semifreedom— this was what was not enough for me. *I myself*, that which I am conscious of as my self, as my own person…I myself wish to be independent—not dependent on another and not by means of another, but instead to be something for myself [*nicht an einem anderen, und durch ein anderes, sondern für mich selbst Etwas seyn*], and as such, I want to be the final cause of my destiny. The role that every originating natural force takes up in that body of thought I want to take up myself, with the only difference being that the means of expression is not determined by other forces.[10]

The seat of this first cause lies in Fichte's own "thinking and willing." He concludes that "my active natural force should only be under the command of my will."[11] The self-positing I thus becomes its own self-determined natural force. In this way it is completely free and its own first cause: free of all determination by external forces.

A subtle accusation of narcissism lurks in the humor and irony of Schleiermacher's review of *Vocation of Man* that is a response to Fichte's rejection of natural necessity:

> Why did [the I] startle so powerfully when confronted by that system of natural necessity? Because it would cause it to lose its love, its interest in itself, in its personality as a finite being, because it simply did not want to be dependent on another, and not for another, but instead to be something for itself [*nichts an einem andern und für ein anderes, sondern nur etwas an und für sich selbst sein wollte*].[12]

---

[10]Ibid., 191.
[11]Ibid., 192.
[12]*KGA*, I/3, 246. Although Meckenstock noted many of the places in Fichte's text on which Schleiermacher drew for his review, this example was one that he did not find.

The subtlety of this criticism lies in talking of the I that can at the same time be read as being Fichte. This approach masks Schleiermacher's personal contempt for Fichte that here lurks behind the recounting of the essential arguments of *Vocation of Man*. But, while on one level Schleiermacher is accusing Fichte of self-infatuation, on another, he is questioning the validity of so absolutely rejecting natural necessity. Schleiermacher will resolve the case of freedom without recourse to an absolutely independent self-posited I.

Two conclusions can be drawn so far concerning Schleiermacher's dispute with Fichte about freedom and nature. As seen just above, Schleiermacher believes that Fichte's recourse to the self-positing I may merely be grounded in a profound preoccupation of Fichte with Fichte. This accusation of narcissism humorously undermines Fichte's motivation for seeking a break from nature's causal chain and makes the enterprise seem fundamentally lacking in solid philosophical grounds. Additionally, Fichte's "natural way of thinking" contrasts with a "philosophical" approach to this issue that Fichte rejects as "brooding and ponderous argumentation." Fichte's "natural way of thinking" results in the harnessing of that force of cause and effect that is so evident in nature and making it reside in the thought and willing of the self-positing I. Schleiermacher rejects this absolute way of arguing to autonomy and resolves the issue of freedom in a way that is argued philosophically but still remains practical at the same time.[13]

4.2. Natural Law from Fichte's *Some Lectures on the Vocation of the Scholar*

In order to discuss Schleiermacher's discourse on freedom in the *Essay*, it is first important to start with Arndt's claims that the *Essay* can be understood to be taking

---

[13] At this point it is important to interject that the consequences of this rejection are enormous and go well beyond the scope of this study on Schleiermacher's *Essay on a Theory of Sociable Behavior*. The relationship between Schleiermacher's notions about consciousness and feeling, for example, have relied all too often on a Fichtean reading of Kant's notion of apperception. This complex theory has been subjected to a new careful and clarifying reading by Karl Ameriks, who makes definite distinctions between Kant's original and modest claims for apperception and those of Fichte and modern readers of Fichte who fail to distinguish between the Kantian and Fichtean notions of apperception. Ameriks, *Kant and the Fate of Autonomy: Problems in the Appropriation of Critical Philosophy* (Cambridge: Cambridge University Press, 2000), esp. 234–64. I leave further exploration of this important distinction for a future examination of Schleiermacher and consciousness.

its lead from the second doctrinal proposition of the practical section five of the *Doctrine of Science*.[14] Arndt has provided the most insightful and philosophically cogent arguments that exist concerning Schleiermacher's early work and concerning the *Essay* in particular. He is always careful to distinguish Schleiermacher's thoughts from those of Fichte and, in doing so, has provided some of the most in-depth analysis that there is on specific points of Schleiermacher's philosophical argumentation. However, I believe that a more clearly differentiated reading of the development of philosophy from Kant to Fichte is possible, and thus, the age in which Schleiermacher is making his critical approaches to idealism can be read quite differently.[15] True, the difference between Arndt's and my theses can in some senses be seen as a small one. Still, I am more inclined to look at the contrast between Schleiermacher and Fichte when Schleiermacher claims that "[w]ithin idealism...one cannot make a greater contrast than between him [Fichte] and me," whereas Arndt tends to emphasize the commonalities between the two that might be drawn from emphasizing the word "within."[16]

Arndt's claim that Schleiermacher draws on §5 of Fichte's *Doctrine of Science*, which is the latter's second doctrinal proposition (*Zweiter Lehrsatz*), rests on Schleiermacher's use of reciprocity as the limiting and determining factor of the sociable sphere. Arndt recounts that Fichte wanted to resolve the conflict between determining and being determined by declaring the conflict to be mere appearance: imagination could resolve the conflict by playful synthesis. Arndt maintains that Fichte's conflict within appearance is made real by Schleiermacher by the latter's placing it in the practical realm of society. To make this case, Arndt differentiates carefully between the Fichtean I and the not-I and compares those with the I and you of Friedrich Heinrich Jacobi. Arndt sees Schleiermacher's resolution derived analogously from Fichte's second doctrinal proposition, in which the oscillation between the I and not-I facilitates self-discovery in others.

Certainly, Arndt characterizes the practical nature of Schleiermacher's

---

[14] Arndt, "Geselligkeit und Gesellschaft," 59.

[15] I have already presented this thesis in Foley, *Heinrich von Kleist und Adam Müller. Untersuchung zur Aufnahme idealistischen Ideenguts durch Heinrich von Kleist* (Frankfurt am Main: Peter Lang, 1990). Ameriks has independently placed this differentiation on a solid philosophical foundation in many articles and in his recent book, *Kant and the Fate of Autonomy*.

[16] Schleiermacher to F. H. C. Schwarz, March 28, 1801. Cited after Arndt, "Gefühl und Reflexion," 110.

solution correctly. Furthermore, in seeing Schleiermacher's approach as one that develops the work of Fichte beyond Fichte's own thinking, Arndt provides an elegant solution to the problem of the evident use of Fichte's terminology by a thinker who privately expresses strong misgivings about Fichte's approach.

However, the connection between Schleiermacher's thinking and this particular section of Fichte's work is tenuous. Section five of the *Basis of the Entire Doctrine of Science* manifests one of the most vigorous affirmations of Fichte's philosophy of the I and not-I, and throughout the various manifestations of the *Doctrine of Science* (Fichte published numerous works with "*Doctrine of Science*" in the title) relies ultimately on the positing of that "natural way of thinking" and "general perspective" that Schleiermacher opposed. By evincing his support for Fichte's clarity and dialectic method, Schleiermacher gave himself the right to use the terminology of Fichte's philosophy, and it is this language that leads interpreters to seek affinities with the content of Fichte's works. More precisely, however, Fichte should be seen as setting a challenge for Schleiermacher to surmount. In this sense Arndt's ultimate characterization of Schleiermacher, achieved by looking at the real case of society and at societies as practical instances of a reciprocity used in Fichte's works, fits well with what I shall discuss in the following. The challenge for Schleiermacher's inquiry into the subject of "free sociability" comes not from Fichte's *Basis of the Entire Doctrine of Science* but from his *Basis of Natural Law*.

In section seven of *Natural Law*, Fichte states that jurisprudence is founded on the question of (his emphases) "*how can a community of free beings, as such, be possible?*"[17] The question is, of course, a perennial one, but one that Fichte seeks to solve by means of the principles of the *Doctrine of Science*. He sees a fundamental conflict between individual freedom and the making of the will of the individual subordinate to the structure of the state. In practice people find a way to work around this conflict: "It turns out that each member of the community limits his personal external freedom in his thoughts by means of internal freedom to such an extent that all other members of the community can remain externally free alongside him."[18] This practical strategy is achieved by means of the reciprocal relationship between members of the community. As rational beings, each of the members has the obligation to realize his or her "free effectivity" (*freie Wirksamkeit*). Action or

---

[17]*Grundlage des Naturrechts*, in *Fichtes Sämmtliche Werke* vol. 3, 85.
[18]Ibid., 9.

activity plays the functional role here, whether by acting or choosing not to act, because either of these is a free decision. In ascribing free effectivity to itself, a rational being must simultaneously ascribe it to others. Thus, free effectivity both describes and defines the existence of the external world in terms of the existence of other freely effective rational beings:

> The concept presented here is that of *free reciprocal effectivity* [*freie Wechselwirksamkeit*] at its most precise: it is nothing other than this. For any freely occurring effect, I can think of a free reactive effect as *accidental*, but that would not be the required precise concept. If the concept is to be determined precisely, *effect and reactive effect* cannot be thought of independently of each other... Something of this nature now has to be postulated as the necessary condition for the self-consciousness of a rational being.[19]

There is a process here by means of which self-consciousness of the individual reveals others to that rational being. Free reciprocal effectivity provides the concept that leads Fichte into a discussion of society, and the method and the concepts that it provides are very close to those used by Schleiermacher in the *Essay*.

Fichte develops this move toward others in his §3, the Second Doctrinal Proposition of *Natural Law*: "*The finite rational being cannot ascribe free effectivity to itself without ascribing it to others; this means assuming the existence of other finite rational beings other than itself.*"[20] The concluding definition at the end of this section defines humanity by means of this very reciprocity: "Only free reciprocity [*freie Wechselwirkung*] through concepts and according to concepts, only giving and receiving knowledge, is the authentic character of humanity, through which every person inexorably hardens themselves into a human being."[21]

Reciprocity is precisely the term Schleiermacher uses in the *Essay*: "Reciprocity thus reflects upon and completes itself: the concept of reciprocity contains both the purpose and the form of sociable activity, and that reciprocity also determines the entire nature of society."[22] Fichte's *Natural Law* shows clearly how this notion of reciprocity is derived and how it fits with the *Doctrine of Science* as a

---

[19]Fichte's emphases. Ibid., 34.
[20]Ibid., 40.
[21]Ibid.
[22]*KGA*, I/2, 170.

whole. However, the formulation of Fichte's concept of reciprocity in his *Einige Vorlesungen über die Bestimmung des Gelehrten* (*Some Lectures on the Vocation of the Scholar*)—in the second lecture in particular—resonates even more strongly with Schleiermacher's development of reciprocity as a concept that helps formulate free sociability.

Fichte sees his *Some Lectures on the Vocation of the Scholar* of 1794 as a propedeutic to a thoroughgoing work on natural law.[23] By clearing up questions concerning other beings and the body, this brief work covers some of the same ground as *Natural Law*. After defining society as "the relationship of rational beings to each other,"[24] Fichte goes on to explore reciprocity as in *Natural Law*. As in *Natural Law*, reciprocity in *Vocation of the Scholar* comes from the relationship with rational beings other than the self-conscious I. Again, this notion is derived from free activity. However, in *Vocation of the Scholar*, Fichte makes it clear that the term is derived from Kant: "This leads me to take advantage of Kantian terminology; a *reciprocity according to concepts*; a purposive community (*Gemeinschaft*): and this is what I call society (*Gesellschaft*). The concept of society has now been fully determined."[25] In this passage, we see the difference between Fichte and Schleiermacher, who in his third footnote of the *Essay* makes it clear that there is a need to distinguish between community and society. In talking about "the concept of the free sociability of society in its truest sense," Schleiermacher makes clear that it is "society" for its own sake and not "community" for some other purpose that constitutes true free sociability:

> The word should only be understood in this way. In every social gathering that is bound and defined by some external purpose, the participants have something *in common*. Such gatherings are *communities*, κοινονιαι; here, they actually have nothing in common; rather, everything is reciprocal, in effect at variance with each other; these are *societies*, συνουσιαι.[26]

Schleiermacher has taken Fichte's active concepts from *Natural Law* and *Vocation of the Scholar* in particular and has found an inconsistency in that Fichte's

---

[23] *Fichtes Sämmtliche Werke*, vol. 4, 302.
[24] Ibid.
[25] Ibid., 305–6. In the *Critique of Pure Reason*, Kant's table of the categories that describes the "relational category of community" as "reciprocity between that active and the passive". Purposiveness (*Zweckmässigkeit*) is an important feature of the *Third Critique*.
[26] *KGA*, I/2, 169.

indiscriminant use of the term "community" has ultimately led the latter to unnecessarily passive conclusions. Schleiermacher is very clear that he seeks to commit his notion of reciprocity to continued activity. Passivity describes another form of being together that is not characterized by free sociability:

> Those who are gathered in the theater or who attend a lecture together hardly manifest a society. No individual is engaged in free sociability with the artist but rather in bound sociability because the actor is intent only on a specific effect, and the audience is unable to effect a matching return, but rather actually always conducts itself passively [*leidend*]. The true character of a society, then, in terms of the intent of its form, is that there should be a reciprocity [*Wechselwirkung*] that permeates all of its participants but that is also entirely determined and completed by them.[27]

The examples of the theater and the lecture illustrate people gathering for some purpose other than sociability for its own sake. This purpose makes the relationship among the participants very different because of the lack of activity on the audience's part, and the inability of the actors or speakers to enter into a reciprocal relationship with the audience.

When he describes the social drive, Fichte uses the same language as Schleiermacher to make the point that there is a need for reciprocity (emphases are Fichte's): "This drive is oriented toward *reciprocity* [*Wechselwirkung*], *mutual* effect, *mutual* giving and taking, *mutual* passivity [*Leiden*], and doing: not mere causality, it is not just oriented toward activity in reply to which the other would have to behave passively [*leidend*]."[28] Passivity creeps in for Fichte, whereas Schleiermacher would be more cautious about the term in this instance. The latter also sees the same drive and calls it a "natural drive toward sociable crystallization."[29] Clearly, Schleiermacher derives more than just the language for the *Essay* from Fichte; there are important concepts that he is applying in much the same way as Fichte.[30]

There is another significant point of reference in *Vocation of the Scholar* that needs examination, and this reference can act as a transition in showing how

---

[27] *KGA*, I/2. There are errors in the original published text as well in the notes in the *Kritische Gesamtausgabe*. See notes on the translation below.
[28] *KGA*, I/2.
[29] *KGA*, I/2, 182.
[30] I would like to thank Prof. Michael Vater (Marquette University) for urging me to read Fichte with a subtle eye.

Schleiermacher dealt with the inconsistencies in Fichte's conceptual scheme. Just preceding the passage from *Vocation of the Scholar* regarding the social drive, Fichte sums up his discussion of man and society using the term "Geschicklichkeit": "Thus—and this is the outcome of our whole discussion so far—man is meant for society; sociability (*Gesellschaftlichkeit*) belongs among the aptitudes (*Geschicklichkeiten*) that he is meant to develop according to his vocation as discerned in the previous lecture."[31] "Geschicklichkeit" can best be translated as "adroitness," "aptitude," or "skill." However, we do have a specific problem in translation as this "Geschick" can also mean "fit" and "to put a matter right" and allows it to relate to "schicklich" and "Schicklichkeit" of the *Essay*, in which these terms mean "appropriate" or "propriety." Both can be seen to overlap in the area of being "fitting" or "apt." However, it is important not to deny the difference in terms here, as it also marks an important difference in the way Schleiermacher and Fichte approach the problem of society.

In lecture 1 of *Vocation of the Scholar*, "Geschicklichkeit" is part of a process of culture. In order for culture to come about, there is a need to acquire this skill:

> Acquiring this skill [*Geschicklichkeit*], partly to suppress and eradicate misguided inclinations that preceded the awakening of our reason and feeling of independent action, partly to modify the things outside ourselves and to alter them in accordance with our own concepts—the acquiring of this skill [*Geschicklichkeit*], I say, is called *culture*.[32]

"Geschicklichkeit," then, has a twofold character for Fichte. It is that function of reason that takes us beyond the animal inclinations, and it is also an interaction with the things around us so as to modify them. This twofold meaning is a fundamental necessity for the I as it establishes itself with recourse to the things around it, thus allowing the I to establish its essential unity:

> If the I is to be always unified with itself, then it must strive to have an effect on those things upon which the feeling and the representation of the human being depends. The human being must seek to modify those things and to make them agree with the pure form of his I.[33]

Fichte has a firm notion of the I as being established absolutely; all talk of interaction

---

[31]*Fichtes Sämmtliche Werke*, vol. 6, 308.
[32]Ibid., 298.
[33]Ibid.

and activity is grounded in this notion of the identity of the rational being: "The ultimate vocation of all finite rational beings is, therefore, absolute unity, constant identity, complete agreement with itself. This absolute identity is the form of the pure I and the only true form of it."[34] Fichte's "Geschicklichkeit," then, is a striving of the I that leads to culture and society. This active function of the I is founded on "absolute identity" of the I. At the same time, this skill (Geschicklichkeit) is also a drive toward sociableness (Gesellschaftlichkeit) that is founded on the kind of identity of the I that Schleiermacher has found a cause to ridicule in his review of Fichte's *Vocation of Mankind* (see above).

In the *Essay* Schleiermacher admits that the term "Schicklichkeit" exists already in normal language.[35] Herder indicates a French origin for the term in a discourse on conversation much the same as Schleiermacher's. When discussing the awkwardness of French comedy on the German stage, Herder points out that the French refer to "propriety and impropriety of expression [*das Schickliche und Unschickliche im Ausdruck*]" as "*laws of taste.*"[36] But, for Schleiermacher, "Schicklichkeit" becomes a philosophical term of central significance to the activity of free sociability. Just like Fichte's "Geschicklichkeit," Schleiermacher's "Schicklichkeit" is an activity of the individual that brings about society. This brings Schleiermacher's "Schicklichkeit" to a place in his system that is similar to Fichte's "Geschicklichkeit," describing the "drive toward sociableness."

4.3. Resolving Fichte's Challenge on Freedom

Fichte reconciles his challenge "*how can a community of free beings, as such, be possible?*"[37] through "propriety" or "Schicklichkeit."[38] Schleiermacher's answer is to formulate a law: "our law is the commandment of propriety and states that nothing should be evoked that does not belong to the communal sphere of all."[39] Propriety

---

[34] Ibid., 297.
[35] Ibid.
[36] Johann Gottfried Herder, *Briefe zur Beförderung der Humanität*, ed. Heinz Stolpe et al., vol. 2 (Berlin: Aufbau, 1971), 164.
[37] *Fichtes Sämmtliche Werke*, vol. 3, 85.
[38] I return to emphasizing the English terms now that I have dealt with the contrast between Fichte and Schleiermacher's similar sounding yet different terms.
[39] *KGA*, I/2, 171.

exemplifies an important step in resolving the fundamental conflict between individuality and the common good that Fichte's question characterizes. If a communal sphere of all can exist, it must do so in a way that preserves individuality. The existence of the term "propriety" indicates that such a sphere can be sought using a skill that we already possess. The resolution is possible by limiting the subject matter of one's discourse, and yet conveying this subject matter in a manner that leaves one's individuality in tact.

However, Schleiermacher's solution does not absolutely limit both of these parts of the resolution in a Fichtean manner but in a dynamical way that differentiates his solution from the ideas of Fichte. Still, Schleiermacher takes from Fichte the idea of making his philosophical arguments dynamic or active in a Fichtean sense. The resolution of the problem of sociability that "propriety" facilitates relies on Fichte's active terminology. In a sentence that sounds altogether as though Fichte could have written it, Schleiermacher declares that sociability is the site at which inherent conflicts between individuality and the common good (such as would result from Fichte's question) can become apparent. But sociability is sadly misconstrued:

> Thus, it is only natural that the requisites of sociability, which are comprised of independent action [*Selbstbsthätigkeit*] and limitation of the self [*Selbstbeschränkung*], are misunderstood in all individual details such that one is made absolutely subordinate to the other because it is not known how to combine the two.[40]

By discussing propriety as an active skill or facility, Schleiermacher develops a solution to this core social problem. By discerning that subject matter determines the character of a society and by calling this character the "tone" of the society, the point above, valid for society in general, is brought to bear on conversational societies in particular:

> By means of this difference, that conflict mentioned earlier is entirely resolved, and the law of propriety now acquires the meaning: I must observe the tone of the society, and with regard to the subject matter, I should allow myself to be guided and limited by that society (this provision was disregarded by those who had proceeded from a one-sided maxim of self-limitation [Selbstbeschränkung]). Nevertheless, I remain at liberty to

---

[40]Ibid., 173.

> allow my individual manner to reign entirely free within this sphere. This boundary was transgressed by those who had demanded to be completely unfettered in society.[41]

By using Fichte's active vocabulary, Schleiermacher finds a new path to mediating between being self-limited and being completely unfettered. He asserts that his solution is no compromise; those that attempt to make a compromise between these poles in no way resolve the problem. After making his point about those that misunderstand the conflict between independent action and limitation of the self, he chides those that grasp for a mere compromise between these two poles:

> Besides these, there is yet a third maxim that with a moderanist spirit avoids the accusation of belonging to one or the other by taking a little from both and depending on the society; whether the former or the latter has the upper hand, the mixture is adjusted until it can, if necessary, be palatable to all. Of course this does not constitute a solution of the contradiction; rather, this pulls it all the tighter together; the one-sidedness is not avoided by doubling it.[42]

The *Essay* takes a different approach to the two opposing poles of the problem of sociability. Using the case of conversational groups and sociable entertainment, Schleiermacher finds a solution to the perennial problem of freedom and society. The solution is to work with both parts of this opposition and to use them dynamically, both in order to discern what society is and to move it forward. Propriety becomes the force that governs the discerning of the limits of society and at the same time is the force that takes society into new realms. In this way the limits are sufficiently dynamic as to permit the inclusion of individuality. Schleiermacher introduces the concept of "character" to facilitate discussion of achieving free sociability by means of a specific variable that defines particular societies:

> The first view contained the rule that we were, not even for a moment, to do anything to go beyond that subject matter that expresses the character of the society. In the second, this character appears itself as something that is never fully determined, and we are commanded to contribute to discerning it more precisely at every moment. Thus, while these two rules really do comprise a whole and are intended to complete the concept of propriety, they,

---
[41] Ibid., 174.
[42] Ibid., 173.

nevertheless, contradict each other. That is why so often only the one is heeded, while the other is, in contrast, entirely neglected. The mistakes that result from this contravene the concept of propriety in its totality, and the improper shows itself in its crassest light to be ridiculous. What can be more ridiculous than someone completely suppressing the natural striving of a conversation to rise up to a higher sphere, always remaining unwaveringly firm at that position at which he or she was at the outset and also seeking to keep others at that point by force.[43]

Propriety means that we have a responsibility both to determine and to further society at the same time. This dual, and seemingly conflicting, duty permits the unification of both the limiting and individual vectors of society that comprise free sociability. We see no compromising of these two aspects with Schleiermacher. Instead, there is a striving to make the society the most it can become by bringing into it appropriate individuality that will allow it to reach as far as it can. This view is a dynamic one of society that demands progress. Early in the *Essay* Schleiermacher says that society must "be observed in a twofold manner, both as being as well as becoming,"[44] thus defining society in a way that could be seen as Romantic (perhaps even constituting what is Romanticism, as Schleiermacher is one of its progenitors); the Enlightenment notion of progress is enhanced by the simple act of being. What we have here is a uniquely liberal view of freedom that requires furthering by always testing its limits but also one in which the sphere of freedom is growing along with its populace.

Two further topics grow out of the discussion so far. The first of these compares the idea of free sociability with the utopian visions of Rousseau in the *Social Contract*. Schleiermacher's approach in the *Essay* attempts to deal with many of the same issues as does Rousseau, especially with regards to the practicalities of realizing liberal freedom; Schleiermacher may, indeed, have been influenced by Rousseau's ideas.[45] The second topic returns to Fichte from whom the dynamic

---

[43] Ibid., 180.

[44] Ibid., 168.

[45] Kurt Nowak has produced a thorough analysis of Rousseau's role in German Protestantism of the eighteenth century, mostly as a foil and clearly rejected by figures such as Teller and Spalding. After making clear Eberhard's discussions of Rousseau, Nowak lists the rather thin remarks on Rousseau by Schleiermacher. Given the lack of serious philosophical attention to Schleiermacher's *Essay* anywhere, it is not surprising that Nowak does not note the reference to Rousseau therein. Kurt Nowak, "Der umstrittene Bürger von Genf: zur Wirkungsgeschichte Rousseaus im deutschen Protestantismus des 18. Jahrhunderts," in *Sitzungsberichte der Sächsischen Akademie der Wissenschaften zu Leipzig:*

figures of Schleiermacher's philosophy are derived but whose solutions do not remain in the dynamic realm and who can be seen to have capitulated to the polarities of the social challenge he set.

4.4. Rousseau's General Will

For Schleiermacher, a condition of war exists when in social gatherings people "insist that everywhere one may contribute and exercise one's entire individuality."[46] Indicating the problems such a state would cause, Schleiermacher says: "If this maxim were universal, it would necessarily cause a state of continual war among the predominant socialites that would have to end with the fall of society itself without achieving any significant result at all."[47] By saying that it is wrong to "exercise one's entire individuality," Schleiermacher emphasizes that people must come together with a concept of and a wish for community that recognize the difficulties of integrating individuality with community. If people come together in a manner that only allows them to consider themselves, such a self-centered motive will produce the equivalence of a condition of social war as presented by Thomas Hobbes in the seventeenth century. Such a gathering does not comprise valid sociability and does not make for worthy society.

Hobbes held the view that man needed to be governed by a strong sovereign. The sword of justice provided the powerful symbol and tool by means of which order could be imposed by government. Hobbes's underlying assumption was that man was essentially driven by base motives that made life without government "a condition which is called war; and such a war as is of every man, against every man."[48] It seems appropriate to speculate that Schleiermacher had Hobbes in mind when he envisioned "a state of continual war among the most prominent socialites" if people merely acted selfishly. Hobbes saw this selfishness as characteristic of society without order, and he projected that in such an unordered state "the life of man [was] solitary, poor, nasty, brutish, and short."[49]

Philologische Klasse, vol. 132, part 4, 5–48, esp. 20–21.
[46] *KGA*, I/2, 172.
[47] *KGA*, I/2, 172f.
[48] Thomas Hobbes, *Leviathan*, ed. Michael Oakeshott (New York: Touchstone, 1997), 100.
[49] Ibid.

In contrast to Hobbes, the eighteenth-century French philosopher Jean-Jacques Rousseau believed that human beings were in essence good and that it was society and its laws as they existed that made them bad. For Rousseau, the first, natural societies were characterized by love, particularly that of the father for his children; here, man is in essence good.[50] An ideal state with good laws would protect and enhance the inherent goodness of human beings. As people are essentially good, Rousseau theorized that it is material things that give rise to trouble between people: "[M]en are not naturally enemies. It is conflicts over things, not quarrels between men which constitute war, and the state of war cannot arise from mere personal relations, but only from property relations."[51] Thus, private interest derived from property was what made people bad. Once common interest and common ownership were abandoned by primitive societies in a state of nature, private interest led to the kind of conflicts Hobbes mistakenly thought were exemplary of people's true nature. However, as there was no property in the state of nature, (a state prior to society), human beings were not bad there.

Rousseau's *Social Contract* of 1762 is based on moral considerations. If people are good and society makes them bad, how can this situation be rectified to produce a morally worthy society? Countering Hobbes, who claims that society can only come about under the rule of a terrifying power, Rousseau writes that society cannot have a moral foundation if it is derived solely from a structure of fear: "To yield to force is an act of necessity, not of will; it is at best an act of prudence. In what sense can it be a moral duty?"[52]

Schleiermacher's approach interprets Rousseau's contention that Hobbes's state of war is achieved by owning property. Schleiermacher insists that interaction based on the profit motive is in itself no moral grounds for socializing: he explains that self-interest in interaction cannot lead to the formation of a valid and moral society. According to Schleiermacher, entire theories of sociability have been based on the reprehensible goal of furthering one's own advantage, and Schleiermacher cites Adolph Freiherr von Knigge's *Über den Umgang mit Menschen* (*On Dealing With People*) (1788) as exemplary of such capitalistic practices. People who promote

---

[50]Jean-Jacques Rousseau, *The Social Contract*, translated and introduced by Maurice Cranston (Harmondsworth: Penguin, 1968), 50f.
[51]Ibid., 55–56.
[52]Ibid., 52.

such self-serving versions of sociability "do not love and honor art for its own sake, but rather focus on the fortune they can have in the world by it, and like craftsmen, they carry out their profession only for profit."[53] For Schleiermacher, then, worthy sociability is desired for its own sake.

Hobbes's practical answer to the problem of transcending this state of war is for people to abandon their natural freedoms and to submit to the authority of a single, severe ruler and sovereign, who will, in turn, guarantee an otherwise equitable civil society. Rousseau wishes to create a totally equitable society in which sovereignty remains with those contracting to become members of society. Rousseau solves this problem by means of what is presented as a democratic institution and concept, the general will, or *volunté générale*.

The most compelling evidence for Schleiermacher's use of the *Social Contract* in formulating his *Essay* is derived from the comparison of the social elements of Schleiermacher's *Essay* and the specifics of the general will. Fundamental to Rousseau's first mention of the general will in the *Social Contract* is the goal of incorporating the individual into the whole without abandoning the independence of that individual: "'Each one of us puts into the community his person and all his powers under the supreme direction of the general will; and as a body, we incorporate every member as an indivisible part of the whole.'"[54] This statement is placed by Rousseau within quotation marks as a conclusion of or established principle for his argument. When discerning his formal and material laws of sociability, Schleiermacher similarly asks the individual to place his or her person into the community, here under the aegis of reciprocity:

> Reciprocity will initially be considered as form and will in this way provide a formal law of sociable activity: Everything is to be reciprocal. Next, it will be considered as substance, thus providing the *material* law: Everyone is to be inspired to a free play of thought by means of communicating what is mine.[55]

Schleiermacher has the same difficulties to deal with here as does Rousseau, and in order to confront them, the formal and material laws of sociability are established as principles that should maintain reciprocity and individuality, respectively, without sacrificing one to the other. It is that very individuality that Hobbes is so ready to

---

[53] *KGA*, I/2, 168.
[54] Rousseau, *Social Contract*, 61.
[55] *KGA*, I/2, 170.

sacrifice to authoritarian rule. The third of Schleiermacher's laws is the quantitative law that states that: "*Your sociable activity should always remain within such limits as to permit a particular society to exist as a whole.*"[56] This law acknowledges the individual's place within society not as a subsumed member, but as a contributing member who should be conscious of acting to remain within the society of which he or she is a contributing member. In this way society can remain an institution common among its members.

Rousseau discusses this issue when pointing out the general applicability of the general will:

> All men constantly wish the happiness of each but for the fact that there is no one who does not take that word "each" to pertain to himself and in voting for it think of himself?... The general will, to be truly what it is, must be general in its purpose as well as in its nature;...it should spring from all for it to apply to all.[57]

The general will is to remain applicable to all, and in order for this universal applicability to be the case, it must also be derived from all.

This generality of the general will, however, can be undermined by the existence of interest groups. Such sectional associations can threaten the cohesion of society by upsetting the balance achieved by opposing individual wills:

> The great number of small differences will always produce a general will and the decision will always be good. But [in] groups, sectional associations are formed at the expense of the larger association, the will of each of these groups will become general in relation to its own members and private in relation to the state.[58]

Sectional interests merely allow private opinion to prevail, and although the generality of debate is still manifest, it is restricted to the discourse among the members of the interest group itself.

Therefore, the general will needs to be kept general. To achieve this goal, Schleiermacher stipulates his commandment of propriety that states that "nothing should be evoked that does not belong to the communal sphere of all."[59] Private

---

[56]*KGA*, I/2, 171. He also rather confusingly refers to it as his first law as he considers it to incorporate the other two (the formal and the material laws).

[57]Rousseau, *Social Contract*, 75.

[58]Ibid., 73.

[59]*KGA*, I/2, 171.

interest does not have a place in the discourse of a society that wishes to preserve itself as a whole. Both Schleiermacher and Rousseau indicate that a sense of community must be preserved, and Schleiermacher seeks this preservation by focusing on his commandment of propriety, thus excluding private interest.

The existence of such a communal sphere is fundamental to both Schleiermacher's and Rousseau's thoughts on society. For each of them this concept of the communal sphere is manifest among individuals as a mutual concept in its own right, and it is not discerned by performing some mathematical operation on the private interests of each individual constituting the society. To make this point, Rousseau contrasts the "will of all" with the general will: "There is often a great difference between the will of all [what all individuals want] and the general will; the general will studies only the common interest while the will of all studies private interest, and is indeed no more than the sum of individual desires."[60] This contention is much like Schleiermacher's rejection of compromise between the polarities of independent action and the limiting of the self. Rousseau's general will successfully expresses the spirit of the community, whereas negotiating and compromising private interest alone totally disregards the possibility of there being any community spirit to be discerned. Schleiermacher identifies this mathematical approach to private interest as a misunderstanding of the process of discerning the communal spirit. Schleiermacher states that such a mistaken approach assumes that "for the good of society one must deprecate oneself and wish to be nothing better than the middle average of the whole."[61]

Limiting the self in this way because others are asserting their private interests, however, in no way solves this issue of discerning the communal spirit. Merely considering more private interests and committing oneself to be restrained by those considerations leads one no closer to the goal of community. If society as a whole will benefit by furthering the common good, then each individual, as a member of that society, will surely also benefit. As Rousseau points out, in attempting to separate one's private will from the common interests, one will become aware that the two are linked: "Each man, in detaching his interest from the common interest, sees clearly that they cannot separate it entirely."[62] Rousseau is admonishing

---

[60] Rousseau, *Social Contract*, 72.
[61] *KGA*, I/2, 173.
[62] Rousseau, *Social Contract*, 150.

the members of society to realize this reality. One must not forget that his is a moral enterprise and that by means of the general will men are supposed to be able to realize their moral potential. Rather than admonishing his participants, Schleiermacher feels that people will be able to grow into the character of society. This character of society (like the general will) has been established out of the common identity and common interest of the group: "I am meant to contribute my individuality, my character, and I am meant to take on the character of the society; both are meant to occur at the same moment, are meant to be one and unified in a single mode of action."[63] Schleiermacher has given Rousseau's social foundation a new reciprocal formulation.

Here, we see also some divergence between Schleiermacher and Rousseau because Schleiermacher seeks to resolve entirely the issue of individuality, not as an issue of will but as one of character. The impulse to assert the self is given its output in the guise of the manner in which subject matter is dealt:

> An individual person is characterized with respect to his or her thinking and action and not at all with respect to the subject matter—the latter is common to many, and it is considered to be something quite accidental. Instead, a characterization follows from the way in which a person handles, combines, develops, and conveys the subject matter. This is the essential element that characterizes an individual, and with respect to the society, we would like to call this *manner*.[64]

It is not what people talk about that makes them individuals; rather, it is how they talk about it. In this way individuality no longer threatens the cohesiveness of the community. Schleiermacher thus moves his considerations into an unresolved realm in Rousseau's thinking. This realm is an area in which much criticism can be leveled at Rousseau's utopian vision. The practicalities of discerning the general will mean that Rousseau must leave a great deal of responsibility to the group that formulates the proposals for the assembly to debate, for this group is also responsible for executing the general will as discerned by the assembly. The power vested in these executive and formulating groups makes the general will wane into insignificance when one becomes aware of the very general nature of the proposals that can be voted on.

---

[63] *KGA*, I/2, 173.
[64] *KGA*, I/2, 174.

However, Schleiermacher is telling us that a society truly does come about among the group carrying out the debates. The focus of Schleiermacher's interest is on the nature of discourse itself. The nature of this debate, when carried out under the correct conditions, has the power to manifest true society. People will not undermine the spirit of community when it is their desire to be members of a true community. Schleiermacher shows us that the parliamentary-style debates that Rousseau says will take place to discern the general will are the very vehicle by means of which the spirit of community becomes manifest. The debate itself, therefore, becomes the factor that forges the harmony and unity of the group.

This process, of course, remains a vicious circle if one assumes that mankind is entirely composed of self-interest as he is in Hobbes's vision of society. But assuming a powerful desire for sociability, and therefore community, as Schleiermacher does, a very different result is obtained. The very opening line of Schleiermacher's *Essay* proclaims the existence of this desire: "Free sociability, neither fettered nor determined by any external end, is demanded vociferously by all educated people as one of their primary and most cherished needs."[65] What results for Schleiermacher is a theoretical discourse on the nature of debate that is also about a vision of good society. Conversation becomes the focus of realizing a social utopia like the one dreamt of in Rousseau's social contract. The pitfalls of Rousseau's utopian vision are counteracted by giving debate the central and focal role of molding society, thus creating a sense of community among the participants.

4.5. Morality and Law

Fichte concludes a very different notion of community from Rousseau. In *Natural Law* Fichte develops the thesis that unity of will is a desirable goal that, in his opinion, is like Rousseau's general will. If all are of one will, then there is a unity of all the wills. This proposition he opposes to what Rousseau rejects as the *volonté de tous* (will of all), which like a mathematical remainder, is the resulting will from a collection of wills in opposition to each other.[66] When society arises, it is the result of the will of those participating, i.e., a positive act as a unity of purpose.

---

[65] *KGA*, I/2, 165.
[66] *Fichtes Sämmtliche Werke*, vol. 3, the footnote on 106f.

Fichte's discussion of this concept from Rousseau is an acknowledgment of how much he feels he owes the latter in the development of his thinking. Without referring to Rousseau in name in the earlier *Vocation of the Scholar*, Fichte makes this unity central to his concept of society: "[T]he final, highest goal of society is complete unity and unanimity among all possible members of the same."[67] While he admits this unity is an unobtainable ideal tending toward the Godly, Fichte's notion of the highest goal for society contrasts sharply with Schleiermacher's notion of bringing one's individuality into the circle. Where Fichte talks of unanimity (*Einmüthigkeit*), Schleiermacher talks of individuality (*Eigenthümlichkeit*). Where Schleiermacher seeks to include individuality in society, Fichte sees individuality as a source of conflict incompatible with life in society in which freedom is of necessity compromised.

Unity for Fichte arises from the law that the members of society can agree on as being applicable to each of them individually. Departure from this scheme occurs at the moment when one individual is oppressed: "Just as certainly as they are all of one opinion, they certainly want the law. As soon as just one of them is to be oppressed, then that one person does not willfully consent, and they are no longer all of one opinion."[68] Previously, in the 1793 *Contribution to the Correction of the Opinions of the Public on the French Revolution*, Fichte stated that he believed the individual had the right to negate a contract at any time: "It is an inalienable right of every individual to void any contract as soon as he wishes, even unilaterally; unalterability and permanent validity of any contract is the most grievous transgression of human law that there can be."[69]

In his *Notes on Contract Law*, thought to have been composed in 1796 and/or 1797, Schleiermacher responded to Fichte's assertion. Effectively Fichte's proposition suspended all contractual obligations:

> Fichte says that a contract is only valid and has legal status if there is a continuing determination of the will of the promisor. But in this way all legal compulsion is suspended... Yes, according to this doctrine the promisor would still have a dominum directum over the matter after he had fulfilled his obligation, and all property rights would be suspended. This error derives

---

[67] Ibid., vol. 6, 310.
[68] Ibid., vol. 3, 107.
[69] Ibid., vol. 6, 159.

from another Fichtean proposition, namely this one, that there can be no everlasting contracts because a person can never promise not to change his or her mind.[70]

This last proposition is the one discussed above from Fichte's 1793 work on the French Revolution. Clearly, Schleiermacher felt that Fichte was making the very idea of contractual obligation impossible by making it rely on fickle human will. For Schleiermacher, Fichte had failed to resolve the problem of how people could live in society of their own free will. In attacking this problem in Rousseau's terms, Schleiermacher reveals that he feels Fichte only allows human society to degenerate into a state that was previous to the making of the social contract and in which there was no property.

Fichte sees the issue of people living in society together as a negative problem with respect to freedom: "But they cannot survive together if each one does not limit his freedom by the freedom of all the others."[71] Law becomes the regulative principle that makes it possible for people to live together:

> And thus we have the entire object of the concept of law: namely *a community between free beings as such...* It turns out that one imagines every member of the society to limit his own outward freedom by inner freedom in such a way as to permit all the other members to be outwardly free also. This then is the concept of law.[72]

This internal regulation makes coexistence possible. Earlier, in *Natural Law*, he indicates that this regulation is a form of self-limitation: "All legal relationships are determined by the proposition: each person must limit his freedom by the possibility of the freedom of the other."[73] For Fichte, freedom has a negative cast that is governed by self-limitation, and it is regulated by the law; indeed, the role of law is to regulate freedom.

The relationship between Fichte's outer and inner freedom is that of law to morality. Again, in *Natural Law*, he makes a clear distinction between the realms of law and morality:

> Only through actions, expressions of their freedom in the sensory world, do

---

[70] *KGA*, I/2, 58f.
[71] *Fichtes Sämmtliche Werke*, vol. 6, 159.
[72] Ibid., vol. 3, 9.
[73] Ibid., vol. 3, 120.

rational beings find a reciprocal relationship with one another: The concept of law, thus, only refers to that which expresses itself in the sensory world; that which has no causality in that world, but rather remains internal to the disposition, belongs before a different judge; namely that of morality.[74]

Fichte's approach must necessarily be different from Schleiermacher's because the latter has a profoundly different evaluation of causality. Fichte's division between morality and law is the same as Kant's, and thus, Schleiermacher is rejecting both Kant and Fichte by developing his own view of causality. Schleiermacher's new concept of causal relationships leads to his unique views concerning the relationships between morality, law, the state, and freedom.

At roughly the same time as his work on the *Essay*, as well as his *On Religion*, Schleiermacher wrote a satirical pamphlet that was in effect a defense of the notion of civil rights for Jews. In his *Letters on the Occasion of the Political-Theological Task and the Sendschreiben (Open Letter) from Jewish Heads of Households*,[75] published in July of 1799, Schleiermacher concludes that Jews are able to be full citizens because they come under the aegis of the same legal and moral laws as Christians. Schleiermacher can reach this conclusion because he makes a fundamental distinction between religion and morality, and this morality cleansed of religion has a more fluid relationship to the law. These distinctions become the basis of Schleiermacher's revolutionary work in *On Religion*, for which he has been quite rightly recognized. But, the very same complex of issues informs both the *Essay* and the *Letters*, and these latter two deal with the secular repercussions of his reformulation of the notion of causality. *On Religion*, on the other hand, works out its religious consequences. I shall argue later that it was the realization of the importance of this reformulation of causality and what it meant to be religious that distracted him from his work on the *Essay*, leaving it incomplete, and to turn to writing *On Religion* instead.

For Schleiermacher, Kant holds a simple binary view of cause and effect and does not break out of a mechanistic view of nature. Even with Kant's view of the ethical agent as a final cause, cause has merely been moved into the realm of thought. Schleiermacher turns to Spinoza and finds a metaphysics that holds that all finite

---

[74]Ibid., vol. 3, 55.
[75]"Briefe bei Gelegenheit der politisch theologischen Aufgabe und des Sendschreibens jüdischer Hausväter." *KGA*, I/2, 327–61.

things inhere in the infinite, thus setting up a much more complex relationship between cause and effect. Julia Lamm's excellent book on Schleiermacher's theological Spinozism labels this development of Spinoza's original scheme as Schleiermacher's "principle of inherency."[76] Despite her very thorough work, all research so far has overlooked the possibility that Schleiermacher's interest in Spinoza may have found impetus in a particular work by Schleiermacher's teacher in Halle Johann August Eberhard that made a suggestion to restore Spinoza to an acceptable philosophical doctrine via this very issue of inherence in a handbook on the history of philosophy for lecturers of 1788.[77] We know that Schleiermacher owned this book and that Eberhard taught Schleiermacher at the time of the latter's own essays on Spinoza. Eberhard's note was intended to rehabilitate a modified Spinozism and to distinguish it from atheism.[78] Via this principle of inherence, Schleiermacher holds a Spinozan world view in which all causes and effects are in a constant, complex flux with varying degrees of immediacy to one another.[79]

Kant maintains that only a will purified of desire can be an ethical will, and in fact the identity of the agent is integrally connected with the will: the true self is that will independent of external forces. Nothing could be more distinct from Schleiermacher's views concerning cause and effect or from his idea of freedom. Identity and moral personhood is much more complex than this for Schleiermacher and cannot be determined by the action or existence of a free will alone. Schleiermacher's reason is more practical than Kant's. Identity is constructed from so many causes in flux: in an essay titled "Brief Exposition of the Spinozan System"

---

[76] Julia Lamm, *The Living God: Schleiermacher's Theological Appropriation of Spinoza.* (University Park, Pa.: Pennsylvania State University Press, 1996), 26.

[77] Bernd Oberdorfer, *Geselligkeit und Realisierung von Sittlichkeit. Die Theorieentwicklung Friedrich Schleiermachers bis 1799*, Theologische Bibliothek Töpelmann, vol. 69 (Berlin: de Gruyter, 1995), gives a wide ranging account of Eberhard but does not note this important potential point of influence.

[78] Eberhard still works with a Cartesian notion of God as perfection. Spinoza can be modified from his inherence argument by saying that "by the visible [world] one understands the most perfect and best epitomization of finite things" ("unter der sichtbaren [Welt] den vollkommensten und besten Inbegriff endlicher Dinge versteht"). Schleiermacher works with this principle of inherence but, like Eberhard, considers its relevance beyond merely the visible world. Johann August Eberhard, *Allgemeine Geschichte der Philosophie zum Gebrauch akademischer Vorlesungen*, (Halle, 1788), 249. This work has been identified in the catalog of Schleiermacher's library (with the title abbreviated to *Allgemeine Geschichte der Philosophie*) as item RA 81,217. See Meckenstock, *Schleiermachers Bibliothek*, 176.

[79] Lamm, *The Living God*, 43.

(1794), he says that "reason individualizes us least of all."[80] In this way Schleiermacher quite happily includes desire and finds no need to extricate himself entirely from the flux of cause and effect in order to discern an ethical life.

Despite such apparent intermingling of causes Schleiermacher can still draw distinctions, most notably between religion and morality, even if in practice such factors are not entirely separable. Schleiermacher's *On Religion* accords morality and religion their distinct spheres:

> should [these feelings of religion] cause actual actions and incite you to deeds, then you find yourselves in an alien realm. If you hold this to be religion, however rational and praiseworthy your action may appear, you are absorbed in an unholy superstition. All action should be moral and it can be too, but religious feelings should accompany every human deed like holy music; we should do everything with religion, nothing because of religion.[81]

Thus, religion should play no role in motivating action. Morality and religion are not absolutely linked. There is no need for God-given free will, and it plays no role in the measure of the moral worth of our actions. Religion and rationality are not coincident either. It is a terrible mistake to place them all together and to link them so unequivocally as Kant intends. Religion is a downright interference in what sounds like rational and moral action, as Schleiermacher says later: "Ask the moral, the political, and the artistic person, and all will say that this is their first precept; but calm and thoughtfulness are lost when a person permits himself to be driven to action by the powerful and disturbing feelings of religion."[82]

Schleiermacher agrees with Kant on the moral law, but he disagrees with him about freedom. Albert Blackwell has examined this issue in detail with respect to Schleiermacher's early work, especially *On Freedom* (1790). Blackwell suggests that Schleiermacher disagrees with transcendental freedom because he holds to a system of causality, much like the one I have delineated above. Kant's transcendental freedom postulates an ability to ground action outside the sensuous world's natural causality, and he separates motivation (or causation) by a good will in the intellectual world from causation of actions by things in the sensual world. The latter for humans

---

[80]"die Vernunft individualisiert uns am wenigsten," *KGA*, I/1, 574. Cited after Lamm, *The Living God*, 44.
[81]Schleiermacher, *On Religion*, 29f.
[82]Ibid., 30.

often is manifest in inclination that Kant rejects as a valid ground for discerning morally good action.

I would like to build on Blackwell's theses and their excellent characterization of Schleiermacher's early philosophy. I disagree with Blackwell regarding his reading of Kant, but much less so concerning his ultimate conclusions concerning Schleiermacher's stand on the issues. I shall make the case that Schleiermacher is somewhat closer to Kant's ideas mostly because Kant has been misread, and I will point out some of Schleiermacher's reasoning on freedom and morality that has been overlooked because the *Essay* has not been treated seriously as a philosophical work. Schleiermacher's notions of causality clearly make the case for rejecting Kant's transcendental freedom. In the following discussion, I shall argue even more strongly than Blackwell that Schleiermacher agrees with parts of Kant's discerning of the moral law.

I wish to disagree with a very small point made by Blackwell that Schleiermacher is distancing himself from Kant's respect (*Acht*) for the law when the former talks of respect (*Achtung*) for the law in *On Freedom*. Schleiermacher was quite capable of misquoting when he relied on memory, as he does with: Goethe's "The Fisherman" in the *Essay* (noted below). Blackwell gives a translation of a section from *On Freedom* that discusses Kant's idea of morality and the feeling of respect for the law that it involves:

> The realization of a command of reason involves a feeling, and with it, an impulse [Trieb] relating immediately and solely to practical reason, which it represents in the faculty of desire. *This impulse must have exactly the same relation to the faculty of desire as every other*. Upon the existence of this impulse rests the entire possibility of the idea of responsibility, for it is through this impulse alone that reason is joined to the faculty of desire. In earlier moral systems one called this impulse the moral sense; in the more recent it is called esteem for the moral law.[83]

This passage follows exactly Blackwell's translation. However, I would say that the very fact that Schleiermacher is giving this information as a historical labeling indicates that his intention here must be to cite what Kant intended for that label. Schleiermacher's use of the term "Achtung" instead of "Acht" is too inconsequential

---

[83]Cited after Blackwell, *Schleiermacher's Early Philosophy of Life*, 44.

and is more likely another example of Schleiermacher's inaccuracy, rather than evidence for claiming that Schleiermacher is thereby "deliberately avoiding identification with Kant's term for the incentive of the moral law."[84] Still, Blackwell's conclusions concerning the way in which desire and reason are joined for Schleiermacher remains valid. Blackwell goes on to examine how closely Schleiermacher's earliest philosophical works mirror some of Friedrich Schiller's ideas on this topic, and I shall have to turn to a similar examination for the *Essay*.

4.6. Kant's Kingdom of Ends

Now that we have seen that Schleiermacher does not explicitly reject Kant's morality, it is first necessary to examine some Kantian moral notions that play an absolutely central function in the *Essay*. In trying to show that Schleiermacher rejects Kant, I contend that Schleiermacher's employing of important and key Kantian moral philosophy has been missed.

Schleiermacher opens the *Essay* with an affirmation of sociability as an ethical enterprise, thus fulfilling the statement of the project in his *Notebooks*: "Right at the start, [an] elegy on society as the embodiment of the ethical condition."[85] And, indeed, the first two pages of the original version cover only this subject as a discourse on ethics modeled on ideas from Kant's *Groundwork of the Metaphysic of Morals*. The statement in the *Notebooks* and his discourse place ethics as the starting point of a publication on a social phenomenon. The theoretical, ethically ideal space Kant creates, but does not explore to the extent Schleiermacher does, Kant calls the "kingdom of ends," and through this key notion, ethics and the social sphere are brought together by Schleiermacher with a uniquely Kantian cast.[86] Schleiermacher's use of Kant has been much explored, and Kant has previously been drawn on to explore Schleiermacher's *Essay*, but as yet, the *Essay* has not been considered as an

---

[84] Ibid.
[85] *Gedankenhefte*, KGA, I/2, 29.
[86] Immanuel Kant, *Groundwork of the Metaphysic of Morals*, translated and analyzed by H. J. Paton (New York: Harper and Row, 1964), 100f. Hereafter cited as *Groundwork. Grundlegung zur Metaphysik der Sitten*, ed. Paul Menzer, published by the Königlich Preußischen Akademie der Wissenschaften (Academy Edition), vol. 4 (Berlin: de Gruyter, 1903), 385–463. Hereafter cited as *GMS*.

attempt to bring into practice a sphere that manifests Kant's kingdom of ends. In considering the *Essay* in this way, I will make it clear that Schleiermacher diverges from Kant's ethics, although the kingdom of ends clearly functions as the point of departure for Schleiermacher's ethical and social considerations in the *Essay*.

Arndt has come the closest to acknowledging the importance of this aspect of Kant's ethics to the *Essay* by citing Schleiermacher's opening to show that Schleiermacher is applying what Kant discerned as autonomy in the ethical. According to Arndt, Schleiermacher concludes that Kant's ethical autonomy cannot assert itself fully in all spheres of ethical life because it is too abstract and theoretical.[87] However, Kant himself would not have characterized real ethical life as abstract and theoretical. His discerning of the essence (or as he calls it the "groundwork") of ethics required him to carry out abstract theorization. Schleiermacher acknowledges the absolute necessity of theory for his own considerations of sociability, and it seems more likely that he determined a course that deviated from Kant not because of a rejection of Kant's principles, but because he found himself able to develop them in different directions. Schleiermacher's broad discussion of the value of theory in the *Essay* indicates that he was very well disposed toward theorizing and that he considered himself to be engaged in a theoretical enterprise as the title of the *Essay* exhibits.[88]

My first task is to establish firmly that Schleiermacher is dealing with Kant's kingdom of ends as presented in the *Groundwork*. Once this is established, I will survey the ways in which Schleiermacher develops Kant's ideas to examine sociability. This examination will show the relationship to Schleiermacher's thinking on society and social philosophy displayed in the *Essay*.

Schleiermacher concludes the opening of the *Essay* by stating that the initial text delineates the ethics of free sociability: "This is the moral (*der sittliche Zweck*) of free sociability."[89] In Kant's moral system, the distinction between means and ends is fundamental to a moral realm, or his kingdom of ends:

> I understand by a "*kingdom*" a systematic union of different rational beings under common laws. Now since laws determine ends as regards their universal validity, we shall be able—if we abstract from the personal

---
[87] Arndt, "Geselligkeit und Gesellschaft," 52.
[88] *KGA*, I/2, discussion of theorizing especially around 166.
[89] *KGA*, I/2., 165.

> differences between rational beings, and also from all the content of their private ends—to conceive a whole of all ends in systematic conjunction (a whole both of rational beings as ends in themselves and also of the personal ends which each may set before himself); that is, we shall be able to conceive a kingdom of ends which is possible in accordance with the above principles.
>
> For rational beings all stand under the *law* that each of them should treat himself and all others, *never merely as a means*, but always *at the same time as an end in himself*. But by doing so there arises a systematic union of rational beings under common objective laws—that is a kingdom.[90]

These points are Schleiermacher's very considerations in seeking the sociable sphere, and we shall have to consider further his conclusions in resolving the problems attendant to what Kant identifies as "the personal differences between rational beings." The difference between treating others as means and treating them as ends, however, remains central to creating this moral realm. In accordance with Kant's description of what constitutes a moral realm, a fundamental assumption of Schleiermacher's free sociability is that society is seen as just this form of moral end: "However, one must assume that all regard society as an end in itself and that they seek nothing in it other than society for its own sake."[91] Taking sociability seriously in this way and by discussing it as a moral issue, Schleiermacher necessarily moves the discussion of sociability (*Geselligkeit*) to talk readily about society (*Gesellschaft*). The term "Gesellschaft" in German can both refer to sociable or fashionable society (to use an English phrase connected with this concept) or to society in general. In seeing sociability as a moral issue that contrasts treatment of people as a means with that of people as an end, Schleiermacher is making a distinct departure from previous writers on sociability who have failed to note the moral reprehensibility of writings on sociability that encourage treating people as a means.

The responsibility for the moral degeneration of sociability can be laid squarely at the feet of those who present sociability from a perspective of advantages to be gained. Writers of such works Schleiermacher labels as the virtuosos who entirely disregard the true ethical end of sociability:

> Such collections stand all the concepts on their heads, and to add to that, they distort the whole thing by means of the most mistaken opinions. This is

---

[90]*Groundwork*, 100f. = *GMS*, 433.
[91]*KGA*, 1/2, 176.

because the supposed virtuosos do not love and honor art for its own sake, but rather focus on the fortune they can have in the world by it, and like craftsmen, they carry out their profession only for profit.[92]

Schleiermacher cites Knigge's famed work *Über den Umgang mit Menschen* as a prime example of such writing. Knigge and other writers see how people may ingratiate themselves to further their own standing, and thus, they promote the use of other people as a means to social or material success. Such approaches to sociability fail to see the fundamentally moral tenets that should ground social interaction, and consequently, they miss the whole point of sociability as an end in itself. The status of sociability as an art will require further examination, but Schleiermacher's rejection of approaches like that of Knigge as being based on false tenets is clear from the above passage.

Kant calls this issue a "practical imperative…: *Act in such a way that you always treat humanity, whether in your own person or in the person of any other, never simply as a means, but always at the same time as an end.*"[93] This imperative establishes that a person has the moral responsibility to treat others as ends, not means, and moral personhood is constituted in being such an end oneself.

Schleiermacher's sociability manifests this imperative in a social form, by making sociability an end in itself:

> If sociability is sought for its own sake (and it is itself nothing other than its own moral tendency), then the fulfillment of sociability can be manifest in nothing other than the ability to assemble socially, truly forming a society wherever the physical possibility for it is given, and where it already exists to maintain it.[94]

Schleiermacher identifies sociability for its own sake as the moral tendency that links it to Kant's moral philosophy. Schleiermacher moves Kant's philosophy further by placing the moral distinction between a means and an end into the sphere of the sociable circle, but this stance is in fact the very kingdom of ends that Kant stipulated as the ideal moral space; the realm in which each rational individual treats the other as an end in itself. By furthering Kant's ideas in this manner, Schleiermacher remains Kantian at least in the first step of his arguments.

---

[92] *KGA*, 1/2, 168.
[93] *Groundwork*, 96 = *GMS*, 429.
[94] *KGA*, 1/2, 168.

The founding of this first step on Kantian moral principles is evident in the fundamental notion of the individual as his or her own lawmaker. This principle defines moral responsibility as well as moral autonomy. For Kant, freedom lies in the capacity to formulate the universal law. This law is derived from the application of rationality to actions and by observing that the maxim on which action is based is morally worthy if it can be universalized to all other rational beings. Kant states that, when a rational will can do this operation, it is then the author of the moral law that it follows: "The will is therefore not merely subject to the law, but is so subject that it must be considered as also *making the law for itself* [*als selbstgesetzgebend*] and precisely on this account as first of all subject to the law (of which it can regard itself as the author)."[95] As the author of the law that it follows, the rational, and thus moral, will is free. This will is pure and acting morally when it is free from pressures exerted on it externally or even internally, i.e., when it is free to be acted upon because there are no other forms of interest involved "because the Idea of making universal law...is *based on no interest* and consequently can alone among all imperatives be *unconditioned.*"[96] Kant's autonomous will, unconditioned by other forces, is based on a law of which it is the author and with which it complies as an autonomous moral (rational) being.

This principle is of central importance to Schleiermacher's formulation near the end of the opening section of the *Essay* in which, immediately after stating the "moral end of sociability," he acknowledges the value of this Kantian unconditioned state:

> Sociable life also has forms that pressure it and has contingent matters that are at variance with its purpose. Here, too, one can despair everywhere at the awkwardness and malice of individuals; there is much to eliminate, a good deal to alter. Only here, owing to the inherent lack of civil authority, everyone must be their own legislator [für sich selbst Gesetzgeber seyn] and must look to it that the common good sustains no damage. All improvement must proceed from this principle and can only really be brought about by every individual adjusting his or her behavior in accordance with that common

---

[95] *Groundwork*, 98f = *GMS*, 431. The emphases are given in the original. I have corrected Paton, who omitted "for itself" from the emphases.

[96] *Groundwork*, 99 = *GMS*, 432. The emphases are given in the original.

goal.[97]

Schleiermacher's ideal sociable state then depends upon Kant's notion of the self as its own legislator in formulating "society as the embodiment of the ethical condition." The sociable sphere has the advantage over society in that it has no external legislating authority, and thus, the participant is placed in the position of legislating for himself or herself. Within this restricted environment, a unique opportunity arises to bring about Kant's kingdom of ends.

The ideal moral sphere in which rational beings treat each other not merely as a means but as an end can only be achieved if the moral sphere can be discerned by removing all interfering elements as just discussed. This discerning needs to take place by theorizing, and Schleiermacher is in agreement with Kant's mode of progress in this regard:

> In brief, seen from this vantage point, the case for sociability stands entirely on the same footing as that for ethics and law. Taking this into consideration, seeking out a theory is a challenge one cannot shirk. Without such a theory, every exercise is but blind, disjointed empiricism.[98]

Schleiermacher bases this insight on Kant's fundamental tenet, as stated in the preface to the *Groundwork*, that there is a need for a pure moral philosophy free of distraction by the empirical: "Do we not think it a matter of the utmost necessity to work out for once a pure moral philosophy completely cleansed of everything that can only be empirical and appropriate to anthropology?"[99] And, yet, Kant knows that his philosophy and theoretical enterprise stands in stark contrast with those who propagate popular philosophy: "For if we took a vote on which is to be preferred, pure rational knowledge detached from everything empirical—that is to say, a metaphysic of morals—or popular practical philosophy, we can guess at once on which side the preponderance would fall."[100] This observation is the very same problem that Schleiermacher faces in developing his ideas in the face of those supposedly practical works by the so-called "virtuosos" like Knigge, who are in fact the very same popular philosophers who rely on the empirical world, i.e., their experience. These people have missed the whole point of sociability because they

---
[97]*KGA*, I/2, 166.
[98]*KGA*, I/2, 167.
[99]*Groundwork*, 57 = *GMS*, 389.
[100]*Groundwork*, 77 = *GMS*, 409.

"themselves admit they are only founded on the viewpoint of common empiricism."[101]

Schleiermacher discerns that sociability can potentially realize Kant's kingdom of ends because it manifests a realm that does not rely on the empirical. When discussing the moral agent, Kant specifically labels this realm as the "intellectual world": "as regards whatever there may be in him of pure activity (whatever comes into consciousness, not through affection of the senses but immediately) he must count himself as belonging to the *intellectual world*."[102] In formulating the moral end of sociability, Schleiermacher places the participants of free sociability squarely in a world of pure activity that is liberated from the nuisances of ordinary living, and he also calls this the intellectual world:

> Here, a person is completely within the intellectual world and can act as a member of it. If one's powers are left to their own free play, one can develop them harmoniously. Subject only to those laws one places upon oneself, one depends only upon oneself to cast off the limitations of domestic and civil circumstances for a time. One can do this to a degree that is in accordance with one's inclinations. This is the moral purpose of free sociability.[103]

This contention fits entirely Kant's notion of the requirements for understanding morality: Schleiermacher's sociable sphere suits all the Kantian prerequisites of a morally ideal sphere. However, in working through the social phenomenon of this realm, Schleiermacher develops these ideas and, in many ways, goes beyond what Kant maps out.

4.7. Reciprocity and Schiller's Free Play

The focal point of Schleiermacher's movement beyond Kant lies in the former's understanding of sociability as an art. Schleiermacher develops his understanding of this phenomenon again with the help of another writer. Here Schiller's "Form" and "Stoff" become central to resolving the dilemmas that arise from the laws on sociability that come from what is effectively a progressing dialectic in the *Essay*.

---

[101] *KGA*, I/2, 172.
[102] *Groundwork*, 119 = *GMS*, 451. Kant's own emphases.
[103] *KGA*, I/2, 165.

Schiller and Schleiermacher both address the dissonance between the intellectual and the sensual spheres that characterizes Kant's discussion of the struggle for morality. Schiller's *Letters on the Aesthetic Education of Mankind*, originally composed in 1793, develops a way to bring these two poles of human motivation together. Just as he provided a dynamic model to resolve the difficulties of Rousseau's and Fichte's freedom and self-limitation, Schleiermacher seeks to overcome the dichotomy between the intellectual and sensory worlds. The language of the *Essay* already suggests that Schleiermacher found useful terms in Schiller's *Aesthetic Education of Mankind*, but the relationship goes further than a borrowing of terminology as Schleiermacher uses Schiller's response to Kant's ethics as a model for his own assimilation of substantial elements of those same ethics.

The affinity between Schleiermacher and Schiller extends back to Schleiermacher's earliest writings that predate the publication of Schiller's works on aesthetics. Blackwell has pointed out that there is no evidence of mutual influence in the earliest period, but by 1799, and *On Religion*, this original affinity has led Schleiermacher to a familiarity with Schiller's works on aesthetics.[104] Schiller's *Aesthetic Education of Mankind* is a contribution to moral theory, and aesthetics are central to this world, inasmuch as the aesthetic sense coincides with the faculty that can be developed (or educated) to make a person's inclinations coincide with moral duty. It is this understanding of the *Aesthetic Education of Mankind* that allows us to make sense of Schleiermacher's use of Schiller's work in the *Essay*.

Kant states in the introduction to the *Groundwork* that "human reason can in matters of morality...be easily brought to a high degree of accuracy and precision even in the most ordinary intelligence."[105] Kant imagined the development of reason to achieve accuracy in moral decision making, so that, while reason is a priori, its application and right decision making are dependent on appropriate development. Thus, reason relies on experience to come to its full flowering. But, if reason is a priori, how can it rely on experience to be developed? To make sense of this conflict, we have to understand that it is *the application of reason* that requires education.

This proposition is only a minor aside in Kant's theory and illuminates an issue that often leads to misinterpretations of Kant. Kant is often thought of as propagating a moral theory that requires people to act as some form of automata

---

[104]Blackwell, *Schleiermacher's Early Philosophy of Life*, 178.
[105]*Groundwork*, 59 = *GMS*, 391.

when making moral decisions. Reason alone is regarded as the arbiter of morality by Kant, but this belief is not the same as saying that action imbued with any other motives besides reason (e.g., inclination) are not good. What Kant is saying is that any motive other than reason is irrelevant in deciding whether an action is or is not morally correct. The only element that decides the morality of an action is its motivation by reason. This conclusion, however, does not discount motives that contain as contributing motives other elements: these elements are merely irrelevant in deciding on the action's morality. There is a common misconception of Kant's moral actor struggling against her inclinations in order to act out of a purely rational sense of duty. Kant would only draw on such an example to adumbrate the rational as the only valuable motive: examples from real life would contain a much more complex web of rational motives (including motives from inclination) struggling with one another.

Schiller grasps upon the notion of inclination leading the moral actor astray and sees the need to fulfill Kant's idea that accuracy in moral decision making can be developed. The former's *Aesthetic Education of Mankind* takes on the project of discerning how, by means of education, inclination may be brought into line with rationality. If such a project were successful, then this education would permit the very accuracy and precision in moral matters that Kant suggests may be achieved. This program, then, would be an education in Schiller's sense and would fulfill Kant's suggestion that morality may, at least to some degree, be developed through education. Schiller received public recognition from Kant for being in agreement with him on "the most important principles,"[106] and in the following, I shall examine how Schiller explores this aside of Kant's.

In the fourth letter of the *Aesthetic Education of Mankind*, Schiller acknowledges the issue of free will and the (Kantian) moral dilemma of the will residing between duty and inclination: "Human will is completely free between duty and inclination."[107] Schiller's goal (like that of Schleiermacher's sociability) is to produce a moral state, and he attacks the conception that what is natural has to be sacrificed for ethics. He states that it would always "be the sign of an inadequate

---

[106] Immanuel Kant, *Religion Within the Boundaries of Mere Reason and other Writings* (Cambridge: Cambridge University Press, 1998), 48.

[107] Friedrich Schiller, *Sämtliche Werke*, Auf Grund der Originaldrucke, ed. by Gerhard Fricke, Herbert G. Göpfert and Herbert Stubenrauch (Munich: Carl Hanser, 1962). vol. 5, 576. Hereafter cited as Schiller, SW.

education if ethical character could only assert itself by sacrificing natural character."[108] If natural character is to persevere in the face of the ethical character asserting itself, one of these must change through education. The whole purpose of education, then, would be to bring natural character (that of the sensuous realm) into line with ethical character (that of the intellectual realm). These realms coincide with the poles between which the will has freedom; inclination, and duty, respectively. A lack of education will result in the misconception of Kantian moral philosophy in which the moral actor struggles against his inclinations. With the appropriate education, there would be no need to suppress the natural character (inclinations), and duty and inclination would coincide. In Schiller's schema this coincidence is manifest in the striving toward harmony.[109] His schema is worked out by first identifying various human drives that permit themselves to be developed.

Schiller calls the first drive the "sensuous drive," and he says that it "proceeds from the physical being of the human or from his sensuous nature"[110] and that it is through this state that "physical being announces itself."[111] The second of these drives, the "formal drive;" is founded in reason, and it "proceeds from the absolute being of the human or from his rational nature, and strives to set him free, to lend harmony to the variety of his appearance, and in all these states of change to assert his personhood."[112] In Schiller's system these two drives are at work simultaneously and can be understood to be in competition with each other to the point where one or the other could become overemphasized.

For Schiller, the role of culture is to restrict these drives each to their appropriate sphere; otherwise, personality or freedom might be at risk:

> The role of culture is to watch over each one of these drives, and culture owes both of these an equal measure of justice, and should not merely protect the rational drive from the sensuous one, but should also support the latter against the former. Thus culture has a double task; in the first instance it is to protect the sensual from attacks on freedom and in the second it is to secure

---

[108]Ibid., 577.

[109]Steven D. Martinson, *Harmonious Tensions: The Writings of Friedrich Schiller* (Newark: University of Delaware Press), 173. As the title of this work indicates, it contains broad references to harmony in Schiller's works. The reference here is to the *Letters on the Aesthetic Education of Mankind*.

[110]Schiller, SW, vol. 5, 604. Schiller's emphases.

[111]Ibid.

[112]Ibid., 605.

personality from the power of sensation.[113]

If the project is to be successful, it is not merely to be a furthering of the rational capacities. Schiller embraces and defends the physical and the sensuous as part of human freedom and the rational as a determining factor of human personality.

According to this schema, each of the drives has its appropriate sphere: "[T]he sensuous drive compels us physically and the formal drive morally."[114] As a physical drive, the sensuous is called the material drive. To be human is to combine these two necessitating forces:

> Based on transcendental foundations reason creates the following demand: there must be community between the formal drive and the material drive, i.e., a play drive. That is because only the unity of reality with form, accident with necessity, suffering with freedom can complete the concept of humanity.[115]

The polarity of the distinction between the formal and material drives extends to numerous spheres, but they all combine to define humanity and to define it as manifest in the play drive. Fulfillment of humanity is achieved by combining the fundamentally dualistic nature of humans in the play drive.

Beauty coincides with this dualistic nature of humanity inasmuch as it similarly seeks balance between the material and formal[116] and by its being "the common object of both drives, that is the play drive."[117] The fifteenth and sixteenth letters discuss this activity, but by the last (twenty-seventh) letter, Schiller's use of beauty to turn toward the realm of appearance has him in trouble with commentators who dismiss this connection as an inconsistency derived from his own struggle with the failed ideals of the French Revolution.[118]

Arndt similarly argues that Schleiermacher turns toward aesthetic appearance following Schiller's use of appearance (*Schein*). For Arndt, the fundamental dialectic

---

[113] Ibid., 606.
[114] Ibid., 613.
[115] Ibid., 615.
[116] Ibid., 619.
[117] Ibid., 615.
[118] Detlef Gaus discusses this turn in *Geselligkeit und Gesellige*, 72. Those who made this argument earlier are Käte Hamburger, "Schiller's ästhetisches Denken," in Friedrich Schiller, *Über die ästhetische Erziehung des Menschen* (Stuttgart: Reclam, 1965), 149, and Helmut Koopman, *Freiheitssonne und Revolutionsgewitter. Reflexe der Französischen Revolution im literarischen Deutschland zwischen 1789 und 1840* (Tübingen: Niemeyer, 1989), 29.

of Schleiermacher's *Essay* is a Kantian antinomy between, on the one hand, being determined by others and determining others in the realm of appearance and, on the other, the reality of lived sociability that rises triumphant from the antinomy.[119]

I agree with Arndt that lived sociability is the practical solution to the dialectic that Schleiermacher sets up, but below, I take a closer look at the use of Schiller's terms in the *Essay* to demonstrate that, with such a precise evaluation of the details of Schleiermacher's dialectical approach, there is a diverging interpretation. Just as in the above section on Kant, the interpretation I offer goes beyond Arndt's broadly correct analysis showing that Schleiermacher is examining Kant's notion of moral autonomy: more precisely, the *Essay* examines the possibility of realizing Kant's kingdom of ends.

Schiller's work clearly reveals a strong Fichtean influence. Much of the absolutizing language, Schiller applies shows that he derives a good deal of his thinking from Fichte rather than directly from Kant, even referring to Fichte in notes. Scholars who approach Schleiermacher's work with a philosophical training that has steeped them in a Fichtean interpretation will not seek to differentiate these strains, but instead, will treat the work of Fichte as a legitimate interpretation of Kant's philosophy.[120] At this point, I will have to defer a complete treatment of this issue for Schleiermacher. Still, I offer, at least, an approach to Schleiermacher's use of Schiller's terms that shows a clear differentiation of Schleiermacher from a philosophical world often not even conscious of its absorption by and into Fichtean thinking.

Schleiermacher's formal law of sociability states that "[e]verything is to be reciprocal."[121] With this primacy of reciprocity, Schleiermacher is framing this aspect of his thought with Fichtean dynamism, while avoiding its descent into absolutes as discussed earlier. But this formal law is only part of the "two views of reciprocity"[122] that he separates in his analysis of the concept of society. After dealing with the formal law, Schleiermacher turns to the view of society as substance: "Next, it will be considered as substance [*Stoff*], thus providing the *material* law: Everyone is to be

---

[119] Arndt, "Geselligkeit und Gesellschaft," 58f.

[120] Ameriks has made this point for Kant's theory of apperception. Ameriks, *Kant and the Fate of Autonomy*, 234–64. I have also discussed this point with regard to interpretations of the use of idealist philosophy by the author Heinrich von Kleist. Cf. Foley, *Heinrich von Kleist und Adam Müller*.

[121] *KGA*, I/2, 170.

[122] *KGA*, I/2, 170.

inspired to a free play of thought by means of communicating what is mine." Consequently, there are two laws of sociable activity derived from reciprocity, and they correspond with Schiller's formal and material drives. The resulting inspiration to "free play" also corresponds with Schiller's play drive that is the consummation of the form and material drives.

Schleiermacher returns to the Kantian origins of the disparity between the intellectual and sensuous realms when he talks about sociability enabling people "to remove themselves from their civil circumstances and to give room to a free play of their intellectual activities."[123] This injunction sounds as though the material side of that equation must be removed to move into the Kantian pure realm of the intellectual sphere. Schleiermacher's solution is different, though, from Kant's. The former works with a Fichtean notion of reciprocity to permit a practical and realistic relationship between the polarities of the rational and the natural that follows Schiller's division into form and material drives. Free play is the solution to this problem, and it appears very early in Schleiermacher's *Essay*. In the midst of his introductory section that describes the ethical realm that sociability will realize, Schleiermacher describes the person acting as a member of the intellectual world (i.e., the kingdom of ends) and states that "[i]f one's powers are left to their own free play, one can develop them harmoniously."[124] Here, in the Kantian delineation, lies a Schillerian caveat: the moral individual can develop his or her inclinations so that freedom is not compromised between duty and inclination. These powers are the ones that motivate, and for Schleiermacher, freedom depends on neither being compromised. This very harmony can be achieved if development proceeds as a reciprocal relationship. Schleiermacher understood this harmonization to be commensurate with Kant's moral thinking, and from this understanding he developed his own theories of sociability to maintain this reciprocity and the resulting unique idea of freedom.

---

[123] *KGA*, 1/2, 176.
[124] *KGA*, 1/2, 165.

5. The Unfinished *Essay*

Schleiermacher originally had planned to write two additional parts to his *Essay on a Theory of Sociable Behavior*. In this chapter I will offer a number of suggestions to explain why these did not materialize (5.3). Before doing so, however, I will examine the notes Schleiermacher wrote down that may have been intended to be incorporated into parts two and three. In what follows, after first providing a précis of his *Essay on a Theory of Sociable Behavior* (5.1), I will include an English language translation of the relevant portions of Schleiermacher's *Notebooks of Thoughts* (5.2.1) and an overview of the arguments of these uncompleted portions (5.2.2).

All attempts to reconstruct the unwritten portions of the *Essay* from Schleiermacher's notes must remain speculative, at least to some degree. Given the survival of Schleiermacher's notes on the uncompleted portions of the *Essay* it seems reasonable to carry out this speculative task. Such speculation can never be exhausted, and I present below a collection of translations of Schleiermacher's notes so that others may follow my arguments and draw their own conclusions with the notes before them. There is material in the notes that may well never have found its way into the published version. Any attempt at a reconstruction has to rely on Schleiermacher's notes, and as he was working on more than one project at the same time, it is not always possible to tell what belongs to the *Essay* or to other works, let alone to tell exactly where his sometimes vague notes belong in the *Essay*. Indeed, there are various bon mots in the notes that would lend themselves to a more lengthy and humorous exposition as found in his *Letters on the Occasion of the Political Theological Task and the Sendschreiben (Open Letter) of Jewish Heads of Households* (1799),[1] but these items seem not to have been included. Such omissions

---

[1] "Briefe bei Gelegenheit der politisch theologischen Aufgabe und des Sendschreibens jüdischer Hausväter." *KGA*, I/2, 327–361. There is a fine English translation available: Friedrich

indicate that the project had become more limited in its execution than in its planning. Thus, in attempting an outline of the uncompleted portion, I have taken the liberty of neglecting notes that may not have formed the backbone of the argument. The notes represent an early form of Schleiermacher's ideas (perhaps, at times, even mere musings) on sociability and are but a station along the way to formulating his published comments. With that proviso, it should prove possible to offer some informed speculation concerning the contents and arguments of the uncompleted portions of the *Essay* based on Schleiermacher's *Notebooks* from the period.

I start this speculative project with a definite footing by presenting a précis of the arguments of the completed portion of the *Essay*. Following Schleiermacher's notation in the *Notebooks of Thoughts*, I refer to the two printed articles constituting that we have come to know as the *Essay*, as 'Part I.' Schleiermacher refers in the notes to 'II' and 'III' and these are the parts that I attempt to reconstruct below in the same fashion as my précis of the arguments of the completed portion. My précis of the arguments of Part I (the two articles that constituted the printed *Essay*) is followed by a grouping of the notes that would have constituted 'Part II' and 'Part III' of the *Essay* had they been written. In order to complete the speculative project, I follow this translation up with a projection, in the manner of my earlier précis for Part I, of what the arguments of Part II and the Part III could have been.

5.1. Précis of the Completed Arguments

The page numbering refers to the standard edition of Schleiermacher's works, the *Kritische Gesamtausgabe*, volume I/2, used throughout for the *Essay*. These pages are also referenced in the translation of the *Essay* in the Appendix.

Pages 165–66: Society as the embodiment of the ethical condition
Sociability is first and foremost determined by ethics. Schleiermacher applies Kant's ethics as delineated in the *Groundwork of the Metaphysic of Morals*. (In Kant's system no ends other than morality itself should be the motivating force of ethical

---

Schleiermacher, *Letters on Occasion of the Political Theological Task and the Sendschreiben (Open Letter) of Jewish Heads of Households*, trans. and intro. by Gilya G. Schmidt (Lewiston: Edwin Mellen Press, 2001).

action. For Schleiermacher, the sociable corollary of this argument is that sociability cannot be determined by any end external to itself. For Kant, to be in an ethical state one needs a world that is made up of individuals who treat each other as an end and not as a means to some other goal. This world is what Kant calls the "kingdom of ends.") The intellectual world is one in which the faculty of reason can reign, but it is, of course, hampered by the realities of the physical world. The social body politic is, thus, an embodiment of the ethical condition, or at least, it has the potential to be so. The ethical end of sociability relies upon the human will being freely determined by nothing other than morality as its goal. (The intellectual world of Kant's kingdom of ends manifests this ethical end of sociability.) Even if in reality the situation is very different, things may be improved by each individual acting in accordance with this prescription. The lack of any public enforcement means that, in the case of sociability, each person is his or her own lawgiver. (Again, this is in accordance with Kant's ethics, which make the reasonable [or rational] laws of behavior the subject of each individual's own law making. In Kant's system this practice preserves freedom because one is only subject to laws of which one as a rational agent is the coauthor. In free sociability one has a special social situation in which Kant's kingdom of ends is realized.) This opening section is also a fulfillment of Schleiermacher's note 110 in the *Notebooks of Thoughts*: "Right at the start [an] elegy on society as the embodiment of the ethical condition."

Page 167: The need for a theory of sociability
The intention is to produce a complete theory of sociability, at least in outline. (Schleiermacher's work remains a fragment, comprising about the first third of the whole theory.) Sociability is a practical matter and cannot, therefore, be brought about by means of a theory. A theory is, nevertheless, useful in that it will lay out the stages that one must go through in order to attain sociability.

Page 167: Feeling, the analogies to ethics and justice and beyond to art
To those who might say that sociability should rest on a feeling that is grounded in human nature, there is only one reply: this feeling indicates that there is some kind of basic concept of sociability that is held in common and lies in nature. This observation is just like the natural rules of justice, so that justice and ethics rest on the same foundations as sociability. Without a theory of sociability, any exercising of

sociability is a rather inward looking, or blind, experiential event. By adding a theory of sociability, its practitioners can be taken beyond this blindness into the realm of art, and thus, of conceiving what he or she is doing in the broader society as a whole. (Friedrich Schiller is the theorist who produces a social theory that seeks its fulfillment in society as an art form in his *Letters on the Aesthetic Education of Mankind*.)

Pages 167–68: Sociability as its own natural tendency versus the advantage to be gained by it

So-called virtuosos of sociability seek only the advantages to be gained by sociability, as if it were some marketable skill. In contrast, Schleiermacher treats sociability as a natural (or innate) tendency. This tendency is accompanied from the outset and, in its original manifestation, by an end (or goal) and a form of its own. All the laws of sociability can be derived from this natural tendency. Those that see sociability differently write books of etiquette that give rules allowing one literally to "win friends and influence people." Treating sociability in this manner is a distortion of an existing human moral tendency that needs to be developed and not misrepresented merely to give someone particular advantages.

Pages 168–69: The double approach to sociability

A practical approach to this theory of sociability can be attained by acknowledging the existence of society while at the same time seeking to develop that society. By both maintaining and creating sociability, one can say that it is always in a state of being as well as becoming. For a theory of sociability, this state means that one must derive one's rules from the original, naturally occurring sociability and that sociability must be constructed by putting these rules into practice.

Pages 169–70: Reciprocity and the laws of sociability

True society is manifest wherever interaction is reciprocal. This reciprocity is the essence of society, and it provides two laws of sociable activity. 1) The formal law: Everything is to be reciprocal. 2) The material law: Everyone is to be inspired to a free play of thought by means of communicating what is mine. These combined laws result in a third principle, the quantitative law: One's sociable activity should always remain within such limits as to permit a particular society to exist as a whole. These three laws encompass everything that can be derived from sociability as it exists and that can be drawn on for sociable behavior. In fact the third of these, the quantitative law, is the prerequisite of the first two, so that Schleiermacher rather confusingly calls it the first law and uses it to launch the next phase of the *Essay*.

Pages 171–72: Further analysis of the quantitative law
What one can and should not say in order to maintain the communal sphere of all is called appropriate. Schleiermacher introduces "propriety" (Schicklichkeit) as a technical term that designates this appropriate discourse. The existence of the term begs the question of how this communal sphere of all is to be determined.

Pages 172–73: A contradiction and two false maxims
The demand to remain within the communal sphere contradicts free sociability. If one were to leave part of oneself behind so as to be able to fit into a particular society, then one would no longer be the individual that defines who one is. Consequently, people in real life often do one of two things: either they emphasize themselves too much and think they can ignore any rules and just impose their individuality on other people—according to their lights, society is thus increased by fitting into it as much as it can possibly handle—or they hold themselves back, never rising above the average, to which they believe all society is striving, as if to fulfill some natural law. These behaviors constitute two contradicting and false maxims that are inimical to every principle of free sociability. Too much imposition of one's individuality or too much self-restraint are both anathema to sociability and lead either to accusations of arrogance or banality. Sociability is indeed made up of self-activity and self-limitation, but these actions are altogether misunderstood. Trying to find a compromise between these two, so as to please everyone, is also no solution. Instead of compromising, we need to unify these two principles.

Pages 173–76: Resolving the conflict
This conflict can be resolved by looking at the way in which societies are characterized. The manner of dealing with subject matter, rather than subject matter itself, characterizes people. Tone is the term that can be used to describe how subject matter characterizes different societies. The law of propriety now reads: I must observe the tone of the society, and with regard to the subject matter, I should allow

myself to be guided and limited by that society.

Two conclusions may be drawn from this law:

1) One must remain within one's particular element, and even if some range too freely, one must not allow oneself to be taken into realms in which one is uncomfortable. Schleiermacher cites Goethe's poem "Der Fischer." We are to understand that the reader is not to be drawn into the deep (i.e., not Siren-like), but rather we are to understand the poem as an ironical admonition not to fall foul of being drawn into the wrong sphere.

2) Use one's manner in all discourses; do not let it be dampened by particular subject matter.

Pages 176–77: Start of the determination of the communal sphere of all
"Secondly" refers back to page 172 that introduced the discussion concerning how to meet the demand of keeping within the communal sphere. The current section contains some introductory remarks that lead into an examination of how this sphere is to be determined. Schleiermacher again works dialectically by discerning a conflict: There is a group gathered; they want to be sociable. The first part of this proposition presents who the group members are in civil society, and the second describes their intention to remove themselves from civil society. The problem is where to start with these two parts of the proposition. This polarity leads again to two false maxims. Schleiermacher ends the first published portion of the *Essay* on this dialectical cliffhanger by not naming the maxims.

Pages 177–80: Finding the character of the society
The first false maxim is the use of people's positions in society to determine the communal sphere of all. Although this ranking is a very convenient way of determining what people might have in common, it reduces them to what they are in virtue of their professions. Social position really only represents the very minimum of what a person can be, and thus, such a starting point restricts the freedom of the people to be more than their mere appearance offers. Women are the worst off, laboring under an all-too-common assumption about their social roles and interest. Men at least are freed from the domestic sphere when discussion revolves around work, but for women there is no such possible escape from the domestic sphere if society's discourse is founded in this way. Such a maxim restricts society to an

unnecessarily low point.

The second false maxim arises from the proposition that those coming together want to form a society and that one can assume a receptivity for the very best one can give. Unfortunately, someone operating under this misapprehension will determine the tone of society and will exclude others because of it because giving one's best in this way will exclude too many others as they will have no understanding of the material being discussed.

The need to determine the communal sphere can only be resolved by combining the two precepts (i.e., that the group gathered wants to be a society and that they are determined by their civil circumstances). The two precepts can be used as mutually limiting. To find that measure of material that a particular combination of people is capable of handling, one must start with that material that the civil world necessarily understands as being available to them. However, one must also assume that he or she has developed this material to make it appropriate for sociable use. On the other hand, instead of just giving the best about what one knows the best, limit oneself by what another in the group does not know anything about. One of these approaches gives the inner limits and the other the outer limits to this sphere. The sociable imperative is, then, to determine the sphere of the society ever more precisely by moving between these limits. Schleiermacher gives the label "*refinement* of conversation" to the ability to carry out this determination well.

Page 181: Summary of what has been done so far
1. Both sides of the quantitative law have been examined.
2. Those things that complete sociable behavior (as furthered by 1) have been determined.
3. The character of society as to size has been derived from 2.
Now the two halves must be combined to make a whole.

Pages 181–82: The double tendency that resolves the conflict
A contradiction lies in saying that we must not go beyond some limits that are never fully determined. Schleiermacher discerns what he calls a "double tendency" that resolves this contradiction. One must, on the one hand, participate properly and consciously, while on the other, one must add comments that may not work in order to see if others will follow the lead and take the conversation higher.

Schleiermacher's defense of innuendo and persiflage (and indecently irony and parody) is given as a method to allow for this second, uncertain pursuit.

It is important for me to point put here that Schleiermacher's double tendency represents an entirely revolutionary notion of freedom in society. In general, liberal notions of freedom allocate to the individual only so much freedom so as not to restrict anyone else's freedom. Schleiermacher's notion of freedom includes a responsibility on the part of the individual to test the limits of what the society can tolerate. Schleiermacher's free sociable individual should use his or her speech to push sociable society to the limits of what society can handle. This also fulfills the dynamic demand that society is always becoming as well as being.

Pages 182–84: An appendix to the first part
The ways in which people come together give rise to varying responsibilities for the participants regarding making sociability come about. There are three ways for people to gather: a) by accident; b) by communal will; or c) by the will of one individual. What one does with people of differing abilities gathering depends on how they came together. First, if they gathered by accident, then it should be possible just to let sociability crystallize as best fits the situation; under such circumstances, there would be no responsibility to try to include anyone of lesser sociable ability by reducing sociable pleasure to a lower level. Second, there would be no cause to make a smaller, covert society among the bigger one if the group gathered by the will of all; responsibility is evenly shared, and one would be expected to make concessions to include those present. Finally, in practice people are not usually really looking for true sociability, as is most frequently the case when an individual has invited others and when that individual has the responsibility to make it possible for these others to follow the law of propriety without sacrificing their sociable pleasure. In such a situation, one can bring about a parallel sociability as long as it is not to the detriment of the others: it may even be a covert one if the host is merely reciprocating on a sociable debt that he or she owes others by inviting a particular guest, then that guest can do what he or she wants. Sociability was not a factor in this invitation, and people can behave as if they were brought together by accident. Even innuendo and persiflage have an appropriate role in such a situation.

Page 184: Final words

This proposition is a theory and merely indicates the ideal toward which reality must tend.

5.2. Schleiermacher's Notes for the *Essay*

Schleiermacher's *Notebooks of Thoughts* must be the foundation of any attempt to reconstruct the unwritten portions of the *Essay*. In order to be comprehensive in my approach to this reconstruction, and for comparison with the text, I offer first the notes that provided Schleiermacher with his working material for the published *Essay*. These are followed with the notes as he grouped them for the subsequent, missing portions of the *Essay*.

5.2.1. Translations From the *Notebooks of Thoughts*[2]

Part I of the *Essay*

[Note 84.] The good way of life has a negative and a positive part: contradictions govern the latter just as much as the former.

[Note 96.] Knigge deals with absolute contradictions as if they were a negotiation in which everyone makes some concessions.

[Note 97.] Be what you are, always and completely (Knigge), is a principle of what absolutely never occurs in society. Instead, one must only say: Avoid being no part of yourself. What is very interesting, though, is the inner society with the self that one is not allowed to be at that moment.

[Note 99.] Following the most terrible elementary rules and the most unethical maxims of freedom, Knigge asks very naively: to what extent might women be able to act according to these rules?

---

[2] *KGA*, I/2, 25–39.

[Note 102.] As soon as one uses society merely as a means for one's own egoism, everything must go awry and go badly.

[Note 104.] One has reason to be cheerful in poetry and morals that practice need not wait for theory; in society that theory need not wait for practice.

[Note 105.] Knigge treats people like Jews: One is supposed to discount more than half of their opinions concerning others.

[Note 106.] In the good way of life, there is only as much practice as there is theory; individual observations are always missing certain perspectives and connections.

[Note 110.] Right at the start, [an] elegy on society as the embodiment of the ethical condition.

[Note 112b.] One has to be the reflection of the whole society and yet an individual. to 144

[Note 119.] Knigge has behaved like a bad host by placing what little there is of value in his book in the poorest of company.

[Note 136.] Some behave in society like insoluble[3] chemical substances. They always settle to the bottom. to 29[4]

[Note 137.] Most of the casuistic issues regarding the good way of life lie in the antithesis between feeling and concept. Here, too, the imperative of feeling is intended for manner and that of the concept for tone.

---

[3]Schleiermacher mixes similes here. He uses the term "unzerlegbar," a natural sciences word used to connote an entity that cannot be analyzed by breaking it into its constituent parts.

[4]29 reads: "Disputes are the finest reagent for illiberality." The language appropriate to chemical reactions links these two. These are the very kind of witticisms that Schleiermacher might have wanted to include in a longer version of the *Essay*. He reaches back to 29 for its potential as such a witticism, but 29 does not appear to belong to the original sketched ideas of the *Essay*.

[Note 143.] The fundamental antithesis is that everyone is end and means at the same time,[5] and it is from this antithesis that the above mentioned concept proceeds: namely, my end should solely be an activity, and my activity should only be a savoring, i.e., the better it is, the nearer this activity approximates a work of art.

[Note 144.] What was said in 112b comes from every part of a whole having to be homogeneous with respect to the genus, namely that one person cannot be of the latter and another of the former species. This antithesis cannot be resolved other than this: that which is characteristic of a society does not have to be characteristic of an individual (this is the subject[6] or the tone) and vice versa (this is the manner). This antithesis does not occur in the state because one is not exactly a member as much as one is an individual. The good way of life amounts to this: that one can present all subjects and bear all manners.

[Note 146.] Reciprocity occurs only when every action of the one is the effect of the other. That includes the activity of the listener while listening; thus, he or she needs only to comprehend—but now his or her activity should be a free development of his or her humanity. I should thus put him or her into such a state that he or she can do nothing but comprehend and in such a state that he or she can do nothing other than wish to comprehend. The latter does not have to be caused by the subject,[7] but rather by the form; [it] should not be Pretiosity,[8] [it should not be an] addiction to saying masses of interesting things, but rather an interesting lecture; otherwise, I can never be certain that this will is my effect. The former unavoidable comprehension need not be due to the lecture, but rather needs to be a result of the subject[9]—need

---

[5]This statement is the very crux of the ideal moral sphere of the kingdom of ends that Kant elucidates in his *Groundwork*.
[6]Stoff.
[7]Stoff.
[8]Heinrich von Kleist uses this supposedly French term when discussing the salons of Berlin in 1801: "In Gesellschaften komme ich selten. Die jüdischen würden mir die liebsten sein, wenn sie nicht so pretiös mit ihrer Bildung täten. An dem Juden Cohen habe ich eine interessante Bekanntschaft gemacht, nicht sowohl seinetwillen, als wegen seines prächtigen Cabinets von physikalischen Instrumenten." "I hardly go to socials. The Jewish ones would be my favorites if they did not deal in such a 'pretiös' manner with their education. I have made an interesting acquaintance with the Jew Cohen, not so much on his account but rather for the splendid cabinet of physical instruments he owns." Heinrich von Kleist to Ulrike von Kleist, 5 February 1801. Von Kleist, *Werke*, vol. 4, 193.
[9]Stoff.

not be affective—overburdening of this unavoidable comprehension with multivalence; otherwise, comprehension is not activity, it has to be precision.

[Note 147.] If the comprehending of the listener is to be an activity, then it must have some effect on the speaker. Passivity must be active. This continues *ad infinitum* and is society's mute game. The higher the power to which this is raised,[10] the more the good way of life comes to dominate.

[Note 148.] Talking needs to be an effect of the one listening. Of course, this is only possible in a divinatory way, namely such that he or she adopts it as his or her effect right away. At the same time, each act of talking should be an expression of my essence. Consequently, two one-sided maxims: One that is to talk with everyone concerning one's profession: one that is to talk in accordance with one's own wishes. The former addresses manner, the latter, tone. [This] only accounts for initial talk as what follows needs to be the effect of the average. after 144.

[Note 166.] The concept of propriety must be produced anew each time; the belief in its preexistence is the aristocratism of the good way of life.

[Note 168.] Reciprocity has no end other than itself. Round tables are a wooden measure against isolation.

[Note 169.] Because a society can deteriorate of its own accord at any moment, whoever entertains one also makes it. Asking a group to gather does as yet not constitute a society. Bad asking is good practice. The English have no society because they ask so homogeneously.

[Note 161.] To what extent do games constitute a society. Valediction on lomber.[11] Dance is not a society but rather only a dialogue. English dancing is as such very consistent as it is for the English who absolutely do not want to socialize with the opposite sex.

---

[10]Following the mathematical-sounding discussion of infinity, I have rendered "potentiierter" using *potential*, signifying the order of a number.

[11]A card game referred to in German by its Spanish name "L'hombre."

[Note 189.] Large societies are absolutely tasteless and at the same time an insult because the host only uses the sociability of the others as a means to another end. On Kant's limit to societies. The limit is far more individual and cannot be determined by some mystical number (by doing this Kant has done something that he himself rejects as superstition).

[Note 190.] The complete unity of a society is always merely an idea.

[Note 191.] One cannot pay off a poor host better than by making his or her society into a caricature to as great an extent [as] possible.

Part II of the *Essay* (never written)

[Note 90.] Sources of antimony in the good way of life are as follows: those against the individual and against the whole, the natural and the positive, treatment as means and ends, of the letter and the spirit.

[Note 100.] Society has something ethical but also something juridical: namely one must presume everyone to be a poor socialite.

[Note 101.] It is entirely untrue that one can be much without understanding the ways of the world.

[Note 107.] It is presumably only among organic products that two different substances combine in a nuanced way—with elemental substances, this presumably occurs in stages. Likely because with the former there really is no full homogeneity.

[Note 111.] The hypotheses of physics that posit substances as manifestations of purely physical ideas and those laws that are posited as explanations of things exhibited have a completely different status in the other fields of academic inquiry and have to be handled completely differently regarding their relationship to the facts. Schelling handles those of the first type as if they were those of the second.

[Note 113.] Poor living lies in the material because it is vulgar as it does in tone because it is misanthropic.

[Note 114.] Knigge only recommends a fine tone so as to bring that inner gold into circulation under its auspices.

[Note 115.] In Knigge's opinion, there is no need for rules governing interactions with orphans or the titled.

[Note 118.] Reciprocity must occur according to particular laws, and yet, one is supposed to feel free. The antithesis between the natural and the conventional proceeds from this.

[Note 120.] There are two ways for a theory to come about, emanating from the center or from the limits inwards. The second way for empirical matters.

[Note 142.] Measured flattery is just as unpleasant in society as unmeasured disapprobation; it really has to be a concert not monotony, and in order to bring this about—this is also always a just act—one may have to deny one's nature.

[Note 145.] Ideal activity accompanied by the real is the state of enjoyment. That state in which ideal activity follows the real is mental labor; that in which the ideal cannot follow the real is physical labor.

[Note 149.] Actually, I prove that there is no such thing as a bad way of life, rather that everything is part of the good one, and therein lies a great deal of the good way of life.

[Note 150.] One must attend to the individual and to the whole. It follows from this that the narrative needs to be entirely dialogical and that the dialogue has to be epidemical.

[Note 151.] The individual should be an end to me—not a means too?

similarly 2 mistaken maxims.[12]—he or she should never be a means for me (the cowardly maxim)—everyone must have to bear being treated as a means. (the arrogant maxim). Combining: being a means to me, the individual must also be an end to me. The joke has to be such that the individual is him or herself pleased and aroused by it—and in such a way that he or she remains in a social condition, i.e., I must not force him or her back into his or her familial or civil condition.

[Note 156.] The good way of life is not intended to be an interim institution that destroys itself when the people have become clever enough or sufficiently well known, but rather, it should persevere: its goal is actually the domestic or civil condition.

[Note 157.] As there are thirsty natures, no one must be prevented from setting down his or her water, but it should occur in an appealing form either as persiflage or as courtesy. The former is to be preferred. For the truly fluid, no form is fitting.

[Note 158.] No matter how poor its reputation, wit is absolutely necessary in order to make hearing active. The universal addiction to delivering even poor material wittily indicates the necessity of this requirement.

[Note 159.] A good dialogue should be lapidary in style but without commentary.

[Note 160.] Those present can also be objects, i.e., means. Contradicting maxims. Some exaggerate sanctity to the point that they feign the absent as present.[13]

[Note 162.] Among those states that require protection is the state of being a woman.

[Note 163.] A story needs to be evaluated like a lecture or a text. The

---
[12] I maintain Schleiermacher's lower case and numeral, thus indicating the note form of this text.
[13] This witticism is typical of Schleiermacher, in this case being at the expense of Catholic and other high church doctrines that see the Eucharist as manifesting the real presence of Christ.

storyteller is a dictator.

[Note 164.] The good way of life needs to be lively.

[Note 165.] It is imperative that people are stimulated from every angle. to 142.

[Note 167.] Legal duties to the rear behind the hedonistic ones. The poor way of life on the outside necessarily attracts the good one powerfully from the inside.

[Note 170.] Friendship converges toward individuality in the infinite and thus is infinitely divisible and perfectible and merely an approach to itself.

[Note 171.] Every real act of communication is a driving back of what is one's own toward the interior, and each time one addresses another one imparts a feeling of one's limits. These are the main points of the third law. This is also the source of the antithesis between the spirit and the letter.

[Note 172.] Kant *Anthrop.* 42 also sees only bad appearance in the sociable accomplishments and judges them as such.

[Note 188.] Within the law of reciprocity, there also has to be an antithesis between the way this reciprocity assumes the society is and the way it intends to bring about the society.

Part III of the *Essay* (never written)

[Note 92.] Even in the good way of life, there is a conflict between essence and appearance—namely that feeling at ease should be the way an expression of free humanity manifests itself. Striving for this manifestation, no matter in which way, is appearance. The spirit is striving for free reciprocity; the letter is holding oneself back. to III

[Note 95.] ["]Give others the opportunity to shine["] belongs to the letter and

141

presupposes that one assumes them to be originally passive so that they require stimulation. to III

[Note 98.] ["]All people want to be amused["] is the principle of appearance. to III

[Note 103.] Whoever fails to resolve the antimony between dealing with people as means and as ends correctly cannot avoid becoming aware of the insufferable principle that one has to exercise patience and allow people to be boring. to III

[Note 108.] The principle of the conventional is that you must use all available means to indicate that the current social order is the optimal one. to III

[Note 109.] It is unrefined to assume that someone has the spirit of the party and the sect and that he or she is merely a representative. to III

[Note 116.] The antimony of essence and appearance comes about by means of the [following] antithesis: whether each individual should become conscious of his or her own humanity through his or her free activity or rather he or she should become aware of the humanity of others through its effect. to III

[Note 117.] The antimony of the spirit and the letter comes about by means of the antithesis that reciprocity should exist and be free because one is only free to the extent that one does not feel one's limitations, i.e., shining. III

5.2.2. The Arguments of the Uncompleted Portions

The published portion of the *Essay* ends in what it calls "an appendix to this first part."[14] Therefore, the two published sections of the *Essay* should be seen as constituting part one. The notes clearly indicate that selected entries are to be included in part three because they are marked "to III." If the entries that are dealt

---
[14]Ibid., 182.

with in part one are subtracted, the remaining entries concerning sociability must consequently refer to a part two that was also not written. The organization of the notes—many here translated for the first time—reflects this conclusion.

It is important, however, to reiterate that this enterprise involves speculation, even if it is founded on a close familiarity with the text. I base my selection of particular notes mostly on Meckenstock's own suggestions in the *Kritische Gesamtausgabe* and have been able to propose that some further entries be considered as relevant for the ensuing parts of the *Essay*. Important previous work on the *Essay* by Katherine Faull and Andreas Arndt has also drawn on Schleiermacher's *Notebooks*, and I have been influenced by their analyses that have incorporated those notes with the *Essay* proper. When I have found occasion to differ with this earlier scholarship, I have made a special mention of it. The following, then, is a sketch of Schleiermacher's arguments in parts II and III of the *Essay* based on an analysis of the relevant entries in his *Notebooks*.[15]

Part II: The formal law: everything to be reciprocal

Note 90: The dialectical process
Schleiermacher indicates that his argument will once again proceed dialectically. The antitheses that drive this dialectic are stated in note 90 and are derived from Part I as well as new ones being introduced. Similarly these antitheses can be pursued into Part III (171: antithesis between the spirit and the letter) making the whole work dialectical in nature.

Note 118: The fundamental reciprocity between nature and convention
Already in Part I, Schleiermacher had indicated that there was an antithesis between the state of nature and the process of following laws. In note 90 he introduces this antithesis as being between "the natural and the positive," and in note 118 it is referred to as being between "the natural and the conventional." The considerations describe an arc that reaches from Part I all the way forward to Schleiermacher's discussion of positive religion at the end of *On Religion*, a project that, as I will argue at the end of this section, distracted him sufficiently to lead him away from

---

[15]*KGA*, I/2, 25–39.

completing the *Essay*. The antithesis remains within the sphere of an all-important reciprocity, as he delineates it in Part I; self-limitation is represented by the conventional or positive, and self-activity by the natural. Note 118 indicates that considerations of society as a whole (beyond the restricted realm of dialogue in the salon) are Schleiermacher's concern. "[T]he good way of life" (90) has an antinomy that drives Schleiermacher's account of society and sociability. The whole of society is built upon the very idea that one should feel free and yet act according to some laws. This action would be the moral tendency of sociability as it appeared in the opening of Part I (110).

Notes 151 and 160: The reciprocity of means and ends
In note 151 Schleiermacher equivocates on his initial use of Kant's idea that no one should be a means. He calls Kant's maxim "the cowardly maxim" (151) and contrasts it with Knigge's principle that sees everyone as a potential means, that is, "the arrogant maxim"(151). Schleiermacher proceeds as in Part I by combining these two mistaken and contradicting maxims (160) to create a way of characterizing the sociable condition. Effectively reciprocity is achieved only through reliance on others. This conclusion is Schleiermacher's joke in note 151; Kant's unequivocal rejection of using people as a means becomes a sort of necessity in setting up the morally ideal sphere (kingdom of ends) because one needs them to become involved; otherwise, that world will never come about. This observation works for every individual who is stimulated to become involved in this ideal sphere. Sociability is successful by drawing people out of their limited (domestic or civil) condition into the wider sphere of people interacting. This enterprise has to be realistic, and it depends entirely on those actually present: it would be a mistake to make concessions (a limiting factor) for those who are not really there. This proscription leads to a witticism about the real presence at the expense of Catholic doctrine.

Notes 149, 150, and 156: The whole of society dealt with in the good way of
Sociability of the good way of life is not just an interim solution for those seeking entertainment or evenings of good conversation (156). Again, the seeming joke is that the goal of good sociability is to make life as it exists better: the domestic and civil conditions (seen as so limiting elsewhere in the *Essay*) themselves can be improved through good sociability. When applied correctly, good sociability (the

good way of life) can improve the whole of society. All of society can fit into the good way of life (149). When reciprocity works correctly, one has a society; there really is no such thing as society or a way of life at all when there is no reciprocity between members. The whole concept of humanity is that it should be together. There would be nothing more antithetical to humanity than a hermit. This observation is why Schleiermacher says that "[o]ne must attend to the individual and the whole" (150). While his attention in note 150 is again on dialogue, the antithesis between the individual and whole (as stated in note 90) is one of the sources of the antinomy of the good life that drives his dialectical arguments about society.

Notes 120, 170, and 171: The antithesis between the letter and the spirit[16]
Very likely at the end of Part II in 171 Schleiermacher connects with Part I concerning the quantitative law (the third law) and looks forward to Part III that will concern itself with the spirit and the letter (92) as a way of examining the formal law. On the level of method of progress (just as at the end of Part I he reflected on a theory only being an attempt to reach the ideal) here he looks at the way in which a theory can come about (120). A similar reflection on friendship (such an important theme of the section of the *Nicomachean Ethics* Schleiermacher translated) has a outward ranging relationship with itself (170) that relates to the outward and inward focused ways for theories to come about (120).

Relying on the theme of reciprocity, Schleiermacher presents the issue of discerning limits for the sociable group as deriving from the feeling of one's limit one conveys in every address to another (171). This is not so much a self-limitation as a discerning of limitation by means of interaction. In this way what he says about limitation links with the outward and inward focused ways for a theory to come about (120). The antithesis between the spirit and the letter results from feeling the limit

---

[16]Schleiermacher's debt here to Origen has not previously been noted. Origen (ca. 185–254), perhaps the greatest Christian scholar before Augustine, discerned three levels of meaning in biblical texts: the literal (of the letter), the moral, and the spiritual. The literal meaning concerned outer or ephemeral (physical) meaning. The moral concerned its value for us in the present, while the spiritual provided us with access to the divine. Schleiermacher's division between the letter and the spirit does not neglect the moral. The overarching subject of the *Essay* is society in the here and now, and it opens with "society as the embodiment of the ethical condition" (110). Furthermore, Schleiermacher pursues the division between the moral and the spiritual explicitly in his *Letters on the Occasion of the Political Theological Task and the Sendschreiben (Open Letter) of Jewish Heads of Households* and less explicitly in *On Religion.*

when you are trying to transcend it. This is merely stated in 171, but is developed in Part III, and thus makes the transition to Part III.

Part III: The material law: everyone to be inspired to a free play of thought by means of communicating what is mine

Notes 95, 103, and 117: Antinomy of the letter and the spirit; feeling freedom's limits
The idea that people must be given the opportunity to give their best (95) comes from attempting to avoid impressing the feeling of limitation from the outside. But, such a literal interpretation ("of the letter") of free sociability does not fully take the spirit of sociability into consideration. As Schleiermacher has pointed out in Part I, people can be too literal and can impose themselves too much. The bon mot about means and ends (103) is an aside that is an admonition to respect others and to exercise patience.

Notes 92, 98, and 116: Essence, appearance, and humanity[17]
If one's striving is toward feeling at ease, then one does not yet have the essence of the good life (92). Striving should instead be toward free reciprocity, and with an acknowledgment of the arguments of Part I, this notion contrasts with holding oneself back. Such self-limitation follows the letter of what should be sociability and would work if in fact all people were passive (95). The truth of the matter is that many individuals are not passive and that sociability demands reciprocity. If one were just to make everyone feel at ease, then one would be creating a principle that would accord with mere appearance by assuming that everyone wanted to be amused (98). To achieve the reciprocity for which Part II argues without falling into traps of mistaken ideas of sociability, such as holding oneself back, one must do more than merely amuse people or just provide them with stimulation. Interaction is required: this interaction is Schiller's free play from Part I.

---

[17]This section is perhaps one of the most complex and challenging for any reconstruction of Schleiermacher's arguments, and I shall differ somewhat from Arndt's conclusions about essence and appearance. He writes that "dialectical appearance of the antinomy resolves itself in the truth of lived reality." Arndt, "Geselligkeit und Gesellschaft," 59. Arndt relies on sources from Fichte's §5 of the *Basis of the Entire Doctrine of Science* 1794/95 to make this argument, and I have rejected this approach in chapter four. Arndt's speculations are, of course, entirely valid and cogently argued. In itself, his suggestion merits serious consideration; however, my understanding of Schleiermacher's rejection of Fichte does not support such proximity to the absolute I, even if modified by a reading of Friedrich Heinrich Jacobi, as Arndt suggests. Ibid.

In Note 116 Schleiermacher offers a particularly ponderous and complex proposition that characterizes the whole of sociability. If free play is truly successful and brings about free sociability, then people will become aware of humanity. Schleiermacher leaves us to consider the free reciprocity of Part II promoted to the level of free play in Part III by leaving it open as to whether our awareness of our own humanity comes to us through our own free activity or whether we become aware of the humanity of others through the effect of our free activity. Once the antinomy has reached this level of quandary, then we are in the realm of free sociability at last.

5.3. Abandoning the *Essay*

Schleiermacher left us no explanation as to why he failed to produce the second and third parts of the *Essay*. There is only one remark in a letter of February 15, 1799, to Henriette Herz in which he despairs of his ability to write on sociability: "I have read one of Plato's dialogues, I have done a little piece on religion, I have written letters. In short, I have tried everything but the good way of life—and what should I do with that without company? But it's all rather mediocre."[18] Schleiermacher's comment that he cannot pursue work on "the good way of life" for lack of company indicates that it is his *Essay* that he is abandoning.[19]

Below, I explore a hypothesis that the cause for Schleiermacher's abandoning of the *Essay* goes beyond the mere ennui of isolation. It seems to be a valid dramatic gesture to make company a necessary prerequisite to writing about sociability, but I argue that, once he surmounted his initial loneliness and took up writing again, Schleiermacher was instead drawn into writing about religion because the ideas on sociability in the *Essay* were of great consequence for his understanding of religion. Thus, in speculating on Schleiermacher's reasons for abandoning the *Essay*, I draw on some themes from the *Essay* that Schleiermacher pursues in *On Religion*. I believe that he became distracted by their relevance for what he saw as the more significant

---

[18]*KGA*, V/3, 10.
[19]Meckenstock makes this point in his commentary on the *Essay*: *KGA*, I/2, lii. I agree with his contention that this comment refers to the missing continuation rather than to the piece itself, as Wilhelm Dilthey originally assumed. Wilhelm Dilthey, *Leben Schleiermachers. Vol. 1: Denkmale* (Berlin: Reimer, 1870), 89.

project on religion.

In his *Letters on the Occasion of the Political Theological Task and the Sendschreiben (Open Letter) of Jewish Heads of Households*, Schleiermacher discerned that being Christian was not a requirement in order for someone to count as a moral and worthy member of society. In the *Essay* he finds the root of true humanity in society and sociability. In *On Religion* these two threads come together to enable Schleiermacher to see the necessity of sociability for religion.

Many treatments of *On Religion* see the "Fourth Speech: On the Sociable in Religion: or on Church and Priesthood" as ancillary to the work's main arguments.[20] While that speech may indeed be less significant for the theoretical discourse on religion, it contains considerations of the social and ministerial institutions of religion that have a powerful practical relevance. Indeed, sociability is an essential path toward the religious, and the fourth speech explores this vital role for sociability.

In light of his Spinozist view of causal linkage between all elements of life, society and religion are inseparable for Schleiermacher. This connection however, makes no case for forcing the link between society and religion upon those who are not inclined toward it of their own accord. Thus, Schleiermacher argues that there would be no call for some general proposition of religion to be required of all citizens. Quite the contrary, he argues for determined and specific religion because "nothing at all can be given and communicated anywhere in the form of something general and indeterminate, but only as something individual and thoroughly determined."[21] Schleiermacher argues similarly against a weakened form of Christianity as an acceptable approach for Jews toward full membership in civil society. His arguments for giving Jews civil rights (formulated also at this time) hold that Judaism is preferable to a watered-down Christianity.[22] Echoing in *On Religion* Spinoza's famous dictum "a nihilo nihil fit," Schleiermacher remarks that such

---

[20]Gunther Wenz, *Sinn und Geschmack fürs Unendliche. F. D. E. Schleiermachers Reden über die Religion an die Gebildeten unter ihren Verächtern von 1799* (Munich: Verlag der Bayerischen Akademie der Wissenschaften, 1999), 6f. Wenz cites several influential works that outline *On Religion* in various ways but that generally follow his interpretation that the third and fourth speeches are "lediglich Zwischenstücke" [merely bridging].

[21]Schleiermacher, *On Religion*, 77.

[22]Cf. Peter Foley, "Der Jude als moralisch zurechnungsfähiger Bürger. Schleiermachers philosophische Erwiderung auf die Frage der Bürgerrechte für Juden," *Theologische Literaturzeitung* 126 (2001) 7/8: 721–34.

general arguments "would not be something, but actually nothing."[23]

Despite rejecting forcing Christianity upon society, Schleiermacher holds that religion suffuses a very diverse set of activities and institutions. The taste for religion is derived from encountering religion in the everyday experiences of practical life: "In the course of their domestic and civil life, in the greater arena of occurrences where they are spectators, much is naturally encountered that must affect even a slight portion of religious sense."[24] Such slight presentiments of religion ultimately lead to a desire for fuller religion, but it is here that religion can be first encountered.

The secular sociability of the *Essay* presents an ideal form of sociability that will draw people out of their limiting spheres:

> This must be one that enables an individual's sphere to be intersected as variously as possible so that each of his own points of limitation will afford a view into a different and strange world. In such a manner, all manifestations of humanity will become known, one after the other, and the most alien temperaments and relationships can also become familiar and similarly intimate to that individual. This objective is realized by rational people engaging in mutual self-education when they keep company freely.[25]

As the origin of religious sensibility lies in ordinary daily activities, it would be wrong to divide the domestic or civil spheres from the religious ones. In fact doing so creates religious institutions that do not fit with Schleiermacher's understanding of religion and, thus, opens up these institutions to criticism for which Schleiermacher shows acute understanding. Sociability brings people into contact with humanity, and this humanity will form an essential feature in Schleiermacher's arguments on religion.

The secular sociability of the *Essay* is built upon the notion of reciprocity. As Schleiermacher states in the *Essay*: "The true character of a society, then, in terms of the intent of its form, is that there should be a reciprocity that permeates all of its participants, but that is also entirely determined and completed by them."[26] In *On Religion* Schleiermacher proclaims that religion must by nature be social, and this selfsame reciprocity is required for religious sociability:

---

[23] Schleiermacher, *On Religion*, 77.
[24] Ibid., 80.
[25] *KGA*, I/2, 165.
[26] *KGA*, I/2, 169.

> Once there is religion, it must necessarily also be social. That not only lies in human nature but also is preeminently in the nature of religion.... In the continuous reciprocity, which is not only practical but also intellectual, in which he stands with the rest of his species, [a person] is supposed to express and communicate all that is in him.[27]

This claim, too, is the pattern of the *Essay*, inasmuch as it struggles to permit a person to carry out this communication between the poles of "independent action and limitation of the self."[28] But, for religious sociability, Schleiermacher makes the distinction that this communication comes to be of some higher order, even if the same thinking on society underpins his considerations. Ordinary society may well serve as the starting point, but even society must progress as this new religious vein develops: "The communication of religion must occur in a grander style, and another type of society, which is especially dedicated to religion, must arise from it."[29]

Given fertile, receptive ground such a society will develop. This religious form would then be the perfection of Schleiermacher's dictum in the *Essay* in which he describes society as in a state of being and becoming: "However, as the object of the theory of sociable behavior, society must be observed in a twofold manner, both as being as well as becoming, both as the condition of sociable perfection as well as being determined by it."[30] There is a progression from secular sociability to religious sociability; this progression does not mean that all sociability will become religious, but there are ingredients in secular sociability that will lead to religious sociability. This realization, I suggest, led Schleiermacher away from his *Essay on a Theory of Sociable Behavior* into the realm of religion and his more significant and highly popular *On Religion*.

The religious sociable utopia projected by *On Religion* takes on the dimensions of Augustine's *The City of God*.

> I wish I could draw you a picture of the rich, luxuriant life in this city of God when its citizens assemble, all of whom are full of their own power, which wants to stream forth into the open, all full of holy passion to apprehend and appropriate everything the others might offer them.[31]

---

[27]Schleiermacher, *On Religion*, 73.
[28]*KGA*, I/2, 173.
[29]Schleiermacher, *On Religion*, 74.
[30]*KGA*, I/2, 168.
[31]Schleiermacher, *On Religion*, 74. Crouter makes the point that Schleiermacher's original "Stadt

Only in this realm of religious sociability can sociability achieve all it can be. The awkward restraints of secular sociability can be dropped so as to welcome all that others can offer. This end is the fulfillment of the reciprocity from the *Essay*. This openness toward others allows people to transcend themselves and become humanity:

> The more each person approaches the universe, the more he communicates himself to others, and the more perfectly do they become one; none is conscious of himself alone, but each is simultaneously conscious of the other. They are no longer merely people, but also humanity; going out beyond themselves, triumphing over themselves, they are on the way to true immortality and eternity.[32]

In this way the Christian ideal of immortality is incorporated into Schleiermacher's unorthodox theology. From the starting point of reciprocity, his arguments reach toward the fundamental humanity of the individual that allows him or her to transcend the self, leaving the self behind and gaining the universe and immortality. Note 116 from the *Notebooks* emphasizes the role of humanity and the consciousness of humanity when free sociability is fulfilled: "The antimony of essence and appearance comes about by means of the [following] antithesis: whether each individual should become conscious of his or her own humanity through his or her free activity or rather he or she should become aware of the humanity of others through its effect."[33] This proposition must be read with reference to the above quotation from *On Religion*. In doing so, it becomes clear that religious sociability is the logical consequence of a full reciprocity between individuals: consciousness of humanity plays a focal role in permitting Schleiermacher's sociability of 1799 to achieve complete fulfillment, and it can do so only in the realm of religious sociability.

Consequently, note 116 constitutes a realization that the pinnacle of sociability will be achieved only when humanity attains full reciprocal consciousness. In *On Religion* Schleiermacher can readily pursue this matter in the religious context to which he knows sociability will lead. By the time he came to work on his notes to transform them into a text on secular sociability, his thinking had developed, and he knew that his ideas could only be fully accounted for by expounding his theories in a

---

Gottes" is an allusion to Augustine and to Revelation 3:12 (Ibid.).
[32] Ibid., 94.
[33] *KGA*, I/2, 30.

text on religion. There is, therefore, a logic to his abandoning of the *Essay* because he had found a more reasonable venue for his arguments on sociability in *On Religion*.

Appendix

Essay on a Theory of Sociable Behavior[1]

by
Friedrich Schleiermacher

Free sociability, neither fettered nor determined by any external end, is demanded vociferously by all educated people as one of their primary and most cherished needs. Whoever is merely thrown back and forth between the burdens of domestic life and the enterprises of civil life[2] merely has the pace increasingly slowed at which one approaches this higher goal of humanity, the more faithfully the pattern is repeated. A profession confines the activity of the spirit to a limited sphere: no matter how dear or worthy of approval it might be, it will always hold fast to a single point of view in its action and perspective on the world. Thus, the best and most involved profession, just like the simplest and lowest one, will bring about one-sidedness and narrow-mindedness. Domestic life brings us into contact with very little and always

---

[1] Ed. note: The original has been reproduced in *KGA*, 1/2, 165–84. This translation is the second into English. Jeffrey Hoover's very readable "Toward a Theory of Sociable Conduct" appeared in *Friedrich Schleiermacher's Toward a Theory of Sociable Conduct, and Essays on its Intellectual-Cultural Context,* ed. Ruth Drucilla Richardson. *New Athenaeum/Neues Athenaeum*, vol. 4 (Lewiston: Edwin Mellen Press, 1995), 20–47. His translation has a small number of errors, most of which are insignificant. I have made corrections in the following translation, which has benefited greatly from the existence of Hoover's preceding version. The numbers in square brackets refer to the page numbers in the standard German edition of Schleiermacher's "Versuch einer Theorie des geselligen Betragens," *KGA*, 1/2, 165-184. All emphases in the text are Schleiermacher's.

[2] Ed. note: Henriette Herz complained that many Jews were unable to keep up with the kind of learning required for the learned sociability to which they aspired. They did not have the time to read because their efforts were concentrated on their commercial enterprises. *Herz*, 61.

with the same: in this circle even the highest requirements of etiquette will quickly become familiar to someone of an alert nature. With each passing day, his or her spoils in the manifold outlooks of humankind and its actions will become ever less, the more completely the economy of etiquette is established and the more correctly everything proceeds. There must, then, be a state that complements both of these. This must be one that enables an individual's sphere to be intersected as variously as possible so that each of one's own points of limitation will afford a view into a different and strange world. In such a manner, all manifestations of humanity will become known, one after the other, and the most alien temperaments and relationships can also become familiar and similarly intimate to that individual. This objective is realized by rational people engaging in mutual self-education when they freely keep company. Here we are not concerned with a matter of a single subordinated goal; the activity of the higher powers is not curbed by the attention that must be paid to the tasks of the lower powers when there is a desire to affect the external world. Here, a person is completely within the intellectual world and can act as a member of it. If one's powers are left to their own free play, one can develop them harmoniously. Subject only to those laws one places upon oneself, one depends only upon oneself to cast off the limitations of domestic and civil circumstances for a time. One can do this to a degree that is in accordance with one's inclinations. This is the moral end[3] of free sociability; of course, in its present condition, it is as far from its goal as domesticity and the bourgeois club are from [166] theirs. Sociable life also has forms that pressure it and has contingent matters that are at variance with its purpose. Here, too, one can despair everywhere at the awkwardness and malice of individuals; there is much to eliminate, a good deal to alter. Only here, owing to the inherent lack of civil authority, everyone must be their own legislator and must look to it that the common good sustains no damage. All improvement must proceed from this principle and can only really be brought about by every individual adjusting his or her behavior in accordance with that common goal.

    I am far from suggesting that this could be achieved by means of theories; however, it is certain that one cannot approach a goal with any constancy unless one has grasped it and knows the necessary ways to approach it. Thus, there can also be

---

[3] Ed. note: An alternative would be: "moral purpose." As the term "Zweck" is translated as "end" in translations of Kant's works I have chosen "moral end" here, in order to reflect Kant's language consistently.

no improvement without theory. It is to this end that this essay aspires to make a contribution by representing a system of sociable behavior that is at least complete in outline.

It seems to me unavoidable that every attempt made concerning this subject that aims to produce a theory consisting of concepts will necessarily offend the virtuosos as well as the dilettantes. The latter delight in affording profound admiration and applause to the patterns of acting on the world's stage that they love to emulate. In this they wish to be as little disturbed by the criticism of the theorist, who has perhaps not even tried his hand in this area, as do the lovers of art in the smaller theater where the actor amuses and exhilarates us. The dilettantes will say nothing goes more against the grain of polite behavior than does being presumptuous, and nothing is as presumptuous as formulating all-encompassing rules on this very subject. I suggest to them that the theorist does nothing more than enhance the virtuosos. The latter always avoids giving, or forgets to give, an outline of the whole and a place to every individual. In as much as the virtuosos construct rules out of general concepts, they forgo virtuosity and happily take advantage of the former esteemed authorities,[4] namely the theorists. The virtuosos themselves [167] tend to have a low opinion of universally valid rules expressed as formulae. To them, all refinement of sociable behavior appears to be particular, and the best of every individual situation to be dependant upon so many minor circumstances that one cannot trust general rules; all personal perfection must proceed from the emulation of tried patterns or from personal feelings. Precisely because every action, with its manifold contents and the circumstances that have defined it in a particular way and no other, makes, so to speak, an infinity, reflection that precedes emulation must abstract from some elements and be directed toward others. Thus, if this infinity is not to rely upon some feeling, there have to be some rules according to which I can judge from what to abstract and upon what I should reflect. Even feeling itself proves the necessity of a theory, only in an alternative way. In matters of sociability, one has recourse to this feeling with the same confidence as one has recourse to conscience in matters of ethics. In every educated individual,[5] feeling is set up as adjudicator over

---

[4] As Hr. Garve very modestly attaches a very nice theoretical discourse to a sentence from Rochefoucault.

[5] Ed. note: Schleiermacher declines the term "Individuum" correctly for the Latin as "Individuo," thus giving it some emphasis and rhetorical power when placed into the context of being educated. The need for the term to stand out is noted in note 20 below. Its use there warrants greater

particular judgments or special rules that have been found. This state of affairs serves as abundant proof that one considers such a feeling a general feeling founded in the essence of human nature. One demands that a law that is appropriate to this should be acknowledged as if it belonged to a system founded on irrefutable principles. Even conventional rules that are more or less universally accepted point to a mutual, fundamental concept founded in nature, just as visibly as positive laws point to a natural rule of law. In brief, seen from the vantage point of this argument, the case for sociability stands entirely on the same footing as that for ethics and law. With this argument as a prerequisite, seeking out a theory is a challenge one cannot shirk. Without such a theory, every exercise is but blind, disjointed empiricism. It is the theoretician who stands on the highest vantage point for this entire inquiry. He alone seeks the key to the puzzle and the final causes of actions. He alone wants to construct sociable life as a work of art, where virtuosos often perceive it only as a beautiful fantasy. By directing it to its place in the system, he alone wants to give final fulfillment to what the virtuosos say is beautiful and appropriate. Mainly because all of these theoretical considerations have so far been so woefully absent, those who have lived with intellectual spirit in the world and who have studied the art of society have only been able to set down pointers and comments here and there. These are, as it were interrupted pieces of a whole that only the critic can envisage and that cannot be compiled without the addition of the critic's own complementary portion. All the tomes that are written with pretensions to a system are only formless collections in which the rules and limiting guidelines of sociable communication are thrown together with [168] regulations that belong in little books of etiquette for children. Such collections stand all the concepts on their heads, and to add to that, they distort the whole enterprise by means of the most mistaken opinions. This is because the supposed virtuosos do not love and honor art for its own sake, but rather focus on the fortune they can have in the world by it, and like craftsmen, they carry out their profession only for profit.[6]

In contrast, the following will view free sociability as a natural tendency that can not be circumvented. The point of departure will be merely the initial concept of sociability that is available of its own accord in every person. The original characteristics of end and form are already combined here as a means by which this

---

emphasis.
 [6]As evidence for this description, see for example Knigge's *Umgang mit Menschen überall*.

concept is to be reached. An attempt will be made to derive all the laws of sociable behavior from this combination—a combination that always has to be understood as complete and pure.

If sociability is sought for its own sake (and it is itself nothing other than its own moral tendency), then the fulfillment of sociability can be manifest in nothing other than the ability to assemble socially, truly forming a society wherever the physical possibility for it is given, and where it already exists to maintain it. The forming and maintaining of company cannot be separated from one another and must be thought of as one.[7] For the presence of several people in a room for the purpose of being sociable is only the body of the company. This body needs to be brought to li by the activity of each individual, and because it is an entirely free activity, this life can only be maintained by an uninterrupted continuation of this activity. However, as the object of the theory of sociable behavior, society must be observed in a twofold manner, both as being as well as becoming,[8] both as the condition of sociable perfection as well as being determined by it. The original idea of society must come first because it is only through this idea that the laws of behavior can be conditioned and determined. However, because in practice behavior must come first, there still have to be rules of application for these laws of behavior. The coming into being of society by means of this application of the laws must be similarly theoretically prefigured. In order to be complete, the inquiry must then take a double path. First, the requisite regulations are to be derived from the concept of society, and then [169], by making these active in the mind, society itself will be constructed.

If we analyze the concept of the free sociability of society in its truest sense,[9] then we find that several people should affect each other and that this affecting is by

---

[7] Ed. note: "Unterhalten" is the word used here, and it can mean both "to entertain" and, in a now somewhat archaic use, "to maintain." The context necessitates the latter usage. However, Schleiermacher could also have intended the reader to reflect upon the other meaning of the term, for the aim of good sociability is to provide successful entertainment; the *Essay* discusses this very topic.

[8] Ed. note: "Being and becoming" allows Schleiermacher to integrate the notion of progressive human development (*Bildung*) as it was defended by such writers of an earlier generation as Herder, Goethe, and Schiller with the notion of living in the moment. Along with Schleiermacher, younger writers, such as Novalis, improved the idea of Bildung. Combining "becoming" with "being" can be understood as a quintessentially Romantic teaching.

[9] The word should only be understood in this way. In every social gathering that is bound and defined by some external purpose, the participants have something *in common*. Such gatherings are *communities*, κοινωνιαι; here, they actually have nothing in common; rather, everything is reciprocal, in effect at variance with each other; these are *societies*, συνουσιαι.

no means permitted to be one-sided.[10] Those who are gathered in the theater or who attend a lecture together hardly manifest a society. No individual is engaged in free sociability with the artist but rather in bound sociability because the actor is intent only on a specific effect, and the audience is unable to effect a matching return but rather actually always conducts itself passively. The true character of a society, then, in terms of the intent of its form, is that there should be a reciprocity that permeates all of its participants but that is also entirely determined and completed by them. This argument does not mean that a ball is a society; each dancer is actually only in contact with the individual who is at that moment his partner, and both view all others as means or tools. This neglect of the others also accounts for the custom of the English that dictates that each dancer remain united with his or her counterpart for the duration—a more consistent practice than our own. Gaming could more readily fall under the latter characterization because, in reality among the more rational beings, reciprocity includes all participants to a similar extent. However, the latter do not entirely determine this reciprocity because, of course, everywhere chance—which in many genuine societies naturally has an equally significant role— is the third or fourth player. If we take a look at the purpose that is to be achieved by means of this thoroughgoing reciprocity, then it becomes patently obvious, as a result of the predicate of freedom itself, that one should not even speak of a single and determined purpose because the latter determines and limits activity according to material and objective rules. No finite action is to be carried out communally, no undertakings completed in unison, no insight attained methodically. The purpose of society is certainly not to be thought of as lying outside of itself; each individual's effect should be on the activity of the rest, and the activity of each individual should be his or her influence on the [170] others. However, there is no other way to influence a free being other than to stimulate it to self-motivated activity and to offer it an object. Following from the above, this object can in turn be nothing other than the activity of the one offering the challenge; in other words, it can aim at nothing

---

[10]Ed. note: The original text has an error here: κοινονιαι should likely read κοινωνιαι (as opposed to κοινυνιαι as suggested in *KGA*). I am grateful to Hermann Patsch (Munich) and Alan Speight (Boston) for their discussions of this Greek term, which also relates to early monasticism, with its being used in the later Coptic lives of the desert fathers. It is further worth noting a potential relationship to Martin Heidegger's "Mit-sein," or συνουσιαι (*Synousia*), that follows Schleiermacher's preferred alternative here. Heidegger could have been learned of Nohl's discovery of the *Essay* at an early date through a common student. I would like to thank John G. Moore (Lander) for making this latter connection for me.

other than the free play of thoughts and feelings by means of which all members excite and animate one another. Reciprocity thus reflects upon and completes itself: the concept of reciprocity contains both the purpose and the form of sociable activity, and that reciprocity also determines the entire nature of society. However, these two views of reciprocity shall require separation in the following investigation. Reciprocity will be considered initially as form and will in this way provide a formal law of sociable activity: Everything is to be reciprocal. Next,[11] it will be considered as substance, thus providing the *material* law: Everyone is to be inspired to a free play of thought by means of communicating what is mine.

From this concept of society, very generally conceived such that anyone could concede it, the nature of sociability in general can thus be determined. Because we wish to provide a sound theory and will thus need to think of particular actual societies, our law-making is as yet incomplete. Every society must have a certain measure of this nature and exists as an individual only insofar as it bears this. The way in which people stimulate one another is generally speaking limitlessly manifold, and the sphere of their free comments is also limitless. Those who are supposed to form a society together bear only a certain finite measure of this infinite. If this is not grasped and extracted from the remainder, no real society can come about. Each society has its own outline and profile; whosoever fails to contribute to creating this, whosoever does not know how to remain within the confines of this, is as good as not there for this society, even if he or she had completely internalized the two laws mentioned above. In addition to the formal law and material law of sociability, we thus obtain yet a third: the *quantitative* law. These three laws must truly encompass everything from the characteristics originally unified within the concept of free sociability that can be deduced for behavior in this situation. These laws will thus now require closer analysis and determining of their content. We must necessarily begin with the latter as the most recently discovered law indeed manifests the prerequisite of the applicability of the other two, and if it could not be defined, it would make our entire inquiry [171] futile because an object was missing.

First, or quantitative, law: this is founded on the limitation of those who wish to approach one another in a state of free sociability and runs as follows: *Your*

---

[11]Ed. note: Jan Rachold reads "denn" as "dann" in his *Friedrich Daniel Ernst Schleiermacher, Philosophische Schriften* (Berlin: Union Verlag, 1984), 41–64. This interpretation has been followed here.

sociable activity should always remain within such limits as to permit a particular society to exist as a whole. We shall analyze this law more closely in order to see what it encompasses.

As a finite being, every individual has his or her definitive sphere in which he or she alone can think and act and thus also impart himself or herself. The sphere of one individual is not fully that of another, just as certainly as he or she is not that other individual, and everyone—this includes each and every member of a society—has something in his or her sphere that is not included in that of the others. If in the course of social intercourse, only one person touches on a point contrary to another, such that it cannot be found at all in the sphere of that other individual, he or she thus excludes either the latter or himself or herself from the community, depending on which of the two the others declare themselves. If two discuss a matter between themselves that, although they have it in common, is unfamiliar to the others, they make a society of two but have severed themselves from the rest. In every such case, the society ceases to be a whole. Remarks that have such consequences can be very pleasant of themselves. Yes, they can even be excellently appropriate to sociable communication because such interaction can conform entirely to its qualitative laws, but they cannot find space in the present sphere; they are in some disparity of size or type. In short, they do not acquiesce to their surroundings. Accordingly, language itself indicates the name *proper*[12] to us for this concept. According to its content, our law is the commandment of propriety and states that nothing should be evoked that does not belong to the communal sphere of all. We now need to determine how this is to be achieved. The method by which we shall have to approach this is already given. In order to grasp our law fully, we must make the initial assumption (as settled upon above) that a society is given and that its recognition, which is a necessary prerequisite for becoming a society, is already determined. We will also need to ask how the demands of the law can be met in this case. Secondly, we shall have to proceed from the demands of the law and ask how the communal sphere of all is to be determined in each individual case. [172]

Firstly, the communal sphere is assumed to be known and the question is raised as to how the demand to keep me within it can now be met. It becomes

---

[12]Ed. note: The original here is "des Schicklichen," which can either mean "appropriate" or "agreeable." It also connotes "skill" or "adeptness." Further context and use as a technical term, however, make "proper," or "propriety," the most adequate translations.

apparent that this demand is irreconcilable with the goal of free sociability. This goal is pertinent for nothing less than the whole person. Someone is not a member of a society by virtue of possessing this or that quality or piece of knowledge or belonging to a particular class. Instead, that person should contribute his or her very individuality or uniqueness, and the free play of thoughts and feelings, which should constitute that individual's activity in the society, is founded solely in this uniqueness. A human is an individual only in as much as everything is connected within him or her, has a center, and is mutually determined and explained. Deprive that person of some part of his principles, opinions, mode of expression, and behavior and his individuality is lost and he is no longer capable of presenting to us his own view of mankind. In other words, that I should omit some part of my sphere from society means as much as that I should be compelled to cease existing as an individual in the same. The latter is at variance with the goal of the former. This subject will occur often in the course of our inquiry, and I would like to take advantage of this first opportunity offered here to note to what great extent this circumstance obliges us to judge contemporary society charitably. One surely cannot expect the resolution of contradictions that are internal to the object by those who themselves admit they are only founded on the viewpoint of common empiricism. But few can be so fortunate as to have a capacity for premonitions to guide them through these reefs. We wish to regard as excused in advance those who for this reason with the best intentions have, nonetheless, been unable to live up to the law of ethics.

This contradiction leads to two contradictory false maxims, both of which are very frequently put into practice in ordinary life. Quite a few hold to a general precept and insist that everywhere one may contribute and exercise one's entire individuality and that one has permission to ignore the limitations set by society in this matter to as great an extent as possible. Of course, the idea in that is that they themselves want to be the focal point and that the size of a society need only be determined by the number in the group who are capable of being drawn by their attractive powers. If this maxim were universal,[13] it would necessarily cause a state of continual war[14]

---

[13]Ed. note: The language here comes very close to that of Kant's terminology in his *Groundwork*.

[14]Ed. note: This language sounds like that of Thomas Hobbes and his social theory.

among the [173] predominant socialites[15] that would have to end with the fall of society itself without achieving any significant result at all. On the other hand, others hold to a special law and maintain that "for the good of society one must deprecate oneself and wish to be nothing better than the middle average of the whole to which, according to a general law of nature, everything everywhere is aspiring anyway. Whatever meets the eye beyond this middle average is unseemly and would require sanding down like rough edges. All idiosyncrasies would have to be kept in and really would not have to be there at all for society. Everything would depend on a smooth surface that would yield to the slightest pressure and would nowhere offer resistance by means of gauche friction." This maxim completely suspends the final goal of society and strives toward that emptiness that is complained about the most frequently in the highest and the finest circles, simply in order to make it big enough so that the entire nobility might fit in. Similarly, the latter maxim tends to be evinced by courtiers and the former maxim tends to be evinced by the young people who with claims to spirit and a striving for freedom step into the arena of society[16]—often straight out of the halls of the muses.[17] In this spirit we will find a recurring opposition between these parties that level mutual accusations of arrogance and paltry insipidness at each other. Thus, it is only natural that the requisites of sociability, which are comprised of independent action and limitation of the self,[18] are misunderstood in all individual details, such that one is made absolutely subordinate to the other because it is not known how to combine the two. Besides these, there is yet a third maxim that with a moderantist[19] spirit avoids the accusation

---

[15]Ed. note: I differ from the *KGA* here in not correcting Schleiermacher's original "socialites" (Gesellschaftern). The *KGA* instead has "societies" (Gesellschaften).

[16]Ed. note: "Enter the lists of society" is an older phrase that would also convey the overtone of accepting a challenge associated with this use of "in die Schranken der Gesellschaft treten."

[17]Ed. note: This statement appears to refer to the young authors who became members of salons and were accepted into society owing to their literary accomplishments.

[18]Ed. note: The tendency for translators is often to create new vocabulary out of German original texts. Such creation gives the work a more scientific flavor. However, this practice is artificial because the terms are not new creations in the original German, and if they are highlighted in such a way, they thus detract from a true reflection of the original text. This type of translation has been avoided here, although a case could be made for dealing otherwise with the compound nouns "Selbstthätigkeit" (independence of action) and "Selbstbeschränkung" (limitation of the self). The preoccupation with the self in the *Essay* gives a Fichtean ring to the language. This Fichtean echo is further strengthened by the reference to absolute subordination of concepts.

[19]Ed. note: Hoover notes that this term is used pejoratively and that it concerns the Moderate party of the French Revolution. Hoover, 28.

of belonging to one or the other by taking a little from both and depending on the society; whether the former or the latter has the upper hand, the mixture is adjusted until it can, if necessary, be palatable to all. Of course, this does not constitute a solution of the contradiction; rather, this pulls it all the tighter together; the one-sidedness is not avoided by doubling it.

Yet, how is that contradiction to be resolved in the case under consideration here? If we want to proceed in a general and particular fashion, as required by a theory, then no other option remains but to combine both contradictory positions completely, as the task indicates. I am meant to contribute my individuality, my character, and I am meant to take on the character of the society; both are meant to occur at the same moment, are meant to be one and unified in a single mode of action. If we look at this command more closely, then we will actually find another in it, namely that what [174] constitutes the character *of the individual* is considered in society only to be something accidental and so also that which constitutes the actual character of society is meant to be thought to be accidental *in the individual*.[20] The requirement to unify the two contradictory positions leads to the requirement to think in this way and in no other as the only possible means to fulfill the first of these requirements. In fact we find that this really is the way this matter is considered. An individual person is characterized in respect to his or her thinking and action and not at all in respect of the subject matter—the latter is common to many, and it is considered to be something quite accidental. Instead, a characterization follows from the way in which a person handles, combines, develops, and conveys the subject matter. This is the essential element that characterizes an individual, and with respect to the society, we would like to call this *manner*.[21] However, it is this very subject matter that is used to divide societies into different types and to determine their character. If one wants to describe a society,[22] then one starts by stating whether it concerns itself with news or with moral accounts—generally referred to as *medisance*[23]—with art, with literature, or with philosophizing. Those qualities that

---

[20]Ed. note: Schleiermacher declines "Individuum" according to the rules of Latin grammar. The first instance gives "Individui" for the genitive case, and the second dative, being correctly rendered as "Individuo." The translation places these declensions in cursive script in order to reflect the emphasis Schleiermacher gives to these nouns as Latin and, therefore, as academic or technical terms.

[21]Ed. note: "Manier" is here a technical term that Schleiermacher is introducing and defining.

[22]Ed. note: Here "eine Gesellschaft" refers to the particular sociable circle.

[23]Ed. note: This word "medisance" is the French term used by Schleiermacher in the original.

arise from the manner of the individual members, that allow the society to be described for example as witty, vulgar, calm, vivacious, or noisy, are not regarded as the differentiating factor of the type, but rather as determining the degree of its merit and preeminence within its type. If one compares two societies in which the same subject matter dominates, then one will always say, they are of one type but the one is finer and superior. If one compares two others in which the manner is relatively similar, the subject matter, however very different, then one will say, they are both equally excellent, but the former is of an entirely different character to the latter. I would like to call the character of a society, thus determined by the subject matter, its *tone*.[24] While this is etymologically correct, it is, however, not quite entirely in line with common usage. By means of this difference, that conflict mentioned earlier is entirely resolved, and the law of propriety now acquires the meaning: I must observe the tone of the society, and with regard to the subject matter, I should allow myself to be guided and limited by that society (this provision was disregarded by those who had proceeded from a one-sided maxim of self-limitation). Nevertheless, I remain at liberty to allow my individual manner to reign entirely free within this sphere. This boundary was transgressed by those who had demanded to be completely unfettered in society. From this, the following is derived:

1) The actual object of the proper is not manner at all: instead, the object of the proper is subject matter. With regard to the latter, the crucial issue is to find the limits within which the society must remain confined and to discern with acuity the outlines that are often entangled in each other in an unlikely manner. Thus, politics and history, literature and criticism, theatrical issues and mimic arts are indisputably very closely related subjects. [175] For a great part of very fine societies, an untraversable chasm is, nevertheless, firmly established. Where talk has been of the one, to allude to the others is often an impropriety that, failing appropriate foresight, one only recognizes by its results once it is evinced. By contrast no one should—at least for the sake of propriety—be timid about his or her own distinct manner. It

---

Again, a fashionably French term is applied in a pejorative context. Schleiermacher and Henriette Herz are at pains to distance themselves from certain aspects of French sociability. The word refers to gossip or slander.

[24]Ed. note: The etymology of "tone" is shared with that of "tension," tone being derived originally from Greek via Latin and denoting tension in a rope or string that thus determines the quality of sound. Schleiermacher here refers to the intellectual tension of a salon that is determined by the subject matter preferred there and that, in turn, gives rise to the quality (or type) of the conversation that constitutes the tonal quality of the gathering.

really is essential to the perfection of a society that its members diverge from one another in their opinion on the subject and in their manner of dealing with it in as manifold ways as possible. Only thus can the subject be exhausted in regard to sociability, and the character of the society entirely developed. Shyness in giving one's own approach free range, even if it should be inferior and faulty, is a stupidity that is highly damaging to society. It is, of course, not praiseworthy to be dull in one's marks of respect, to be wide-ranging in speech, and to be bland in one's ideas, but these are not at variance with propriety at all and can only be improved by means of practice and by practice alone. That is why I consider it really necessary that each should strive to make evident what he or she is, both in relationship to the society as well as in regard *to the individuals*[25] themselves. To hold one's disagreeable qualities within bounds is thus the task of the others, and they will surely attend to that. There is hardly a sadder impression than when some of those in a society that are afflicted with such unfortunate qualities give their natures free range and when other similar natures watch half apprehensively, half enviously, and force themselves into an alien mold in which they are still nothing for society. No one should avoid their element. Not as a seductive siren but out of friendly intent, I would wish to call successfully to all those that find themselves in this situation:

> Oh, if you knew how the little fishy was
> so contented on the bottom;
> You'd jump right down, just as you are
> and be healthier than you've ever gotten.[26]

---

[25]Ed. note: See note 20 above. Schleiermacher is using the Latin (neutral plural) here: "Individua."

[26]Ed. note:
O, wüßtest du, wie's Fischlein ist
So wohlig auf dem Grund;
Du sprangst hinunter wie du bist,
Und würdest erst gesund.

This verse is the second half of the second stanza of Goethe's 1779 *Der Fischer*. Hoover also made this discovery. Hoover, "Toward a Theory of Sociable Conduct," 30 note #9. Schleiermacher's version contains some slight variations from Goethe's original, and hence, we may assume that he is quoting from memory:
Ach wüßtest du, wie's Fischlein ist
So wohlig auf dem Grund,
Du stiegst herunter, wie du bist,
Und würdest erst gesund.

2) In conformity with the law of propriety, consummate sociability is comprised of two elements. On the one hand, one needs a certain *elasticity*, a skill to expand and contract the surface that one offers the society as required. One also needs to have numerous subjects at one's fingertips, and if the society is agile, to be able to run through many of the same with ease and speed, but then again, forgetting all else with ease, contentedly abiding with a minor [176] subject and comprehending how to take it patiently through its paces in manifold ways. This elasticity must secondly be connected with a certain *impenetrability*. One's own power and type must be present everywhere to an equal extent and must reveal itself actively and reactively, be the subject matter great or small, familiar or obscure. Taking both together, I can think of no better name to give them than *agility*. No word known to me better expresses the capacity to fit in every space and, yet, to be present and move in one's own form. One is in possession of this virtue to an increasing degree the greater the sphere of differing circumstances in which it reveals itself and the further apart the points on either side lie at which we are no longer in command of these circumstances. The most agile is he or she who is at once the most many-sided and the most unique, who is prepared to engage with any subject matter and who also knows various ways of impressing his or her distinctiveness upon the most trivial and most alien of subject matter.

Second, assuming the demands[27] of the law of propriety now, the question can be asked, how then in each case am I to determine the common sphere to which I am to limit myself? That communal sphere does not come along with the person simultaneously and can only come about in my idea by striving to have a particular circle for the demands of that law. Society comes about only by acknowledging such

---

D. Luke's excellent prose translation reads: "Oh, if only you knew how the little fishes live so snugly down in the depths, you would come down here yourself, just as you are, and you would know true wellbeing then!" *Goethe: Selected Verse*, ed. D. Luke (Harmondsworth: Penguin, 1964), 79.

It is interesting to note that Henriette Herz used this very poem to illustrate the difference between her husband and his Enlightenment sensibilities and her own more Romantic leanings, evident in her sympathies toward Storm and Stress writers. In relating an incident concerning Karl Philipp Moritz, she refers to "Der Fischer." Moritz had asked for an explanation of a line from the poem: apparently Herz's husband was unable to explain it because, according to Henriette, he had never experienced the kinds of emotions expressed in the verse. She leads into this explanation with an example of her husband in a similar situation telling an inquirer, "Go to my wife; she has the knack of explaining such rubbish." *Herz*, 29. Töllner cites this latter story without discovering the connection to "Der Fischer" and Moritz. Töllner, *Die Bedeutung der Geselligkeit in Schleiermachers Leben und Schriften*, 32.

[27]Ed. note: "Forderung" is referred to on page 178 of the *Essay*.

a communal sphere,[28] inasmuch as this occurs to an equal degree for each participant. Thus, if the possibility of a society exists in the gathering of several people, the necessary task then is the proper construction of the measure of sociable subject matter within which only that society can exist. In order to find that unknown measure, one must proceed from the known. Now, nothing is known other than that several people are there and that they wish to become a society. By means of the former, by means of their conviction,[29] nothing is given other than their situation in civil society and such signs given in their external respectability as indicate the level of their education. Nothing is given in the latter other than their intention to remove themselves from their civil circumstances and to give room to a free play of their intellectual activities. However, one must assume that all regard society as an end in itself and that they seek nothing in it other than society for its own sake. These data in fact contradict one another, inasmuch as one indicates their civil circumstances to me, and the other draws me back from them. From which of these two one is meant to proceed is a question [177] that, in the spirit of the previously discerned parts, again leads to two contradictory maxims.[30]

There are some that say: because the task is to find the character of the society to which the present persons are suited, the information that they wish to be a society at all is not of a type to be a starting point. They say this because it is common knowledge that from the general alone one cannot determine the particular that is understood by it. Nothing remains but to go by the appearance of the persons themselves. Thus, the task is reduced merely to seeking what is held in common of the subject matter that each of them offers individually through their appearance and to setting this as the character of the society. This procedure has the indisputable advantage that it very quickly brings us to the determination being sought. However, it also has all the disadvantages of the similar one already examined above, in that it limits the freedom of the individuals unduly and, through this very action, does not allow the society to reach that goal that it could otherwise attain. If I know that one

---

[28] Ed. note: Schleiermacher here uses the term "Spielraum," which connotes "play" as either a "gap" or "leeway," as in room to maneuver, or "participate," as in a game.

[29] Ed. note: Schleiermacher characteristically uses Kantian language here by calling a society that is to be formed an "Anschauung," a conviction he held and Kant mutually held.

[30] Here the first published portion of the *Essay* ends. The second follows immediately in the translation. The heading from the second piece "Essay on a Theory of Sociable Behavior (Continued)" has been omitted and the text has been continued seamlessly in the translation.

person is a merchant, the other a financier, and the third a yeoman, then, of course, that which is communal that follows from these occupations can very readily be found. However, what I know of a person derived from the very idea of their social standing concerning that person's talents, expertise, education is surely but the minimum of that which he or she can be, namely that which he or she must necessarily be owing to the particular profession exercised. How much more knowledge, how many more ideas can these three people yet possess and exchange, none of which belong to their profession at all. If I make it a law for myself to stop at this point and only to view what is communal of this as the sphere that I am not allowed to transgress, then I am limiting the character of the society by means of an operation of sluggish reason, and I restrict the society to an unduly lower level than that on which it potentially could stand. It is a direct consequence of this maxim that the more homogeneous a society is in terms of professions, the more the affairs of their social status constitute the sphere of their conversation. This is because these affairs are the first thing that can be derived from such a determination of the sphere, and they are rich enough in themselves not to require a search for anything else. A direct consequence of this maxim is that the more heterogeneous the members are with respect to professions, the more things will tend toward general political reflections because, despite every difference of class, the situation in a particular state and in the civilized part of the world is yet the last common ground to which a person of such a viewpoint can [178] cling. One sees how commonly this maxim is followed where academics, businessmen, or women come together on their own; the affairs of social status frequently dominate, and in large mixed societies, time and again, it is politics that dominate at first, and once one is tired of this subject, the members crystallize themselves into little circles according to classes as if some unconscious chemical attraction were driving them. This crystallization is certainly to the great detriment of sociability and will certainly never enable it to attain its goal of lifting a person out of the viewpoint of his or her profession for a time. Here I cannot help but make a comment; is it not true that better sociability comes about under the eyes of and upon the direction of women, and that this is, like so many other excellent matters in the affairs of humans, a consequence of exigency? Women namely, are much worse off than men if they follow the maxim criticized here, and their societies organized in this manner must necessarily be the worst and most base. Now, if a man talks of his profession, he nonetheless feels free of one aspect, namely the domestic.

Women, on the other hand, for whom both coincide, feel all their fetters in such a conversation. This drives them away to the company of men where they cannot follow the former maxim because they have nothing to do with civil society; the affairs of states do not interest them. For the very reason that they have no status in common with the men other than that of an educated person, women thus become the founders of the better society.

The second maxim is guided by the concept of sociability having a goal, and that is why it negates the approach of the first maxim. It states that one is not permitted to carry out a determination of the common sphere based on the initial appearance of the people and their civil station because it is these very things that free sociability wishes to transcend. Those who proceed from this point maintain that the precept that everyone together wants to constitute a society is enough of a determinant. They say that this precept already implies the ideal that one needs to ascribe to everyone receptivity for everything that can be of general interest without being the provenance of a particular civil status and that one must trust everyone to have a feeling for the best that each individual can give. Everyone must, then, contribute their best and construct the sphere of the society from the combined sum of that wherein each individual is at their most complete when their professional business is subtracted. This approach has the indisputably laudable final goal of elevating the society to as high a level as possible, but it has the drawback that, by following this method, the society will probably not come about at all. The more anyone wants to concentrate on that in which he or she is preeminent, the more there must be of that into which the others have no insight, even if they are not unreceptive to it. Without this [179] insight, a free play of thoughts is not possible. Whoever remains fixed at this point will necessarily always set a tone with which the others will be unable to harmonize. Actually, nothing communal can be determined without another rule that would have to set how far everyone was permitted to venture into their subject matter. However, there is no data available to set this rule. No matter which of them acts as a point of departure, one inevitably misses the goal of society or the law that is sought.

Again, it will then not be possible to resolve the demand,[31] other than by unifying both given precepts and using them as the point of departure. We do this so

---

[31] Ed. note: This statement refers back to the demands of the law of propriety.

as to make one the requirement or the limit for the other. We start with the appearance of the person, and we allow the final goal of free sociability to limit the result. This union holds the following: in order to gauge the measure of subject matter that a particular union of persons is capable of, one must proceed from the subject matter that the civil situation of the same indicates is necessarily present among them. However, at the same time, one has to assume that they have cultivated that subject matter to such an extent that it is appropriate to the purpose of free sociability inasmuch as they have attained opinions and knowledge of that subject matter that are of general interest and that lie beyond the actual sphere of trade and profession. "These general ideas concerning what is common among those gathered concerning their professional business is that which is then the natural and original subject matter of the society." We could just as well have proceeded from the other point, the final goal of free sociability, and could have limited what was discovered by the first point, namely the opinions of the persons. The second of the maxims criticized demanded that each participant should contribute as completely as possible as the subject matter of the society everything that each could offer that was of general interest. Undetermined as it was, we found this demand to be entirely importune. Our present procedure sets the civil viewpoint of those unified as the limit for this aspiration. Every civil status, insofar as it requires continuous consideration of one subject, necessarily holds those who are tied to it back from those sections of general education that require a diametrically opposed procedure or from those sections most distant from that subject. And thus, the precept now assumes the following form: "In determining the sphere of a society proceed from the total of sociable subject matter altogether, but subtract that of which any single member of the society must almost necessarily be ignorant." By proceeding from each of these two points and being able to limit each by the [180] other one, our unification has in turn thus given us two different rules that are both constructed in accordance with the same rule and thus have the same right to our approbation. The question as to whether we should allow both of these to stand separately or whether we should instead combine them (as was done in the case above) can readily be resolved by noting that the first manifests the concept of something that is the smallest and the other that of something that is the largest. Strictly, we should combine the two, and we can now see that this is indeed possible: namely to use both as points of departure means to hover between the two. With a concept that is determined only in this way, there is actually nothing determined other than its limits. Furthermore, the concept can only be approached rather than ever being discovered precisely. This is, then, the true and final result of our enquiry: seek to determine the sphere of the society between the given limits with ever increasing precision. Sociable perfection that depends upon this determination is thus constituted of moving with ease between the furthest limits of society, which themselves can be precisely determined as discussed above; of touching upon everything that lies in between in such a way that, if receptiveness is there, it will not fail to have an effect and that, if that is missing, no one will find themselves in an embarrassing situation; of noticing from the slightest intimations what is too demanding for one or the other. This is the art that really constitutes *refinement* in conversation.[32]

In accordance with our design, we have now looked at both views of the quantitative law, have determined the perfections of sociable behavior as demanded by those views, and have derived the character of the society in terms of size[33] from that; all that remains is for us to join the two halves and to combine them into a whole. However, this now results in a new difficulty. The first view contained the rule that we were, not even for a moment, to do anything to go beyond that subject matter that expresses the character of the society. In the second, this character appears itself as something that is never fully determined, and we are commanded to contribute to discerning it more precisely at every moment. Thus, while these two rules really do comprise a whole and are intended to complete the concept of propriety, they nevertheless contradict each other. That is why so often only the one is heeded, while the other is, in contrast, entirely neglected. The mistakes that result from this contravene the concept of propriety in its totality, and the improper shows itself in its crassest light to be ridiculous. What can be more ridiculous than someone completely suppressing the natural striving of a conversation to rise up to a higher sphere, always remaining unwaveringly firm at that position at which he or she was at the outset and also seeking to keep others at that point by force. Just as such a procedure if it is observed over the course of an entire lifetime in the field of science or the political world strikes an impartial observer [181] as highly ridiculous

---

[32]Ed. note: "Feinheit der Conversation." "Feinheit" is emphasized in the original, with the Latinized "Conversation" being used as opposed to the German "Unterhaltung."

[33]Ed. note: This statement refers back to the limits discerned earlier, i.e., "something that is the smallest...something that is the largest."

inasmuch as it martyrs the participants, it also causes both effects in the short interval of an evening and on the small stage that is conversation.[34] No less ridiculous is he or she who like the arrogant innovators in those larger spheres consistently strives to drive the tone higher and higher and does not wish to allow the society time to linger with that which entertains it pleasantly. These blunders clearly also lie in taking a half to be the whole, and in order to avoid these too, we must now similarly combine the two commands with each other. This is part of our task anyway, as each of these rules occupies our entire time, and thus, both should be satisfied in one and the same operation: "Not contravening the character of a society, and the more precise determination of this character must be one." Again, two rules lie in this latest command that itself serves as a conclusion to the whole first part of the sociable regulations. First, "[t]he closer determination of the social sphere is intended to constitute not contravene it." That is to say, that in this task I should not proceed from the aforementioned *largest*—as in this manner I would certainly have to pass over[35] much that lies outside of the sphere sought—rather, I should proceed with caution from the *smallest* toward the larger. It is not unusual to see the old adage from Horace exemplified especially gracefully through this anticlimax of conversation, where a discussion starts with higher matters and gradually withdraws to the most common sphere. Second, "the noncontravention of the communal sphere must simultaneously be more precise determination of the same." This and everything that I do in order to maintain the society in accordance with the stipulations of the first view must simultaneously encompass the intention of developing the society in accordance with the stipulations of the second. Consequently, I am not permitted any personal actions and statements at all that would test how precisely the character of the society would allow itself to be determined or how high it can be driven. So that I do not lose my time carrying out potential experiments, this testing must instead remain a subsidiary of that which I

---

[34]Ed. note: "Bühne der Conversation" is a profoundly significant formulation that must necessarily color our perception of the salon as a dramatic space in which participants perform acts of dramatic self-presentation. Feilchenfeldt has identified the salon as a theatrical space. Feilchenfeldt, "Berliner Salons der Romantik," 158.

[35]Ed. note: With "über vieles hinweg," Schleiermacher's choice of words is unusual as he clearly means that extraneous material will be dealt with rather than not avoided as the turn of phrase would initially indicate. The choice of "pass over" preserves this linguistic conflict. Hoover writes "include" here, which while conveying the sense of Schleiermacher's original, diverges from the language used.

am actually doing to maintain the society. All social statements must consequently have a double tendency, a double meaning as it were. This meaning should be one that I should like to call the common denominator, which is related directly to maintenance[36] and which necessarily and unfailingly attains its goal, and another as it were a higher one that is thrown out with some uncertainty to see if someone will pick up on it and pursue the intimations it contains. The multiplicity of ways in which this can take place cannot be recounted here; namely in every way in which ideas or entire fields of ideas can be evoked by being related. Only one thing: in this rule lies the defense of two genres that generally have a poor [182] reputation; in fact though, if they are properly applied, they lie at the pinnacle of propriety; I am talking of innuendo and persiflage. The first is found if, in the manner in which an idea is expressed, there is a relationship to the familiar expression of another idea that lies in another sphere. The latter lies in something being said in a sense that would commonly be held to be serious, while at the same time pointing to another sense in which it is a joke. The usual negative opinion of these utterances and of the lighter types of irony and parody that might well also belong here is based partially on assuming that there is always one person, and probably even one present, who is the object of these. Indeed, if this were the case, which it is not, then it would always remain a punishable enterprise, dangerous to the existence of the society. This negative opinion is undeniably also partially based on this latter fact because in this way a kind of secret society is founded among those who, to the great disadvantage of the remainder, enter into mutual understanding on this point. In order to justify these comments, we need to distinguish between the ways in which people gather in a room for the purpose of sociability, and this will give rise to several ideas that will be best placed as an appendix to this first part.

Following what we have seen, certainly very much depends on the kind of constituent elements available for a society. The sphere of these elements should be something common to *all*, and thus, it necessarily makes a great deal of difference if one or only a relatively small number lags too much behind the remainder in terms of knowledge and education. If they are guided by the laggards, then the better members are incommoded, and disregarding that society's excellent composite elements, the society has to remain mediocre or bad. If they fail to be guided by the laggards, then

---

[36] Ed. note: "Unterhalten" is the German term used here and above (see note 7) and can mean both "to maintain" and "to entertain."

the worse members are out of place. What needs to be done in this situation depends entirely upon the way in which such an uneven society was formed. The composite elements of a society are brought together in three different ways: by accident, by the communal will of all, or by the will of some single individual. If very dissimilar types of people gather in one space by accident—invariably in some public place—that in itself offers as yet no mutual obligation,[37] indeed they have hardly been given occasion to entertain the idea of wishing to comprise a single society. They can yield to their natural drive toward sociable crystallization, and it depends entirely upon them whether they wish to diminish their sociable pleasure for the sake of someone of a lower type who might become too much isolated by this operation. In the latter case, there would be absolutely no reason to resort to such an aid as setting up a smaller secret society within the larger one. There is even less reason for this strategy when it is as a result of communal will that constituent elements of an unequal nature come together in closed societies. Whosoever is there [183] who has to lower his or her sociable pleasure bears responsibility for that him- or herself. That individual has agreed to be drawn into the union, and action, then, has to be appropriate to that union. However, this case will not occur frequently because most closed societies are intent less upon true free sociability than upon some other means of enjoying themselves. This happens most frequently in societies that are brought together upon the instigation of one individual, and that changes the approach entirely. The host is indisputably duty bound to consider in the choice of guests that their ability to follow the commandment of propriety should not be impaired and to bring them together, such that if they should wish to fulfill this axiom entirely, their sociable enjoyment would not be diminished. If the host neglects to do this as a result of ineptitude, then there can be no more polite and friendly aid than to allow unity to constitute itself and secretly to establish a more exquisite and substantial union putting hearts at rest, without disadvantage to the others, even if it is only for fleeting moments, especially as the means are, as such, entirely just, and as there is always simultaneously an overture to the others accompanying this, which, if they were to understand it, would make them feel better about acting in this way. The bigger a society is, obviously the more readily an inept act of this nature will occur. Nonetheless, it does not help to limit oneself to a particular number, as recently Kant has still done in all seriousness

---

[37] Ed. note: "Verbindlichkeit" connotes both "a polite address" or "act of courtesy to another" and "a situation of being combined." "Mutual obligation," thus, alludes to both meanings.

sanctioning the rule that a good society must be limited at either extreme by the number of graces and that of the muses.[38] Whoever calls a society together with pure intentions will always have some in mind as principal figures whom he or she would like to bring en rapport.[39] The host can then readily determine to what extent he or she can complement this with secondary figures by confronting the following question: will the society itself as a quantifiable whole be expanded or contracted by adding this or that individual? –This, of course, cannot be recommended to everyone: who would wish to put so much thought into something that does not amount to more than making a few people richer or poorer for half a day? And how rarely it really is the intention of the host to create an atmosphere of free sociability and to bring about a society. The host just wishes to deal with some outstanding social obligations or to mount an exhibition of his or her taste and household furnishings and thus sets no other limit than that of the size of his or her reception rooms. As soon as [184] some particular makes this apparent, the guests obviously find themselves to be in the same relationship with one another as if they had been brought together by accident since such a foreign and inhumane cause of their predicament might as well have been an accident. As their sociable inclination has actually been highly insulted by this abuse, they are not obliged to take the host into consideration. Thus, they are entirely justified in amusing themselves as best they can, even if it should be by means of a complete splintering of the society into separate parts. In any case, this is the worst that can happen to a host or to the guests (never mind the fact that the former often desires no more than that his elegant house should be treated as an inn and that the latter entertain themselves increasingly, the more the whole affair comes to look like a caricature of itself). Thus, it is much more humane to make this division as unnoticeable as possible. That is surely the worst that can happen if conversation is carried on as innuendo and persiflage for a while.

    Furthermore, it is in the nature of a theory and does not really require explicit evincing that the ideas presented there are ideals that practice is only meant to approach. This is also the case with the concept accomplished here that states that every society should be a unit, should be a whole. Not only will each and every

---

[38]Ed. note: There are three graces and nine muses in Greek mythology. This reference is in Kant's *Anthropology*. Hoover notes this in his "Toward a Theory of Sociable Conduct," n. 11, Hoover, 38.

[39]Ed. note: This "en rapport" (French) equals "in discussion."

society unavoidably have brief moments in which it is actually divided into several parts, but even the most superior of societies will be counted as especially fortunate if it can maintain itself as a true whole for just a while.

Bibliography

Adam, Wolfgang, ed. *Geselligkeit und Gesellschaft im Barockzeitalter: [in der Herzog-August-Bibliothek Wolfenbüttel vom 31. August bis 3. September 1994]*, Wolfenbütteler Arbeitskreis für Barockforschung. Wiesbaden: Harrassowitz, 1997.

Ameriks, Karl. *Kant and the Fate of Autonomy: Problems in the Appropriation of the Critical Philosophy*. Cambridge: Cambridge University Press, 2000.

Antonie, Stefanie. "Bildung und Geselligkeit: 'Zur theorie der Geselligkeit'." In *Gesellige Bildung: Studien und Dokumente zur Bildung Erwachsener im 18. Jahrhundert*, edited by Arnim Kaiser, 223-34. Bad Heilbrunn/Obb.: J. Klinkhardt, 1989.

Aristotle. *Introduction to Aristotle*. Edited by Richard McKeon, The Modern Library of the World's Best Books. New York: The Modern Library, 1947.

Arndt, Andreas. "Gefühl und Reflexion. Schleiermachers Stellung zur Transcendentalphilosophie im Kontext der Zeitgenössichen Kritik an Kant und Fichte." In *Der Streit um die Gestalt einer Ersten Philosophie (1799-1807): mit Texten von Fichte, Hegel, Jacobi, Jean Paul, Reinhold, Schelling u.a. und Kommentar*, edited by Walter Jaeschke, 105-26. Hamburg: Felix Meiner Verlag, 1999.

———. "Geselligkeit und Gesellschaft: Die Geburt der Dialektik aus dem Geist der Konversation in Schleiermachers 'Versuch einer Theorie des geselligen Betragens'." In *Salons der Romantik: Beiträge eines Wiepersdorfer Kolloquiums zu Theorie und Geschichte des Salons*, edited by Hartwig Schultz, 45-61. Berlin: Walter de Gruyter, 1997.

Bahr, Ehrhard. *Was ist Aufklärung?: Thesen und Definitionen*, Universal-Bibliothek 9714. Stuttgart: Philipp Reclam, 1974.

Becker-Cantarino, Baerbel. "Schlegels Lucinde: Zum Frauenbild der Fruhromantik." *Colloquia Germanica, Internationale Zeitschrift für Germanische Sprach- und Literaturwissenschaft* 10 (1976): 128-39.

Becker-Cantarino, Barbara. "Frauenzimmer Gesprächspiele: Geselligkeit, Frauen und Literatur im Barokzeitalter." In *Geselligkeit und Gesellschaft im*

Barockzeitalter: [in der Herzog-August-Bibliothek Wolfenbüttel vom 31. August bis 3. September 1994], edited by Wolfgang Adam, 17-41. Wiesbaden: Harrassowitz, 1997.

———. "Zur Theorie der literarischen Freundschaft im 18. Jahrhundert am Beispiel der Sophie La Roche." In *Frauenfreundschaft-Männerfreundschaft: Literarische Diskurse im 18. Jahrhundert*, edited by Wolfram Mauser, Barbara Becker-Cantarino and Eckhardt Meyer-Krentler, 47-74. Tübingen: Niemeyer, 1991.

Beckmann, Johann Christoph. *Historie des Fürstenthums Anhalt*. Zerbst: Zimmermann, 1710.

Berner, Christian. *La philosophie de Schleiermacher: Herméneutique, Dialectique, Éthique*, Passages. Paris: Cerf, 1995.

Bircher, Martin. *Die fruchtbringende Gesellschaft: Quellen und Dokumente in vier Bänden*, Deutsche Barock Literatur. München: Kösel, 1970.

Blackwell, Albert L. *Schleiermacher's Early Philosophy of Life: Determinism, Freedom, and Phantasy*, Harvard Theological Studies. Chico, Calif.: Scholars Press, 1982.

Bobsin, Julia. *Von der Werther-Krise zur Lucinde-Liebe: Studien zur Liebessemantik in der deutschen Erzählliteratur 1770-1800*, Studien und Text zur Sozialgeschichte der Literatur 48. Tübingen: Niemeyer, 1994.

Bovenschen, Silvia. *Die imaginierte Weiblichkeit: exemplarische Untersuchungen zu kulturgeschichtlichen und literarischen Präsentationsformen des Weiblichen*. Frankfurt am Main: Suhrkamp, 1979.

Brecht, Martin. "Pietismus als alternative Geselligkeit." In *Geselligkeit und Gesellschaft im Barockzeitalter: [in der Herzog-August-Bibliothek Wolfenbüttel vom 31. August bis 3. September 1994]*, edited by Wolfgang Adam, 261-73. Wiesbaden: Harrassowitz, 1997.

Burke, Peter. *The Fortunes of the Courtier: The European Reception of Castiglione's Cortegiano*, Penn State Series in the History of theBbook. University Park: Pennsylvania State University Press, 1996.

Castiglione, Baldassarre. *The Book of the Courtier*, Anchor Books A186. Garden City, N.Y: Doubleday, 1959.

Chadwick, Whitney. *Women, Art, and Society*, New York, N.Y: Thames and Hudson, 1990.

Cicero, Marcus Tullius. *Abhandlung über die menschlichen Pflichten: in drey Büchern aus dem Lateinischen des Marcus Tullius Cicero übersetzt von Christian Garve*. Edited by Christian Garve. Breslau: Wilhelm Gottlieb Korn, 1792.

Conermann, Klaus. "Die Tugendliche Gesellschaft und ihr Verhältnis zur Fruchtbringenden Gesellschaft: Sittenzucht, Gesellschaftsidee und Akademiegedanke zwischen Renaissance und Aufklärung." *Daphnis: Zeitschrift für Mittlere Deutsche Literatur* 17, no. 3 (1988): 513-626.

Davies, Martin L. *Identity or History? Marcus Herz and the End of the Enlightenment*, Kritik GLTCS. Detroit: Wayne State UP, 1995.

Drewitz, Ingeborg. *Berliner Salons: Gesellschaft und Literatur zwischen Aufklärung und Industriezeitalter*, Berlinische Reminiszenzen 7. Berlin: Haude & Spener, 1965.
Edschmid, Ulrike. *Diesseits des Schreibtischs: Lebensgeschichten von Frauen schreibender Männer*, Sammlung Luchterhand 908. Frankfurt am Main: Luchterhand, 1990.
Fambach, Oscar. *Das grosse Jahrzehnt in der Kritik seiner Zeit*, Ein Jahrhundert deutscher Literaturkritik, 1750-1850, Lesebuch und Studienwerk 4. Berlin: Akademie-Verlag, 1958.
Faull, Katherine M. "Beyond Confrontation? The Early Schleiermacher and Feminist Moral Theory." In *Friedrich Schleiermacher's Toward a Theory of Sociable Conduct, and Essays on its Intellectual-Cultural Context*, 41-65. Lewiston, N. Y.: Edwin Mellen Press, 1995.
Feilchenfeldt, Konrad. "Berliner Salons der Romantik." In *Rahel Levin Varnhagen: die Wiederentdeckung einer Schriftstellerin*, edited by Barbara Hahn and Ursula Isselstein, 152-63. Göttingen: Vandenhoeck & Ruprecht, 1987.
———. "Rahel Varnhagens 'Geselligkeit' aus der Sicht Varnhagens: mit einem Seitenblick auf Schleiermacher." In *Salons der Romantik: Beiträge eines Wiepersdorfer Kolloquiums zu Theorie und Geschichte des Salons*, edited by Hartwig Schultz, 147-69. Berlin, Germany: Walter de Gruyter, 1997.
Ferenczi, Sándor. *Sex in Psycho-analysis: Contributions to Psycho-analysis*, Rational Sex. Boston: R.G. Badger, 1922.
Fervers, Kurt. *Berliner Salons; die Geschichte einer großen Verschwörung*. München: Deutscher Volksverlag, 1940.
Fichte, Johann Gottlieb. *Johann Gottlieb Fichte's Sämmtliche Werke*. Edited by Immanuel Hermann Fichte. 11 vols. Berlin: Veit, 1845-46.
Foley, Peter. "Der Jude als moralisch zurechnungsfähiger Bürger. Schleiermachers philosophische Erwiderung auf die Frage der Bürgerrechte für Juden " *Theologische Literaturzeitung* 126, no. 7/8 (2001): 721-34.
———. *Heinrich von Kleist und Adam Müller: Untersuchung zur Aufnahme idealistischen Ideenguts durch Heinrich von Kleist*, Europäische Hochschulschriften, Reihe I Deutsche Sprache und Literatur 1209. Frankfurt am Main: P. Lang, 1990.
Gaus, Detlef. *Geselligkeit und Gesellige: Bildung, Bürgertum und bildungsbürgerliche Kultur um 1800*, M & P Schriftenreihe für Wissenschaft und Forschung. Stuttgart: Metzler, 1998.
Goethe, Johann Wolfgang von. *Unterhaltungen deutscher Ausgewanderten*. Edited by Leif Ludwig Albertsen, Universal-Bibliothek 6558. Stuttgart: Philipp Reclam jun, 1991.
Goodman, Dena. "Enlightenment Salons: The Convergence of Female and Philosophic Ambitions." *Eighteenth-Century Studies* 22 (1989): 329-50.
Göttert, Karl-Heinz. *Kommunikationsideale: Untersuchungen zur europäischen Konversationstheorie*. München: Iudicium, 1988.
Greenblatt, Stephen. *Renaissance Self-fashioning: From More to Shakespeare*.

Chicago: University of Chicago Press, 1980.
Guazzo, Stefano. *La civil conversatione del s. Stefano Gvazzo ... divisa in qvattro libri.* Venetia: G.B. Somasco, 1580.
Hahn, Barbara. *"Antworten Sie mir": Rahel Levin Varnhagens Briefwechsel.* Basel: Stroemfeld/Roter Stern, 1990.
———. *"Im Schlaf bin ich wacher": die Träume der Rahel Levin Varnhagen*, Sammlung Luchterhand 896. Frankfurt am Main: Luchterhand Literaturverlag, 1990.
Harsdörffer, Georg Philipp. *Frauenzimmer Gesprächspiele.* Edited by Irmgard Böttcher, Deutsche Neudrucke, Reihe Barock 13-20. Tübingen: M. Niemeyer, 1968.
Harth, Erica. *Cartesian Women: Versions and Subversions of Rational Discourse in the Old Regime*, Reading Women Writing. Ithaca: Cornell University Press, 1992.
Herbst, Hildburg. *Frühe Formen der deutschen Novelle im 18. Jahrhundert*, Philologische Studien und Quellen 112. Berlin: E. Schmidt, 1985.
Herder, Johann Gottfried. *Briefe zur Beförderung der Humanität.* Edited by Hans-Joachim Kruse and Heinz Stolpe, Ausgewählte Werke in Einzelausgaben. Berlin: Aufbau, 1971.
Herms, Eilert. *Herkunft, Entfaltung und erste Gestalt des Systems der Wissenschaften bei Scheiermacher.* Gütersloh: Gütersloher Verlagshaus Mohn, 1974.
Hertz, Deborah. *Jewish High Society in Old Regime Berlin.* New Haven and London: Yale University Press, 1988.
Herz, Henriette de Lemos. *Henriette Herz in Erinnerungen Briefen und Zeugnissen.* Edited by Rainer Schmitz. Frankfurt am Main: Insel Verlag, 1984.
Heyden-Rynsch, Verena von der. *Europäische Salons: Höhepunkte einer versunkenen weiblichen Kultur.* München: Artemis & Winkler, 1992.
Hille, Carl Gustav von. *Der Teutsche Palmenbaum: das ist, Lobschrift von der hochlöblichen Fruchtbringenden Gesellschaft, Anfang, Satzungen, Vorhaben, Namen, Sprüchen, Gemählen, Schriften und unverselklichem Tugendruhm. Allen Liebhabern der Teutschen Sprache zu dienlicher Nachrichtung.* Nürnberg, 1647.
Hinrichs, Wolfgang. *Schleiermachers Theorie der Geselligkeit und ihre Bedeutung für die Pädagogik.* Weinheim/Bergstr.: Beltz, 1965.
Hinske, Norbert. "Mendelssohns Beantwortung der Frage Was heisst Aufklärung? Oder Über die Aktualität Mendelssohns." In *Ich handle mit Vernunft--: Moses Mendelssohn und die europäische Aufklärung*, edited by Norbert Hinske and Alexander Altmann, 85-117. Hamburg: Meiner, 1981.
Hobbes, Thomas. *Leviathan, or, The Matter, Forme and Power of a Commonwealth Ecclesiasticall and Civil.* Edited by Michael Joseph Oakeshott. New York: Touchstone, 1997.
Hoffmann-Axthelm, Inge. *Geisterfamilie: Studien zur Geselligkeit der Frühromantik*, Studien zur Germanistik. Frankfurt (am Main): Akademische

Verlagsgesellschaft, 1973.
Hoover, Jeffrey. "Friedrich Schleiermacher's Christian Ethics in Relation to His Philosophical Ethics." *Canadian Journal of Philosophy* 20 (1990): 241-60.
———. "Toward a Theory of Sociable Conduct and Introduction." In *Friedrich Schleiermacher's Toward a Theory of Sociable Conduct, and Essays on its Intellectual-Cultural Context. Athenaeum/Neues Athenaeum* 4, edited by Ruth Richardson, 9-39. Lewiston, N.Y: Edwin Mellen Press, 1995.
Kant, Immanuel. *Groundwork of the Metaphysic of Morals*. Edited by H. J. Paton, Harper Torchbooks TB 1159. New York: Harper & Row, 1964.
———. *Kants Gesammelte Schriften*. Edited by Katharina Holger, Eduard Gerreshelm, Ingeborg Heidemann, Gottfried Martin and Paul Menzer. 9 vols. Berlin: Ausgabe der Königlich Preussischen Akademie der Wissenschaften, 1902-.
———. *Religion Within the Boundaries of Mere Reason and Other Writings*. Edited by Allen W. Wood and George Di Giovanni, Cambridge Texts in the History of Philosophy. Cambridge: Cambridge University Press, 1998.
Kantzenbach, Friedrich Wilhelm. *Friedrich Daniel Ernst Schleiermacher in Selbstzeugnissen und Bilddokumenten*, Rowohlts Monographien 126. Reinbek bei Hamburg: Rowohlt, 1967.
Kleist, Heinrich von. *Werke und Briefe in vier Bänden*. Edited by Siegfried Streller and Peter Goldammer. Frankfurt am Main: Insel, 1986.
Köhler, Astrid. *Salonkultur im klassischen Weimar: Geselligkeit als Lebensform und literarisches Konzept*. Stuttgart: M & P, 1996.
Koopmann, Helmut. *Freiheitssonne und Revolutionsgewitter: Reflexe der Französischen Revolution im literarischen Deutschland zwischen 1789 und 1840*, Untersuchungen zur deutschen Literaturgeschichte 50. Tübingen: Niemeyer, 1989.
Lamm, Julia A. *The Living God: Schleiermacher's Theological Appropriation of Spinoza*. University Park, Pa: Pennsylvania State University Press, 1996.
———. "Reading Plato's Dialectics: Schleiermacher's Insistence on Dialectics as Dialogical." *Zeitschrift für neuere Theologiegeschichte / Journal for the History of Modern Theology* 10, no. 1 (2003): 1-25.
Lepsius, Sabine. "Über das Aussterben der Salons." *März*, no. 7 (1913): 227-33.
Lowenstein, Steven M. *The Berlin Jewish Community: Enlightenment, Family, and Crisis, 1770-1830*, Studies in Jewish History. New York: Oxford University Press, 1994.
Martinson, Steven D. *Harmonious Tensions: The Writings of Friedrich Schiller*. Newark; London: University of Delaware Press; Associated University Presses, 1996.
Meckenstock, Günter. *Deterministische Ethik und kritische Theologie: die Auseinandersetzung des frühen Schleiermacher mit Kant und Spinoza, 1789-1794*, Schleiermacher-Archiv 5. Berlin and New York: Walter de Gruyter, 1988.
———. *Schleiermachers Bibliothek: Bearbeitung des faksimilierten Rauchschen*

Auktionskatalogs und der Hauptbücher des Verlages G. Reimer, Schleiermacher-Archiv 10. Berlin and New York: Walter de Gruyter, 1993.

Narciss, Georg Adolf. *Studien zu den Frauenzimmergesprächen Georg Philipp Harsdörfers (1607-1658): ein Beitrag zur deutschen Literaturgeschichte des 17. Jahrhunderts*, Form und Geist 5. Leipzig: H. Eichblatt, 1928.

Neumaier, Herbert. *Der Konversationston in der frühen Biedermeierzeit, 1815-1830*. Bergatreute, 1974.

Newman, Jane O. *Pastoral Conventions: Poetry, Language, and Thought in Seventeenth-Century Nuremberg*. Baltimore: Johns Hopkins University Press, 1990.

Nicolai, Friedrich. *Vertraute Briefe von Adelheid B** an*. Berlin ; Stettin, 1799.

Nowak, Kurt. *Der umstrittene Bürger von Genf: Zur Wirkungsgeschichte Rousseaus im deutschen Protestantismus des 18. Jahrhunderts*, Sitzungsberichte der Sachsischen Akademie der Wissenschaften zu Leipzig: Philologisch-Historische Klasse (SSAWL), 132, 4. Berlin: Akademie, 1993.

Oberdorfer, Bernd. *Geselligkeit und Realisierung von Sittlichkeit: die Theorieentwicklung Friedrich Schleiermachers bis 1799*, Theologische Bibliothek Töpelmann 69. Berlin and New York: Walter de Gruyter, 1995.

Otto, Karl F. *Die Sprachgesellschaften des 17. Jahrhunderts*, Sammlung Metzler, 109. Abt. D, Literaturgeschichte. Stuttgart: Metzler, 1972.

Patsch, Hermann. "Die esoterische Kommunikationsstruktur der Weihnachtsfeier: über Anspielungen und Zitate." In *Schleiermacher in Context*, edited by Ruth Richardson, 132-56. Lewiston, NY: Edwin Mellen Press, 1991.

Philaleth. "IV Zeichen der Zeit: Die Juden." In *Eunomia: Eine Zeitschrift des neunzehnten Jahrhunderts. Von einer Gesellschaft von Gelehrten*, edited by Ignatius Aurelius Feßler, J. G. Rhode and Fischer, 335-37. Berlin: Maurer, 1801.

Plato. *The Republic and Other Works*. Translated by B. Jowett. New York: Anchor Books, 1973.

———. *Symposium*. Edited by Alexander Nehamas and Paul Woodruff. Indianapolis: Hackett Pub. Co, 1989.

Pleger, Wolfgang H. *Schleiermachers Philosophie*, De Gruyter Studienbuch. Berlin and New York: Walter de Gruyter, 1988.

Pockels, Karl Friedrich. *Versuch einer Charakteristik des weiblichen Geschlechts Ein Sittengemählde des Menschen, des Zeitalters und des geselligen Lebens*, Historische Quellen zur Frauenbewegung und Geschlechterproblematik, 40. Hannover: Ritscher, 1799.

Richardson, Ruth. "Schleiermacher's 1800 'Versuch über die Schaamhaftigkeit': A Contribution Toward a Truly Human Ethic." In *Schleiermacher and Feminism: Sources, Evaluations, and Responses*. Schleiermacher Studies and Translations 12, edited by Iain G. Nicol, 49–85. Lewiston, N. Y.: Edwin Mellen Press, 1992.

———, ed. *Friedrich Schleiermacher's Toward a Theory of Sociable Conduct, and Essays on its Intellectual-Cultural Context*, New Athenaeum/Neues

Athenaeum 4. Lewiston, N.Y: Edwin Mellen Press, 1995.
Rohs, Peter. *Johann Gottlieb Fichte*, Grosse Denker, Beck'sche Reihe, BsR 521. München: Verlag C.H. Beck, 1991.
Rousseau, Jean-Jacques. *The Social Contract*. Translated by Maurice Cranston, The Penguin classics, L201. Harmondsworth: Penguin, 1968.
Schiller, Friedrich. *Sämtliche Werke*. Edited by Gerhard Fricke, Herbert G. Göpfert and Herbert Stubenrauch. 3 ed. 5 vols. C. Hanser, 1962.
———. *Schillers Briefe*. Edited by Fritz Jonas and Albert Leitzmann. Stuttgart: Deutsche Verlags-Anstalt, 1892.
———. *Über die ästhetische Erziehung des Menschen in einer Reihe von Briefen*, Universal-Bibliothek 8994/95. Stuttgart: P. Reclam jun, 1965.
Schlegel, Friedrich. *Lucinde: Ein Roman. Mit Friedrich Schleiermachers "Vertrauten Briefen über Friedrich Schlegels 'Lucinde'"*. Edited by Ursula Naumann, Goldmann Klassiker 7632. München: Goldmann, 1985.
Schlegel, Friedrich von. *Studien des klassischen Altertums*. Edited by Ernst Behler, Kritische Friedrich-Schlegel-Ausgabe, 1. Bd. Paderborn: Verlag F. Schöningh, 1979.
Schleiermacher, Friedrich. *Briefwechsel 1801-1802 (Briefe 1005-1245)*. Edited by Hermann Fischer, Kritische Gesamtausgabe / Friedrich Daniel Ernst Schleiermacher, 5. Abt., Briefwechsel und biographische Dokumente, Bd. 5. Berlin and New York: Walter de Gruyter, 1999.
———. *Briefwechsel 1774-1796 (Briefe 1-326)*. Edited by Andreas Arndt and Wolfgang Virmond, Kritische Gesamtausgabe / Friedrich Daniel Ernst Schleiermacher 5. Abt., Briefwechsel und biographische Dokumente Bd. 1. Berlin and New York: Walter de Gruyter, 1985.
———. *Letters on Occasion of the Political Theological Task and the Sendschreiben (Open Letter) of Jewish Heads of Households*. Edited by Gilya Gerda Schmidt, Schleiermacher Studies and Translations 21. Lewiston, N. Y.: Edwin Mellen Press, 2001.
———. *On Religion: Speeches to its Cultured Despisers*. Edited by Richard Crouter, Cambridge Texts in the History of Philosophy. Cambridge: Cambridge University Press, 1996.
———. *Schriften aus der Berliner Zeit, 1796-1799*. Edited by Günter Meckenstock, Kritische Gesamtausgabe / Friedrich Daniel Ernst Schleiermacher 1. Abt., Schriften und Entwürfe Bd. 2 Berlin and New York: Walter de Gruyter, 1984.
———. *Schriften aus der Berliner Zeit, 1800-1802*. Edited by Günter Meckenstock, Kritische Gesamtausgabe / Friedrich Daniel Ernst Schleiermacher 1. Abt., Schriften und Entwürfe, Bd. 3. Berlin and New York: Walter de Gruyter, 1988.
———. *Schriften aus der Hallenser Zeit 1804-1807*. Edited by Hermann Patsch, Kritische Gesamtausgabe / Friedrich Daniel Ernst Schleiermacher, 1. Abt., Bd. 5. Berlin and New York: Walter de Gruyter, 1995.
———. *Werke: Auswahl in vier Bänden*. Edited by Otto Eduard Leopold Braun and

Johannes Bauer. Leipzig: F. Meiner, 1910.
Scholtz, Gunter. *Die Philosophie Schleiermachers*, Erträge der Forschung. Darmstadt: Wissenschaftliche Buchgesellschaft, 1984.
Sedgwick, Eve Kosofsky. "Tales of the Avuculate." In *Tendencies*, 52-72. Durham: Duke University Press, 1993.
Seibert, Peter. "Der Literarische [sic.] Salon; ein Forschungsüberblick." *Internationales Archiv für Sozialgeschichte der deutschen Literatur* 2. Folge, no. Sonderheft 3 (1993): 159-220.
———. *Der literarische Salon: Literatur und Geselligkeit zwischen Aufklärung und Vormärz*. Stuttgart: Metzler, 1993.
———. "Henriette Herz: Erinnerungen: Zur Rekonstruktion einer frühen Frauenautobiographie." *Der Deutschunterricht: Beitrage zu seiner Praxis und wissenschaftlichen Grundlegung* 41, no. 2 (1989): 37-50.
Sherman, Nancy. "Aristotle on the Shared Life." In *Friendship: A Philosophical Reader*, edited by Neera Kapur Badhwar, 92-114. Ithaca, N.Y: Cornell University Press, 1993.
Sorkin, David. *The Transformation of German Jewry, 1780-1840*, Studies in Jewish History. New York: Oxford University Press, 1987.
Spiegel, Yorick. *Theologie der bürgerlichen Gesellschaft: Sozialphilosophie und Glaubenslehre bei Friedrich Schleiermacher*, Forschungen zur Geschichte und Lehre des Protestantismus. München: C. Kaiser, 1968.
Staël, Madame de. *Über Deutschland*. Edited by Monika Bosse, Insel Taschenbuch 623. Frankfurt am Main: Insel, 1985.
Strube, Rolf. *Sie saßen und tranken am Teetisch: Anfänge und Blütezeit der Berliner Salons, 1789-1871*, Serie Piper 1204. München: Piper, 1991.
Tewarson, Heidi Thomann. *Rahel Levin Varnhagen: Mit Selbstzeugnissen und Bilddokumenten*, Rowohlts Monographien 406. Reinbek bei Hamburg: Rowohlt, 1988.
Thomasius, Christian. *Von Nachahmung der Franzosen: nach den Ausgaben von 1687 und 1701*. Edited by August Sauer, Deutsche Litteraturdenkmale des 18. und 19. Jahrhunderts, no. 51, Neue Folge no. 1. Nendeln/Liechtenstein: Kraus Reprint, 1968.
Tieck, Ludwig. *Ludwig Tieck's Schriften*. Berlin: G. Reiner, 1829.
Töllner, Heinrich. *Die Bedeutung der Geselligkeit in Schleiermachers Leben und Schriften*. Erlangen: Junge, 1927.
Unger, Helene. "Ueber Berlin. Aus Briefen einer reisenden Dame an ihren Bruder in Ha." *Jahrbücher der Preußischen Monarchie unter der Regierung Friedrich Wilhelms des Dritten* 2, Mai bis Juni (1798): 17-33, 133-43, 287-302.
Varnhagen, Rahel. "Rahel: ein Buch des Andenkens für ihre Freunde: (als Handschrift.)." edited by Karl August Varnhagen von Ense, 2, 608. Berlin: (Trowitzsch), 1833.
Varnhagen von Ense, Karl August. *Aus dem Nachlass Varnhagen's von Ense: Briefe von Chamisso, Gneisenau, Haugwitz, W. von Humboldt, Prinz Louis Ferdinand, Rahel, Rückert, L. Tieck, u.a.* Edited by Ludmilla Assing.

Leipzig: Brockhaus, 1867.

———. *Literaturkritiken*, Deutsche Texte 42. Tübingen: Niemeyer, 1977.

Vickers, Michael J. *Greek Symposia*. London: Joint Association of Classical Teachers, 1978.

Wenz, Gunther. *Sinn und Geschmack fürs Unendliche: F. D. E. Schleiermachers Reden über die Religion an die Gebildeten unter ihren Verächtern von 1799*, Bayerische Akademie der Wissenschaften. Philosophisch-Historische Klasse, Sitzungsberichte (BAWS): 1999: 3. Munich: Beck, 1999.

Wilhelmy-Dollinger, Petra. *Der Berliner Salon im 19. Jahrhundert: 1780-1914*, Veröffentlichungen der Historischen Kommission zu Berlin. Berlin ; New York: Walter de Gruyter, 1989.

Zeller, Rosmarie. *Spiel und Konversation im Barock; Untersuchungen zu Harsdörffers Gesprächsspielen*, Quellen und Forschungen zur Sprach- und Kulturgeschichte der germanischen Völker, n. F. 58 (177). Berlin: New York, Walter de Gruyter, 1974.

Indexes

Names and Places

Anna Amalie Dowager Duchess of Saxony-Weimar, 44
Aristotle, 72-75, 85, 144
Aspasia, 30, 33
Athens, 30
Augustine of Hippo, 144, 149-150
Barby, 71
Bauer, Hofrätin, 49
Bargagli, Scipione, 35-36, 39
Berlin, 13, 45, 47, 63, 65, 76-79
Boccaccio, 44-45
Brinkmann, Gustav, 23, 85-86
Castiglione, Baldasar, 34, 36, 39, 52-53, 62, 65
Cicero, 34, 60-62
Clausius, Christian Friedrich Gottlieb, 48
Clausius, Minna, 48
Cohen, Ezechiel Benjamin, 46-48, 70
Dante, 36
Derrida, Jacques, 37-38
Descartes, René, 48
Diotima, 29-30
Eberhard, Johann August, 98, 109
England, 44, 136, 153, 158
Ferenzci, Sandor, 65
Feßler, Ignaz, 24, 78
Fichte, Johann Gottlieb, 7-8, 74, 81-98, 105-108, 119, 123, 145, 162
Florence, 36
France, 3, 44, 46-52, 63
Francke, August Hermann, 52
Friendship, 14
Garve, Christian, 61-62, 155
Genlis, Stéphanie-Félicité Ducrest de Saint-Aubin, Countess de, 46, 50
Germany, 2, 35, 51-52, 63
Goethe, Johann Wolfgang von, 44-45, 111, 130, 157, 165-166
Gonzaga, Elizabeth, Duchess of Urbino, 53
Gratian, 51
Guazzo, Stefano, 35-36
Gutzkow, Karl, 62-63
Harsdörffer, Georg Philipp, 36-39, 43, 50-52, 55
Herder, Johann Gottfried, 45, 95, 157
Herz, Henriette, 3, 4, 5, 12, 14-15, 17, 19, 21, 22, 24-72, 75, 78-79, 81, 146, 153, 164, 166
Herz, Markus, 3, 54, 76, 78, 81, 166
Hille, Carl Gustav von, 38
Hobbes, Thomas, 99-101, 105, 161
Horace, 172
Humboldt, Alexander, 76
Humboldt, Wilhelm, 76
Italy, 2, 23, 35-36, 44-45, 52
Jacobi, Friedrich Heinrich, 89, 145

John, Gwen, 15
Kant, Immanuel, 6, 7, 8, 18, 20, 76,
  83-84, 88-89, 92, 108-124,
  126-7, 135, 137, 140, 143,
  154, 161, 167, 174-175
Kleist, Heinrich von, 48, 64
Knigge, Adolf Freiherr von, 51, 100,
  115, 117, 133-134, 138, 143,
  151
Kunth, Gottlob, 76-77
Königsberg, 76
Köthen, 2
La Roche, Karl von, 45
La Roche, Sophie von, 44-45
Lemos, Benjamin de, 21, 70
Lessing, Gotthold Ephraim, 43-44,
  75
Levin, Markus, 21
Maimon, Solomon, 76
Medici, Guiliano de, 53
Mendelssohn, Moses, 20, 24-26, 64,
  70-71, 75-76
Molière, 47
Moritz, Karl Philipp, 166
Müller, Adam Heinrich, 64
Napoleon, 26
Nicolai, Friedrich, 56-59, 61, 74
Niesky, 71
Novalis (Friedrich von Hardenberg),
  157
Nuremberg, 38
Origen, 144
Pericles, 30
Plato, 17, 27-35, 66, 75, 146
Plutarch, 34
Pompadour, Madam de, 30
Prussia, 26, 63
Rambouillet, Madame de, 23
Ringhieri, Innocenzio, 35-36
Rousseau, Jean-Jacques, 98-107, 119
Rügen, 71
Sack, Friedrich Samuel Gottfried,
  60-62
Schelling, Friedrich W. J., 137

Schiller, Friedrich von, 45, 112, 118-
  124, 128, 145, 157
Schlegel, Friedrich, 18, 27, 29, 55-
  62, 64, 70, 72, 81, 83
Schlegel-Schelling, Caroline, 29
Schleiermacher, Friedrich:
  Christmas Eve, 18, 27-28,
  30-34, 71; *Confidential
  Letters on Friedrich
  Schlegel's Lucinde*, 18, 58,
  71-72; *Letters on the
  Occasion of the Political
  Theological Task and the
  Sendschreiben (Open Letter)
  of Jewish Heads of
  Households*, 125, 147;
  Notebooks of Thoughts, 9,
  72-73, 83, 112, 125-127, 133-
  146, 150; *On Freedom*, 110,
  111; *On Religion*, 1, 4, 8, 17,
  83-84, 108, 110, 119, 142,
  144, 146-151
Shakespeare, William, 43
Siena, 39
Smith, Adam, 5
Sophie Elisabeth, Duchess of
  Brunswick and Luneburg, 56
Socrates, 29, 66
Spain, 23
Spener, Philipp August, 2, 52
Spinoza, 82, 108, 109, 147
Staël, Madame de, 49-50
Subenrauch, Samuel, 61
Schwarz, Friedrich Heinrich
  Christian, 83, 89
Thomasius, Christian, 41, 50
Tieck, Ludwig, 55, 63, 65
Tuscany, 36
Urbino, 35, 52-53
Urfé, Honore d', 40
Valadon, Suzanne, 15
Varnhagen von Ense, Karl August,
  12, 42, 53, 64, 70
Varnhagen, Rahel Levin, 12, 14, 21,

23, 25-26, 63, 69-70
Veit, Dorothea (Brendel), née Mendelssohn, 18, 21, 56, 58, 60, 64, 69-70
Vogel, Adolfine Henriette, 64
Weimar, 45
Wieland, Christoph Martin, 44-45
Wilde, Oscar
Willich, Ehrenfried von, 71
Xenophon, 34
Zenge, Wilhemine von, 48

Subjects

Académie Royale des Sciences, 48
Accademia della Crusca, 36, 50
Accademia degli Intronati, 39
Autonomy, 88, 113, 116, 123
Bildung, 4
Catholicism, 139, 143
Causation, 88, 93, 108-111, 156
Character of society, 33, 93, 96-97, 104, 130-131, 148, 163-165, 167-168, 171-172
Coffeehouses, 3
Collegia pietatis, 2, 52
Conversation, 5, 28, 32, 35, 50-55, 63-64, 95, 98, 131, 143, 164, 168-169, 171-172, 175
Dialectic, 86, 142
Enlightenment, 4, 13-14, 34, 76, 81, 98, 166
France, 23, 57
Free sociability, 84, 90-93, 95, 97-98, 113-114, 118, 127, 129, 145-146, 150, 153-154, 156-159, 161, 169, 174-175
Freedom, 82-84, 87-88, 90, 97-98, 106-111, 116, 119, 121-122, 124, 127, 130, 132-133, 145, 158, 162, 167
French Revolution, 106-107, 122, 162
Friendship, 14, 60-62, 66-67, 68, 70-75, 144
Fruit-Bearing Society, 2-3, 36, 38, 39, 43, 50

German language, 50, 57, 75, 81, 114, 136, 153, 157, 160, 162, 173
Homosexuality, 29, 66-68
Inclination, 111, 120, 124, 154, 175
Individuality, 96-99, 101, 104, 106, 129, 140, 161, 163, 165
Jews, 4, 14, 20-27, 43-46, 48, 63, 65, 70, 75, 125-126, 135, 144, 147, 153
Kingdom of ends, 7
Liturgy, 8
Manner of conveying subject matter, 33, 96-97, 104, 129-130, 134-136, 148, 163-165
Mittwochs-Gesellschaft, 24, 77-79
Moral weeklies, 3, 41-42
Moravians (*Herrnhuter*), 3, 52, 71
New Historicism, 11-12, 37, 64
Order of the Golden Palm, 40
Pegnitz Order of Flowers, 37, 43
Pentateuch, 75
Pietism, 2, 42, 51-52
Préciosité, 46-48, 135
Propriety (*Schicklichkeit*), 33, 94-97, 102, 129, 132, 136, 160, 164, 166, 169, 171, 174
Reciprocity, 89-93, 101, 123-124, 128, 135-136, 138, 140-146, 148-150, 158-160
Reformed Church, 3
Renaissance, 34-45, 63-64
Roman Catholicism, 70

Romanticism, 21, 98, 157, 166
Romantics, 8, 56
Social network theory, 15-19
Tone, 33, 96, 129, 131, 134-136, 138, 164, 169
Virtue, 74, 83-84

Virtuous League (*Tugendbund*), 3, 42-43, 45
Virtuous Society, 40
Will, 90, 101-110, 116, 120-121, 127, 132, 135, 174